Aldous Huxley

In the same series

Stendhal Michael Wood
Thomas Hardy: The Poetic Structure Jean R. Brooks
The Nouveau Roman: A Study in the Practice of Writing
Stephen Heath

In preparation

Kafka Franz Kuna
Flaubert Jonathan Culler
Henry James and the French Literary Mind Philip Grover

Aldous Huxley

Keith M. May

BOOKS
10 East 53d St., New York 10022
(a division of Harper & Row Publishers, Inc.)

Acknowledgements

Grateful thanks for permission to quote are due to the following:
Chatto & Windus Ltd for extracts from the works of Aldous Huxley,
the *Letters of Aldous Huxley* (ed. Grover Smith), *This Timeless Moment*
by Laura Archera Huxley, and *Aldous Huxley: Satire & Structure* by
Jerome Meckier; Laura Archera Huxley for an extract from Aldous
Huxley's introduction to his edition of the *Letters of D. H. Lawrence*;
Macmillan & Co. Ltd, and Mr M. B. Yeats for quotations from poems
by W. B. Yeats; Macmillan & Co. Ltd and Mr A. E. Dyson for extracts
(originally printed in the *Critical Quarterly*) from *The Crazy Fabric*
by A. E. Dyson; Laurence Pollinger Ltd and the estate of the late Mrs
Frieda Lawrence for quotations from D. H. Lawrence's *The Rainbow*
and *Women in Love*, and *The Collected Letters of D. H. Lawrence*
(ed. Harry T. Moore); John Farquharson Ltd for quotations from
D. S. Savage's *The Withered Branch*; Curtis Brown Ltd for a quotation from Elizabeth Bowen's *Collected Impressions*; Associated Book
Publishers Ltd for a quotation from Jean-Paul Sartre's *Being and
Nothingness*; The Longman Group Ltd for the British Council for
quotations from *Aldous Huxley* by Jocelyn Brooke; Princeton University Press for quotations from *Anatomy of Criticism : Four Essays* by
Northrop Frye (copyright © 1957 by Princeton University Press);
Faber & Faber Ltd for quotations from T. S. Eliot's *Collected Poems
1909–1962* and *Selected Essays*; The Clarendon Press, Oxford, for a
quotation from *The Oxford Companion to French Literature* (edited
by Sir Paul Harvey and J. E. Heseltine); George Allen & Unwin Ltd
for quotations from : *Memories*, Vol. I, by Sir Julian Huxley, *History
of Western Philosophy* by Bertrand Russell, *Language as Gesture* by
R. P. Blackmur; Martin Secker & Warburg Ltd for extracts from the
Paris Review interview with Aldous Huxley in *Writers at Work*, Vol.
II; William Heinemann Ltd and Mr Ronald W. Clark for
extracts from *The Huxleys* by Ronald W. Clark; The Athlone Press
for quotations from Peter Bowering's *Aldous Huxley: a Study of the
Major Novels*; the *Spectator* for quotations from reviews; André
Deutsch Ltd and Mr Cyril Connolly for quotations from Cyril
Connolly's *The Modern Movement*; Russell & Russell for quotations
from Alexander Henderson's *Aldous Huxley* (London, Chatto &
Windus Ltd, 1936; reprinted New York, Russell & Russell, 1964); the
Editor of the *London Magazine* for quotations from articles by Angus

Wilson, Evelyn Waugh and John Wain in the issue of August, 1955; Edward Arnold Ltd for quotations from E. M. Forster's *Aspects of the Novel*; Calder & Boyars Ltd for a quotation from *Aldous Huxley* (revised edition) by John Atkins; Victor Gollancz Ltd for a quotation from Kingsley Amis's *New Maps of Hell*; the *New Statesman* for a quotation from a review by Leonard Woolf in *The Nation and Athenaeum*; A. D. Peters & Co. and Mr J. B. Priestley for quotations from *Thomas Love Peacock* by J. B. Priestley, reprinted by permission of A. D. Peters & Co.

'I think that fiction and, as I say, history and biography are *immensely* important, not only for their own sake, because they provide a picture of life now and of life in the past, but also as vehicles for the expression of general philosophic ideas, religious ideas, social ideas. My goodness, Dostoevski is six times as profound as Kierkegaard, because he writes *fiction*. In Kierkegaard you have this Abstract Man going on and on—like Coleridge—why, it's *nothing* compared with the really profound Fictional Man, who has always to keep these tremendous ideas *alive* in a concrete form. In fiction you have the reconciliation of the absolute and the relative, so to speak, the expression of the general in the particular. And this, it seems to me, is the exciting thing—both in life and in art.'

Aldous Huxley, *Writers at Work*

'The intellect of man is forced to choose
Perfection of the life, or of the work,
And if it take the second must refuse
A heavenly mansion, raging in the dark.'

Yeats, 'The Choice'

'For the artist or intellectual, who happens also to be interested in reality and desirous of liberation, the way out would seem to lie, as usual, along a knife-edge.'

(Aldous Huxley) Sebastian Barnack in *Time Must Have a Stop*

Contents

TO
PAMELA

A Variety of Fiction

T. S. Eliot, in the course of a short contribution to a memorial volume on Huxley, recalls that at the time of the publication of *Leda* (1920) he was unable to show any enthusiasm for Huxley's verse. Eliot continues : 'After this attempt he wisely confined himself to the essay and the variety of fiction which he came to make his own.'[1]

The phrase, 'variety of fiction', implies that Huxley's longer, separately-published stories ideally should not be called 'novels', and that no satisfactory label for them exists. When Eliot concludes his contribution by asserting that, 'His place in English literature is unique and is certainly assured',[2] we may assume that the unique qualities he is thinking of lie chiefly in the novels.

It would be possible to proceed from acknowledging that Huxley's productions are unsatisfactory by Flaubertian or Jamesian criteria to offering rough parallels from the literature of the past as a means of showing that he nevertheless worked in a worthy tradition. And it is true that a sound preliminary step for those who admire Huxley but are embarrassed by his failure to write a good novel, in the restricted sense, is to remind themselves of what Northrop Frye calls the 'Menippean satire'.

'We remarked earlier that most people would call *Gulliver's Travels* fiction but not a novel. It must then be another form of fiction, as it certainly has a form, and we feel that we are turning from the novel to this form, whatever it is, when we turn from Rousseau's *Emile* to Voltaire's *Candide*, or from Butler's *The Way of All Flesh* to the Erewhon books, or from Huxley's *Point Counterpoint* [*sic*] to *Brave New World*. The form thus has its own traditions, and, as the examples of Butler and Huxley show, has preserved some integrity even under the ascendancy of the novel. Its existence is easy enough to demonstrate, and no one will challenge the statement that the literary ancestry of *Gulliver's Travels* and *Candide* runs through Rabelais and Erasmus to Lucian. But while much has been said about the style and thought of Rabelais, Swift, and Voltaire, very little has been made of them as craftsmen working in a specific medium, a point no one dealing with a novelist would ignore. Another great writer in this tradition, Huxley's master Peacock, has fared even worse, for, his form not being understood, a general impression has grown up that his status in the development of prose fiction is that of a slapdash eccentric. Actually, he is as exquisite and precise an artist in his medium as Jane Austen is in hers.

'The form used by these authors is the Menippean satire, also more rarely called the Varronian satire, allegedly invented by a Greek cynic named Menippus.'[3]

After looking up these words, a critic intent on classifying or defending the novels of Huxley would feel that some progress had been made, but he would still be disconcerted by Frye's placing of *Point Counter Point* among novels and *Brave New World* among Menippean satires. For if *Point Counter Point* is emphatically a novel, it is not the kind of work that theorists of the novel have had centrally in mind.

There are at least three common ways of dealing with this problem. The first way can cheerfully be taken by denigrators of Huxley's novels, but rather miserably by admirers, since it consists of maintaining that he was a congenital essayist who encroached (though brilliantly) on congenital novelists' preserves. Support for this opinion can be gathered by reference to Philip Quarles's well-known jottings in *Point Counter Point* and to Huxley's reply to interviewers for the *Paris Review*.[4] The second way is to hold on to the word 'satire', either applying it with varying degrees of readiness to all Huxley's fictions or applying it only to some and perhaps arguing that the rest suffer from the disuse of natural talents, but in any event making light of the question of his qualities as a novelist. The third way is to talk of the 'novel of ideas', possibly also descrying a kinship between this category and the Menippean satire, and so introducing a nicety which Frye, in his exclusion of *Point Counter Point*, did not entertain. Even the non-satirical, or only partially satirical, 'novel of ideas', such as *Eyeless in Gaza*, might perhaps be related to the Menippean satire, for Frye states that the 'form is not invariably satiric in attitude' but includes such a work as Landor's *Imaginary Conversations*.[5]

None of these three ways of regarding the novels is invalid, but each of them tempts the reader to fail to appreciate Huxley's formal originality. The man who emphatically considers that Huxley attempted the novel proper with only an essayist's gifts is likely to be overlooking Huxley's positive aesthetic achievement. To think of Huxley simply as a satirist is to limit understanding of the purpose of his various devices. The term, 'novel of ideas', is accurate, but needs qualification and should not be allowed to impose the suggestion of a dwarfish offshoot of a grand phenomenon.

Very often, indeed, critics have argued that Huxley ought to have been doing this, that, or the other, instead of holding to his own peculiar course, and the fact that he openly took navigational directions from so many forerunners might sometimes have aided misunderstanding. His technical borrowings are numerous and they range over several arts, but they combine in every novel to form a new, Huxleyan whole. He plundered music, architecture and painting, just as he exploited whatever he required in Petronius as well as in Lucian, in Congreve as well as in Swift, in Anatole France as well as in Proust, to produce specimens of a kind of fiction which, as Eliot says with complete accuracy, 'he came to make his own'. Eliot's emphasis upon the originality of Huxley is an encouragement to consider the novels on their own terms, and while such a consideration will entail notice of Huxley's debts to others, it will chiefly lead us to a clearer understanding of his various meanings as well as a more just assessment of his merits.

It is the meanings, however, that I shall be chiefly pursuing, for a study of Huxley's structural techniques would not be a very fruitful exercise if it did not lead to more accurate and more comprehensive understanding. And the assumption that a novel by Huxley is crystal clear on one comfortable reading is correct only in a limited way. Certainly he is a lucid and repetitious writer whose works contain comparatively few complexities of reference, cross-reference, and allusion (such as we find in Joyce or Nabokov); no preference for presenting human mysteries without intellectually analysing them (in the way of Conrad or of Lawrence), and scarcely any minute awarenesses, demanding contemplation (as in James or Proust). What Huxley is saying, directly or through his characters, is seldom in doubt : he is so consistently intelligible that there are many occasions when a reader might not realize how abstruse the matter would seem in the manner of a less able expositor.

Despite his clarity, Huxley is liable to be misunderstood if his structures are insufficiently or improperly taken into account. If it was for want of some of the true novelist's talents that he poured his meanings into conspicuously ingenious or borrowed moulds, we should not suppose that the moulds can be either disregarded or treated in the spirit of a scholastic game. Nevertheless, one of Huxley's letters may be taken as a warning. To a correspondent who fancied that she had seen a particular connection between form and ideas in *Point Counter Point* he wrote as follows:

'I don't think there was any special significance of the kind you speak of, in the structure of *Point Counter Point* and the others. They represent experiments in the technique of narrative and of the exploration of the mind carried on by one who is not congenitally a novelist and therefore is compelled to resort to devices which the born novelist would never think of using—being perfectly capable of covering the necessary ground without departing from straightforward techniques.'[6]

But what Huxley does not say is that a structure apparently chosen as an expedient may also be or become a vital factor enhancing the meaning of the words of which it is composed. I have come to believe that Huxley's cast of mind was such that whenever he set about the task of communicating through fiction some strong preoccupation, the preoccupation readily assumed a suitable plastic, or pictorial, or musical, or traditionally literary shape, so that his regular methods were not so mechanically willed as the letter might suggest.

At the same time, Huxley's procedures should not be thought of as evasive of experience, because the fine awareness of artistic forms was constantly used to express life's irreducibility to neat patterns. Time and again he caused a character to comment upon the discrepancy between life and art, and some of the blunders of his younger characters arise from ignorance of the discrepancy. For the author, as a craftsman, as a moralist, and as a critic, the conclusion seems to have been that faithful imitations of nature, though sometimes highly impressive, are not the best kind of imitations for every fictional purpose. Let us consider some interesting observations on this matter.

'Mark, at dinner, said he'd been reading *Anna Karenina*. Found it good, as novels go. But complained of the profound untruthfulness of even the best imaginative literature. And he began to catalogue its omissions. Almost total neglect of those small physiological events that decide whether day-to-day living shall have a pleasant or unpleasant tone . . . No mention, next, of the part played by mere sensations in producing happiness . . . Almost equally complete omission of the small distractions that fill the greater part of human lives . . .

'Lying by omission turns inevitably into positive lying. The implications of literature are that human beings are controlled, if not by reason, at least by comprehensible, well-organized, avowable sentiments. Whereas the facts are quite different.'[7]

'The baboons were gibbering as he passed. Pete recalled some of Mr Propter's remarks about literature. About the wearisomeness, to an adult mind, of all those merely descriptive plays and novels which critics expected one to admire. All the innumerable, interminable anecdotes and romances and character-studies, but no general theory of anecdotes, no explanatory hypothesis of romance or character. Just a huge collection of facts about lust and greed, fear and ambition, duty and affection; just facts, and imaginary facts at that, with no co-ordinating philosophy superior to common sense and the local system of conventions, no principle of arrangement more rational than simple aesthetic expediency. And then the astonishing nonsense talked by those who undertake to elucidate and explain this hodge-podge of prettily patterned facts and fancies!'[8]

' "Oddly enough, the closest to reality are always the fictions that are supposed to be the least true." He leaned over and touched the back of a battered copy of *The Brothers Karamazov*. "It makes so little sense that it's almost real".'[9]

'Thought is crude, matter unimaginably subtle. Words are few and can only be arranged in certain conventionally fixed ways; the counterpoint of unique events is infinitely wide and their succession indefinitely long. That the purified language of science, or even the richer purified language of literature should ever be adequate to the givenness of the world and our experience is, in the very nature of things, impossible. Cheerfully accepting the fact, let us advance together, men of letters and men of science, further and further into the ever expanding regions of the unknown.'[10]

The first three of these passages present the thoughts or words of a fictional character, but in each instance Huxley is expressing his own concern. Mark Staithes in *Eyeless in Gaza* complains that even *Anna Karenina* is a falsification of life; Mr Propter in *After Many a Summer* wants explanation rather than description, and Rivers in *The Genius and the Goddess* finds *The Brothers Kara-*

mazov 'almost real' because—he alleges—it fails to make sense. But in his remarks in *Literature and Science* Huxley seems happily to accept that literature is a striving (never wholly successful) to match words to experience. On the one hand there is Huxley the man of science or systematic philosopher, who seeks certainties, and on the other there is Huxley the artist for whom, in Keats's words, there is no 'irritable reaching after fact and reason'.[11]

One peculiarity of Huxley's fiction is the combination of the aims of the generalizing philosopher and the artist. He normally causes his language, his characters, his plots, his structures to signify richly rather than attempt to reproduce the exact multifariousness of personal experience. Particulars of persons, emotions, situations are often presented very clearly, but used (implicitly or explicitly) to illustrate generalities. Thus, the words of Mark Staithes in the above passage are part of a growing portrait of an individual, while they also constitute one of Huxley's ways of including in a work of literature some acknowledgement of the irrelevant physiological events and small daily distractions whose usual absence from literature he is regretting. Similarly, Rivers's assertion that *The Brothers Karamazov* 'makes so little sense that it's almost real' is part of a literary context whose object is to demonstrate the senselessness of life. Negative capability and positive capability conduct in Huxley's novels a partnership that is more often fertile than destructive. His sense of beauty as a great—perhaps as an absolute—good often fashions but never misdirects his search for truth. Conversely, whenever his desire to pursue or propagate a truth seems to run away with him (as in the monologues of Mr Propter) there will always be found some kind of verbal and structural patterning that shows his inability to abandon beauty.

So far I have not completely avoided the danger of causing Huxley to resemble the 'zoological novelist' whom Philip Quarles thinks of placing in his projected novel. The next stage is to modify the picture by filling in detail and by mentioning other features of Huxley's art of fiction. First the aims and methods of his characterization need to be more fully described.

Certainly the characters in the novels, without exception, express attitudes to life so that the author can either show or, in some instances, investigate, the rightness or wrongness of the attitudes. But most of Huxley's people have a good deal of substance. Mark Staithes, for example, is a cynic put up against the pacifism of Dr Miller, and one of his functions is to anticipate the criticism which

Huxley in writing *Eyeless in Gaza* must have expected from sophisticated persons. But Mark is far more than a mere deliverer of sentiments : he is also a distinctive face and voice, the possessor of a family background, the performer of good deeds to an ex-servant and to obscure Mexican revolutionaries; above all he is a man who, with a mixture of stoicism, cynicism and quixotism, struggles through a jungle with a gangrenous knee and finally has a leg amputated without anaesthetics. Staithes is even a 'round' character in that he passes Forster's test of being 'capable of surprising in a convincing way',[12] for the transition from ill-behaved prep-school boy to Marxist undergraduate and thence to embittered middle-aged man is unexpected yet life-like and finally comprehensible.

But the characters of *Eyeless in Gaza* might be counted as exceptions, and it is probably true that Helen Ledwidge in that novel is the most rounded character that Huxley ever produced. What, then, of Mr Scogan, or Lilian Aldwinkle, or Mr Propter, or Vijaya MacPhail? Flat though they are (and Forster says that we must not be too hard on flatness, especially in comedy[13]), each has some degree of livingness; Scogan and Mrs Aldwinkle a rather high degree, Propter a lower degree, and Vijaya a lower still. Even Propter is more than a voice, and his voice, in any event, is neither undistinguished nor incredible; even Vijaya has a certain physical presence. But Propter and most of the figures in *Island* (though not Will Farnaby, the hero) constitute Huxley's worst efforts of characterization. The great majority of his characters are, admittedly, embodied attitudes, but attitudes so thoroughly embodied, so nicely placed in appropriate environments, so attached to persistent imagery, that, as with Dickens's characters (though to a lesser extent), they remain in the memory as distinct individuals. Whoever remembers Myra Viveash or Lucy Tantamount or Eustace Barnack mainly as attitudes to life has read the novels insensitively or perversely.

This point is worth emphasizing here only because in Huxley the composition and disposition of characters are features of form. The characters are figures in landscapes, aesthetic components as well as arguments. Both major and minor characters have—quite realistically—clear features and accoutrements which bear out their natures, but, since they are for the most part comic figures (figures, that is to say, conceived in a comic mode even when they are not actually funny), they continually voice characteristic sentiments, and lack both inconsistency and the less obviously revealing surface of real-life conversation. Just as Dickens's Bounderby, for instance, is forever the 'bully of humility', except when his past is finally disclosed, Huxley's Jo Stoyte is forever blustering, domineering, possessive, except when he finally falls into Obispo's clutches. Of course, Huxley needed to include a high proportion of people who are wittily eloquent about their characterizing ideas, but this need does not seem to have imposed so severe a limitation as Huxley himself imagined. He has Philip Quarles state that the novel of ideas must exclude 'all but about ·01 per cent of the human race',[14] but in practice Huxley's own novels of ideas include a large number of people whose ideas are scarcely more developed than those of numerous unintellectual people in Dickens.

Huxley's techniques of characterization should not be called 'caricature', even if we are prepared to think tolerantly of caricature, because he should be compared not to a cartoonist but to a painter who discerns the stem of a sitter's nature (the ruling passion of avarice, voluptuousness, benevolence, urge to power) and 'brings out' that stem in his portrait, while never seriously perverting the features. The figure 'in the painting', so to speak, is also given the right clothes, placed against the right background, caused to hold the right, disclosing gesture. Thus, Lucy Tantamount is partly made up of the 'tricolor' effect of white face, scarlet mouth, and blue circles around the eyes, the whiff of gardenias, the attachment to Tantamount House, Sbisa's restaurant and the Quai Voltaire. Likewise, Jo Stoyte is partly composed of the barrel figure, the bellowing voice, the castellated house and the absurd, grandiose cemetery. We see most of Huxley's characters, in fact we apprehend them sensuously, and their traits are made plain to us in one way or another, but only secondarily—if at all—do we share their moments of consciousness. The distinction must be clearly appreciated: there are many occasions on which a character's train of thought is given, but in most instances he or she is 'seen' thinking, 'seen' feeling, so that the thoughts and the emotions remain part of a vivid pattern rather than experiences intimately shared. In this way we observe Denis Stone standing on the parapet at Crome and thinking of suicide; in this way we perceive Sebastian Barnack's chagrin over the missing Degas.

It might be objected that, except for purposes of broad comedy, such a procedure is inappropriate to the modern consciousness, that it belongs to the ages in which the minutiae and the fluidity of consciousness had not been acknowledged (or perhaps had not come into being). But it is Huxley who, through the medium of Anthony Beavis's diary, expatiates on the disappearance in modern times of the old clear-cut personality.

'It was left to Blake [writes Anthony] to rationalize psychological atomism into a philosophical system. Man, according to Blake (and, after him, according to Proust, according to Lawrence), is simply a succession of states. Good and evil can be predicated only of states, not of individuals, who in fact don't exist, except as the places where the states occur. It is the end of personality in the old sense of the word.'[15]

The fact that Huxley's own people are personalities 'in the old sense of the word' is again a feature of the curious amalgam of the ways of science (or philosophy) and art. Huxley was interested in the classification of human beings, in the Galtonian, Jungian and Sheldonian categories especially, and he was keenly interested in the broad highways of response to experience. He regularly portrayed hedonists, for example, or cynics, because he wished to question the validity of their responses. Thus, while knowing all about the modern, 'atomized' personality, he yet tended to portray the contours of an individual's consciousness, and to align these contours with physical features, as if he believed that such a procedure is perfectly proper to a work of art, especially when that work includes mention of the true complexity of consciousness. It is safe to say that Huxley knew more about post-Bergson notions of the mind and more about the later developments of scientific psychology than most modern authors, but he did not regard such knowledge as necessarily replacing knowledge gained from the old, unprofessional psychologists, and all was grist to his mill. The evidence suggests (particularly the evidence of the *Letters*) that the formation of Huxley's characters often started with observation of life, after which it was assisted by the author's fascinated musings and sometimes by his recollections of similar traits as portrayed in earlier imaginative literature and as discussed by a psychologist-philosopher such as Pascal, La Rochefoucauld, Fénélon or Newman. The result is commonly an accurate picture which, in lacking naturalistic expansiveness, satisfies the needs both of the generalizing philosopher and of the aesthete.

So the characters are observed and understood. But they are also disposed in patterns which take rise less from narrative or from inner growth than is common with good novelists. Huxley stands at a great remove from, say, George Eliot, in her portrayal of the growing Maggie Tulliver, or, on the other hand, from Dumas, in whose works the wonderful narrative lines largely dictate the patterns. In Huxley both story and characters can be distinguished from the structure. This has always been seen to be true of *Point Counter Point* and *Eyeless in Gaza*, both of which novels people have found it possible to discuss with only subordinate reference either to the characters or to the actions. However, all Huxley's other novels are similarly, though less obtrusively, devised. In every instance the structure, or arrangement, is not a crude imposition but an appropriate complex intimately connected at every turn with its components (which is not to say that the connections are always faultless).

Enough has been said about Huxley's art of characterization to show that the characters are not inclined to smudge, through minute mirrorings of nature, the lines of the patterns. The basis (though not, of course, the whole) of the method is that a character is 'caught' in a series of 'attitudes', many of which are explained by the author. An 'attitude' may be a piece of conversation, a physical action, or even a train of thought, but it possesses a clarity of definition which prevents any blurring of the design of which it forms a part. For instance, it would be possible to take Burlap in *Point Counter Point* as a melody forming part of a larger theme, and to trace the comings and goings of the Burlap melody with the result of knowing more about what Huxley means by Burlap and, indeed, about the meaning of the whole novel.

The 'attitudes' of the characters naturally help to compose the narratives, but the narratives are sometimes susceptible of contemplation in their own right, rather as in a parable or *exemplum*. This is especially true of the stories of the novels from *After Many a Summer* onwards, and while it is certain that Huxley would have derided woodenly earnest contemplation (after the manner of Jane Austen's Mary Bennet, who read great books and made extracts), it is certain that he hoped we would pay due attention to his parables. However, the narratives, like the characters, contribute to structures which are aesthetic as well as moralistic in an uncommon way. In *Island*—to take the extreme example—where the action is feeble and the moralizing ubiquitous, a reader misses much if he fails to absorb, not only the beauty of the settings, but also the movement of the story-line towards an ecstatic climax.

Since in Huxley (as in Joyce, who also had poor eyesight) so much is 'seen', it follows that the ideas are modified by the pictorial images; and both are modified in turn by the larger designs. Therefore, examination of the architecture of any of the novels helps us to understand Huxley's frame of mind at the time of writing.

Consideration of the style in each of the novels also reveals the underlying nature of the author's preoccupations. Amid the constant features of Huxley's use of language there are marked local differences, and these differences arise not from dilettante experimentation but from the need to express changing apprehensions of the world.

Obviously Huxley was very sensitive to words, having in his younger days the enthusiasm for verbal beauty which he gives to Denis Stone in *Crome Yellow*, but there is no evidence that he reflected much upon his style or took great pains over it. Sometimes, indeed, as Cyril Connolly has convincingly demonstrated, he was careless.[16] It does not seem that—after his adolescence, at all events—he paid much deliberate attention to his manner of writing, and it is most unlikely that on conceiving a novel he consciously formed a style for it as he more or less consciously formed a structure. On the contrary, the diction and rhythms emerged involuntarily as a result of the particular attitudes which, at any given moment, he was constrained to formulate.

In the ensuing chapters of this study I select for analysis aspects of the language of a novel when the aspects are peculiar and revealing. In this way it becomes possible to define the difference in mood between *Crome Yellow* and *Antic Hay*, to see more clearly the effect of the variety of styles in *Those Barren Leaves*, to understand what has been gained by the verbal tricks of *Brave New World* and *Ape and Essence*.

Sometimes I approximate to the approach of R. P. Blackmur in his *Language as Gesture*. In Blackmur's terminology, 'gesture' is 'the outward and dramatic play of inward and imaged meaning',[17] so that what one is after, when looking at language in such a way, are the implicit elements in even the most explicit statements. The writer has adopted a certain 'stance' in relation to his material and this 'stance', which is often not identical with the propositions on the page, is what has to be defined. Not surprisingly, an examination of certain peculiar features of the language in a novel by Huxley throws further light upon the architecture of the novel, and examination of the architecture helps us to understand more fully the 'stance' represented by the language. By such means 'inward and imaged meaning' is brought nearer to the surface.

Part One

NOVELS OF EXPLORATION

Seeking Reconciliation of
the Absolute and the Relative

Crome Yellow (1921)
Antic Hay (1923)
Those Barren Leaves (1925)
Point Counter Point (1928)
Brave New World (1932)
Eyeless in Gaza (1936)

I

Crome Yellow (1921)

Since *Crome Yellow* invites comparison with some of the novels of Peacock, it will be interesting and useful to consider as we proceed with our study how Peacockian it is in formal structure, style, and attitude.[1]

Mr J. B. Priestley has noted—in addition to the obvious features of country-house settings and gatherings of conversationalists—two characteristics germane to our purpose of Peacock's 'novels of talk', as opposed to the 'tales', *Maid Marian* and *The Misfortunes of Elphin*. He points out that lovers' relationships are treated flippantly, but in the last two novels 'with a certain seriousness, romantic zest, in spite of their droll setting'.[2] Mr Priestley mentions also the 'Arcadian countrysides and wildly romantic solitudes'[3] which surround both lovers and conversationalists. This background, he asserts, 'gives us a sketch of what ought to go on in the world, of the author's ideal realm'.[4]

Of the observations made by Mr Priestley these are the ones which will be shown to have a bearing on the nature of Huxley's first novel. Another observation which, for the present purpose, should be made is that one of Peacock's idiosyncracies (though it is not equally a feature of all the 'novels of talk') lies in the absence of direct links between narrative and argumentation. *Crotchet Castle*, for example, contains blocks of chapters in which Crotchet's guests eat, drink, and debate, and other blocks in which a love-affair develops. One would guess, however, that readers of this novel who have no overriding preference for 'organic form' scarcely notice the disjunction, because there is unity of theme of which a principle vehicle is the author's voice. There is a predominating voice, characterized by Shelley as having 'lightness, chastity, and strength'[5] : only the tone varies.

In these ways there are rough similarities between *Crome Yellow* and some of Peacock's works. We shall see that Huxley too uses scenery to express a positive value; and we shall be concerned partly with the formal and stylistic features of *Crome Yellow* which secure an alliance—as in Peacock—between a love-relationship and a good deal of seemingly irrelevant talk. It will be necessary to investigate how Huxley welds together, among other matters, the portrait of a young sensitive, the talk of Mr Scogan, the inanities of some of the guests, the 'digressive' chapters from the 'History of Crome', and, after that, to define what kind of a work the welding has produced. I hope to show that the result is, as for instance with *Crotchet Castle*, a kind of 'stance', but one both less assured and more subtly comprehensive than Peacock's.

An elementary step in analysing the form of *Crome Yellow* is to note the arrangement of the chapters. About this arrangement Alexander Henderson has made the following remarks :

'The construction of *Crome Yellow* is of considerable interest. The story of Denis and Anne, played out against a country-house background, is advanced by the most simple events—a meeting after breakfast, a fall in the dark, dancing to a pianola, a sitting for a portrait—the everyday incidents of a country household in the summer.

'Diversifying this story, which we may call the main tune, are a variety of events of different kinds which at intervals interrupt the principal theme. The book is, as it were, a composition in rondo form. That is, if A represents the main tune, and the other letters of the alphabet the other themes, the construction is of the kind : A, B, C, A, D, etc.

'The B, C, D tunes are represented by the speculative discourses of Mr Scogan on a wide selection of topics, by the arrival and departure at Crome of other visitors, Mr Barbecue-Smith and Ivor Lombard, by Mr Bodiham, the parson, and the supremely comic sermon on 'knops', by the two self-contained stories related by Mr Wimbush about his ancestors, and finally, by Crome Fair.'[6]

'Composition in rondo form' is an apt description, but the scheme has not the straightforwardness (and the monotony) which Alexander Henderson's alphabetical illustration suggests. First, it is Denis's state of mind that Huxley is interested in rather than the mere sequence of events in his relationship with Anne Wimbush. A portrait of Denis, therefore, should properly be taken to be the principal theme. He is at least present in twenty-five out of the thirty chapters, and while only ten of these in some fashion advance the story of his relationship with Anne, a few of the remainder reinforce our insights into his nature. Chapter Twenty, for instance, includes an amusing anecdotal discourse by Denis on the nature of words. It seems to be a digression from the principal theme, but, since it illustrates an aspect of Denis's nature by no means irrelevant to his failure with Anne, it is not entirely digressive. A yet clearer example is Chapter Twenty-six whose scene is Crome Fair, but in fact it is also, and more importantly, an account of Denis's reactions to Crome Fair.

If we try to classify the chapters according to whether or not they further the principal theme (I am still using this term in a 'musical' rather than a literary sense), we note at once that there are twelve chapters suitably spaced throughout the novel in which events are chiefly seen through the eyes of Denis Stone, or which otherwise portray his consciousness. The story of Denis is unfolded fairly elaborately in the first four chapters, since Huxley's purpose makes it initially necessary for the reader to become well acquainted with the protagonist (and while doing so to meet most of the other characters and to absorb the setting). This is not in the least the kind of novel whose fascination lies in a gradual discovery of a character's true nature, and it contains many sections in which the hero will be either off stage or in the background. Chapters Ten and Seventeen each contain important incidents in the narrative of Denis's relationship with Anne : the first comprises the dancing scene, in which Denis is the wallflower, and the second includes Anne's fall in the dark, responded to by Denis with characteristic ineffectualness. These two chapters are placed in appropriate positions, a third and about a half of the way through the novel, to keep alive the reader's interest in the principal theme. Chapters Twenty-three and Twenty-four are correctly placed to prepare for the climax of Denis's story, since the first of them contains his declaration of love, received by Anne with some perturbation but no evident enthusiasm, and the second includes his discovery of Jenny Mullion's notebook, and the consequent realization that one is a spectacle to others. The climax occurs in Chapter Twenty-nine in which Denis thinks of suicide. His desperation properly forms the subject of the penultimate chapter, as following digressions, broadly humorous or not, would impair the delicately achieved tone of the novel. There is nothing left for Denis to do in the final chapter but leave.

Those chapters which present what Alexander Henderson calls the 'B, C, D tunes' are themselves skilfully varied. Minor speculative discourses by Mr Scogan and others occur in many chapters, sometimes juxtaposed with events in the story of Denis. In one instance, such a discourse forms part of an event in the principal theme : in Chapter Four Denis speaks eloquently to Anne on the subject of the disparity between ideas and experience. The major discourses which occupy whole chapters or substantial parts of them occur only at intervals. The entire topic of the fourteenth chapter is the 'Tales of Knockespotch' and other imaginary books, while that of Chapter Sixteen is the characters of the first six Caesars as touchstones of human types. Almost the whole of Chapter Twenty is given over to Denis talking about the nature of words; Chapter Twenty-two presents Mr Scogan on the Rational State, and a major part of Chapter Twenty-eight consists of Henry Wimbush disclosing his preference for literature over life.

Another category of chapters forms part of the 'B, C, D tunes' : these are the chapters whose contents are yet further removed from the principal theme, in that the guests at Crome have nothing to do with them except, in some instances, by being members of an audience. I refer, of course, to the two sermons by Mr Bodiham in Chapters Nine and Eighteen; to the extracts from the 'History of Crome', which are properly apart from each other (in Chapters Thirteen and Nineteen) and differ markedly in tone; and, one might add without much distortion, Mr Wimbush's account in Chapter Eleven of the Crome privies.[7]

It is clear that Huxley's aim in the arrangement of chapters was to secure the greatest possible variety, and it is worth noting that to the same end he spaced out the more spectacular scenes, and the arrival and departure of extra guests, while striving to ensure that every chapter should be almost self-containedly of interest. It is not a gross exaggeration to say that *Crome Yellow* is a series of anecdotes, short stories, vignettes and embryonic essays by various means fused into a whole. It seems that Huxley, displaying great literary tact and awareness of his capacities in his mid-twenties, moved smoothly into the form of the novel by utilizing his talents for poetry (four volumes of verse had earlier been published), for the short story (*Limbo* came out in the previous year, 1920), and for the essay, the anecdote and the adaptation of sources.[8]

26

Even those chapters which would seem to demand a different treatment, those telling the story of Denis, often reach a high degree of independence. It is not part of Huxley's purpose to cause the reader to long to know what will happen 'in our next'. Thus, while the first chapter is an introduction of an orthodox kind to Denis, the second, while enlarging on the hero's nature, is primarily an entertaining portrait of another character, Priscilla Wimbush.[9] The third chapter is again more orthodoxly part of a continuing narrative, since it consists of an introduction to several of the guests and informs the reader of Denis's interest in Anne. But Chapter Four, while it develops the main theme, also conveys the rudiments of an essay on a fundamental Huxleyan topic of the disparity between experience and all modes of communicating it.

The pattern of linked independence is to be discerned in several of those other chapters which are chiefly about Denis Stone. It is quite easy, for instance, to imagine Chapters Ten and Twenty-four being removed from this novel, and, with no considerable amount of alteration and linkage, emerging as a short story. In the first of these chapters Denis forlornly watches Anne dancing with Gombauld, and at the same time Jenny Mullion seemingly scribbles in her red notebook : in the second Denis sees the cartoon of the scene which Jenny drew. The combined chapters would make a typical Huxley story; one indeed not unlike 'The Gioconda Smile', the chief element of which is likewise the inscrutable but apparently empty-headed woman who in fact understands the intellectual far more shrewdly than he supposes she does. Similarly, Chapter Seventeen, which is concerned with Denis's failure and Ivor Lombard's success in the gardens of Crome at night, has a unitary quality, as have, taken *en bloc*, some of the concluding chapters whose setting is the fair and its aftermath.

If this self-containedness is perceptible in chapters recounting the story of Denis, how much more clearly can it be seen in the 'B, C, D tunes'. The sketch of Mr Barbecue-Smith in Chapter Six could appear almost inviolate in a magazine (whose regular contributors were not Barbecue-Smiths), while the relationship between Mary Bracegirdle and Ivor Lombard is similarly almost a complete story in itself. Likewise the tête-à-tête between Anne and Mary in Chapter Seven could be regarded as a whole vignette. The sermons of Mr Bodiham are of course total entities; the story of Sir Hercules Lapith has in fact been separately published,[10] and several of the discourses by Mr Scogan, Henry Wimbush, and Denis are basic material for essays. It is in Chapter Five that Mr Scogan predicts aspects of a Brave-New-World society ('In vast state incubators, rows upon rows of gravid bottles will supply the world with the population it requires.'—p. 31); while the other point of this same chapter is merely the telling of a good, and separable, joke: Rowley the labourer's remark, 'Rightly is they called pigs' (p. 29).

So far I have merely drawn attention to the skilful diversification of material in *Crome Yellow*: it is now time to begin considering how homogeneity is established.

At least one critic has been impressed by a pervasive tone.

'Real and yet somehow unreal, somehow a fairy story, a bucolic idyll, *Crome Yellow* haunts the memory like a sunlit wall of peaches seen in childhood, rich with the nostalgic memories of bygone summers. Like the opulent colour of its title, *Crome Yellow* is all of cream and gold.'[11]

What Mr Henderson here attempts to describe is at most only an element in the tone of the novel, but, as I hope to show, he is right to realize that *Crome Yellow* must be grasped, more than is the case with other novels by Huxley, as a kind of embodied mood. The complexities of this mood are what have to be defined.

The conspicuous strand is irony, which is not quite omnipresent, and which varies in depth. One extreme, certainly, is the story of Sir Hercules in Chapter Thirteen, while the other may be represented by Mr Bodiham's sermon in Chapter Nine. The tale of Sir Hercules is a melancholy one whose intrinsic irony is mild and compassionate. But also, the tale is coloured by its surroundings, and urbanely told, so that the reader is aware that any sadness of his own is circumscribed, like the tale itself, by ironic comment. The tone of the whole tale is caught in the poem which Henry Wimbush reproduces in his 'History' as a specimen of Sir Hercules' talents. The theme of this poem is that Man (in particular eighteenth-century man), though he vaunts his soulful qualities, in reality stands but midway between an ancient race of witless giants, and a race to come whose flesh will merely invest, without cloddish superfluity, the soul. Thus Sir Hercules goes some way towards anticipating *Back to Methuselah*, but since the poet is himself a dwarf of much spiritual refinement living in a callous period, the poem is compassionately ironic. It concludes:

'Sad is the fate of those, ah, sad indeed,
The rare precursors of the nobler breed!

Who come man's golden glory to foretell,
But pointing Heav'nwards live themselves in Hell.' (p. 87)[12]

At the other end of the scale Mr Bodiham's sermon is simply funny, an *exposé* of the mind of a parson who aims his sermons towards the satisfaction of his emotions, and is now gloomy because his gloating prediction of Armageddon has not been fulfilled.

I have asserted that irony, though it predominates, is not to be found everywhere, and this fact gives us a direction in which we might look for a definition of the mood of the novel. Most of what happens is absurd and most of the characters have absurd habitual attitudes. There is no need to emphasize Priscilla Wimbush's astrology, Barbecue-Smith's automatic writing, or the dietary habits of the Lapith sisters, but it should be pointed out that very few characters totally escape ridicule. Even Mr Scogan, himself a great mocker, is found to be a compulsive talker.[13]

'In the hall he [Denis] saw Mr Scogan; the man seemed to be lying in wait. Denis tried to escape, but in vain. Mr Scogan's eye glittered like the eye of the Ancient Mariner.' (p. 160)

Ivor Lombard too, though accomplished in many arts, including that of love, is so plainly presented as dilettante and exhibitionistic that he is not to be taken seriously. Huxley comments with reference to Ivor's playing of the piano: 'Small details matter little so long as the general effect is good.' (p. 113)

Gombauld is an interesting case in that, so far as I can discern, he is presented unironically. There is no hint that his striving after the production of a great picture is anything other than the healthy impulse of a sincere and talented artist. He wishes 'to combine prodigious realism with prodigious simplification' (p. 75)[14] and this is seen as a praiseworthy objective, unlike the magniloquent aspirations (unmatched with talent) of Casimir Lypiatt in *Antic Hay*. And yet in the context of this novel Gombauld's very strivings bear by implication at least a hint of absurdity.

Leaving aside the patently silly or inadequate people (Jenny Mullion for all her shrewdness belongs to the latter category), we are left with Henry Wimbush and Anne Wimbush. Henry, who according to Cyril Connolly 'bears a resemblance to Sir George Sitwell'[15] is too unengaged, too withdrawn to be impressive. 'How gay and delightful [he says to Denis] life would be if one could get rid of all the human contacts!'

Anne Wimbush alone seems wholly integrated, the Complete Woman, and yet her personality is not very remarkable. Her conversation lacks the wit and verve of that of Peacock's Clarinda. Nevertheless, she is without the tendency, which afflicts every other character, to wish that things were otherwise. Anne is that perhaps rare creature, the successful hedonist. The first important conversation between Anne and Denis is a central one for the entire novel.

' "I've always taken things as they come," said Anne. "It seems so obvious. One enjoys the pleasant things, avoids the nasty ones. There's nothing more to be said."

' "Nothing—for you. But, then, you were born a pagan; I am trying laboriously to make myself one. I can take nothing for granted, I can enjoy nothing as it comes along. Beauty, pleasure, art, women—I have to invent an excuse, a justification for everything that's delightful. Otherwise I can't enjoy it with an easy conscience. I make up a little story about beauty and pretend that it has something to do with truth and goodness. I have to say that art is the process by which one reconstructs the divine reality out of chaos. Pleasure is one of the mystical roads to union with the infinite—the ecstasies of drinking, dancing, love-making. As for women, I am perpetually assuring myself that they're the broad highway to divinity. And to think that I'm only just beginning to see through the silliness of the whole thing! It's incredible to me that anyone should have escaped these horrors." ' (p. 25)

Anne, says Denis, was 'born a pagan', and the representation of her in a youthful period in her life, for two uneventful weeks only, does not permit Huxley to explore her apparent paganism. His later sirens all pay some price in their search for unalloyed pleasure, and Anne's momentary irritation with Gombauld, when in Chapter Twenty-one he accuses her of flirting with Denis, suggests that her self-knowledge is incomplete. But, that moment apart, she seems so much in harmony with herself and with nature that irony has no target. We are encouraged to assume that it would not trouble Anne to find evidence that one is an object to others; the intelligent strivings of a Gombauld, as much as the self-delusions of a Barbecue-Smith, would seem to her pointless. For the most part this novel is about people or things in some sense affronting nature. Crome itself, says Mr Scogan approvingly, 'makes no compromise with nature, but affronts it and rebels against it' (p. 68)[16]; and in subservience to fashion, the pursuit of verbal felicities, disengagement, nearly all the characters do the same. Nature, beneath constantly summery skies, is seen as flawless, so that only man provides discord. It is at this point that we can see fully the quality of Huxley's irony. It consists in effect of saying: 'Here is the reality; here is the falsehood; and how richly absurd, but also how sad, that there should be a discrepancy.' It is important not to miss the note of regret.

There is a moment towards the end of the novel when Denis, through whose consciousness the theme of discordance is principally conveyed, has a rare, childlike vision.

'Denis peeped at them discreetly from the window of the morning-room. His eyes were suddenly become innocent, childlike, unprejudiced. They seemed, these people, inconceivably fantastic. And yet they really existed, they functioned by themselves, they were conscious, they had minds. Moreover, he was like them. Could one believe it? But the evidence of the red notebook was conclusive.' (p. 188)

This passage (which faintly anticipates much and in particular *The Doors of Perception*[17]) occurs at a point when Denis is hanging back from the clamour of Crome Fair and entertaining a conceit to the effect that his soul is a virginal membrane. But despite this preciosity, perhaps because of it, his perception becomes clear, the usual agents of refraction—reasoning, the search for words, self-consciousness—no longer operating. This is only a step towards that state in which irony, hilarious or regretful, would have no function, but it hints at the underlying reason why *Crome Yellow* is not merely amusing.

These observations are born out and subtilized by examination of Huxley's language whose very evenness, as we shall see, offsets the discordances which it frequently describes. Sometimes, however, the language is evoking conditions of harmony and stability, and it is this function which I propose to deal with first.

Crome is probably to be thought of as situated in Oxfordshire. The house, standing amid gently curving hills, may 'affront nature' but to modern eyes it does not jar with the landscape. We learn that monastic buildings once occupied the site, and that the swimming pool of Crome was once the monks' fish-pond. In fact there are several minor references to the history of Crome as well as the elaborate accounts of that history given by Henry Wimbush. The 'historical-pastoral' backcloth composed of such items as these, and of the several more sharply-focused settings (particularly those in the gardens of Crome), evokes the traditional and the serene. Of course Huxley intends no glib contrast between past and present (the past, as we can tell from the 'History of Crome' alone, is just as susceptible to Huxley's irony as the present) : he merely stages his characters amid scenery which seems enduring and manageable. It is true, if pedantic, to say that this scenery is more 'Arcadian', more reminiscent of Sidney's work, than the Peacockian countryside which Mr Priestley so describes, for Peacock preferred crags and glens. But the function of the landscape is reasonably alike in both authors : that is, to contrast Nature with fallacious human attitudes.

Also even and harmonious is the weather. When we have noted the numerous references to sunshine and its concomitants—white flannel trousers, tea on the lawn, the scent of lavender, evening shadows on the corn—and have likewise observed the details of our sense of background decorum—'sculptured yew trees', 'July borders', the Crome dining room, 'solidly, portwinily English'—we have partly explained Alexander Henderson's apprehension of the novel as 'rich with the nostalgic memories of bygone summers'. However, the important effect to notice is that of a richly-coloured painting in which human posturings, rather ludicrous, are depicted against a somewhat formal landscape.

But the landscape and the posturings are regularly rendered in language that is both decorous and exact. It is not fanciful to suppose that the procedure of Denis Stone is like Huxley's own, and when Denis searches for words that will describe the hills around Crome we are shown that he will be dismayed if the accurate word is not also a euphonious one. Both elements, I suggest, were as necessary to Huxley himself at this stage of his career as they are to his hero. Denis, we are told, 'was enamoured with the beauty of words' (p. 4), and this was surely true of the author. But beauty cannot be allowed to shoulder accuracy aside, and what happens repeatedly in *Crome Yellow* is that keen perceptions of people and places are expressed in felicitous terms.

'That part of the garden that sloped down from the foot of the terrace to the pool had a beauty which did not depend on colour so much as on forms. It was as beautiful by moonlight as in the sun. The silver of water, the dark shapes of yew and ilex trees remained, at all hours and seasons, the dominant features of the scene. It was a landscape in black and white. For colour there was the flower-garden; it lay to one side of the pool, separated from it by a huge Babylonian wall of yews. You passed through a tunnel in the hedge, you opened a wicket in a wall, and you found yourself, startlingly and suddenly, in the world of colour. The July borders blazed and flared under the sun. Within its high brick walls the garden was like a great tank of warmth and perfume and colour.' (p. 22f)

The passage expresses the vision of a representational painter who, obliterating his own concerns, can be undistortedly aware of appearances. And if there is a quality of detachment in the initial observation, this quality is enhanced by the unobtrusively formal arrangement of the sentences. Thus the paragraph is divided almost exactly into two contrasting halves, the first dealing with the cloistral scene on the one side of the yew-trees, and the second describing the walled flower-garden on the other side. The first four sentences depict a scene of black and white; the second four are concerned with brilliant colours. The main feature of the scene described in the first half of the passage is one that perhaps nearly everyone in such a situation would dimly notice, the contrast between silver water and dark yew trees, but not everyone finds such observation at the forefront of his consciousness; and this contrast is repeated, but with much elegant variation, in the second, third and fourth sentences. There is emphasis without monotony. And then, having learned in the fifth sentence about the flower-garden, we are led to it as a visitor would be, via the wicket and the tunnel, led from an apprehension of coolness and shade into one of fragrance and warmth; and the colourful garden is used, appropriately, as the setting for Denis's regrets that he was not 'born a pagan'. The passage also illustrates Huxley's concern for rhythm and one of the methods he habitually uses to achieve it, namely parenthesis in the middle of a sentence : 'at all hours and seasons'; 'startlingly and suddenly'.

With this representative passage in mind it is interesting to note some remarks of Sir Kenneth Clark.

'Should we say that Aldous's gift of perception was not so much a matter of eye, as part of a general sensibility to all forms of orderly or impassioned communication—what used to be called a strong aesthetic sense . . . However, I think that his powers of visual understanding were exceptional, and in support of this I would quote the descriptions in some of his early books.'[18]

In the same connection we might note that Sir Julian Huxley has said of his brother : 'As a child, he spent a good deal of his time just sitting quietly, contemplating the strangeness of things.'[19]

The phrase, 'strangeness of things', should perhaps be taken to include people, for often in the novel we find the characters being presented with a curious perceptive detachment. They are contemplated too, with acuteness, as things seen, and then offered to the reader in precise terms. Here is the most noteworthy example from *Crome Yellow*.

'Next to Mary a small gaunt man was sitting, rigid and erect in his chair. In appearance Mr Scogan was like one of those extinct bird-lizards of the Tertiary. His nose was beaked, his dark eye had the shining quickness of a robin's. But there was nothing soft or gracious or feathery about him. The skin of his wrinkled brown face had a dry and scaly look; his hands were the hands of a crocodile. His movements were marked by the lizard's disconcertingly abrupt clockwork speed; his speech was thin, fluty, and dry. Henry Wimbush's schoolfellow and exact contemporary, Mr Scogan looked far older and, at the same time, far more youthfully alive than did that gentle aristocrat with the face like a grey bowler.' (p. 14f)

This is a fanciful description whether or not Mr Scogan's appearance was based on that of an actual person (in looks he is like Bertrand Russell) but what needs to be noticed is the skill with which the character is presented for the reader's inspection. Scogan's resemblance to a 'bird-lizard' is made vivid not only by the repeated mention of dry, hard features, but also by the mere sounds of most of the passage. For the words in all but the last sentence are predominantly hard rather than flowing, while most of the sentences are either brief or otherwise of abrupt rhythm. Thus, the third, fifth and sixth sentences contain marked caesurae, giving something of the impression of 'abrupt clockwork speed'. It is in respect of sound that the very name, Scogan, admirably fits the appearance and nature of its owner. (Huxley repeatedly shows skill in naming.) For, of course, Scogan—like all Huxley's characters—is what he looks: he is an unyielding little man, resistant to Nature. While Denis, who is Nature's victim, wilts in concentrated sunlight, and Anne, Nature's accomplice, is a 'Hamadryad in white muslin' (p. 22), Mr Scogan chooses an alley of lavender bushes in which to discourse stubbornly on the Rational State.

Most of the characters are presented in a similar way, though less elaborately. There is, initially, a neat description of aspects of their appearances which indicate behaviour and attitude. Thus, Henry Wimbush always wears a grey bowler and his face is 'unageing, calm, serenely without expression' (p. 14), Mary Bracegirdle's face shows 'serious, moon-like innocence' (p. 14) and Gombauld is a 'black-haired young corsair of thirty, with flashing teeth and luminous large dark eyes' (p. 15).[20] As Huxley's descriptions of scenery are those of a landscape painter who happens also to be gifted in the use of words, so his presentations of people are such as might be produced by a painter of portraits who is adept at 'bringing out character'.

In a similar manner people are often discovered in or led to appropriate settings. At the opening of Chapter Seven, for instance, Anne is presented in a lusciously-decorated Venetian bed. (Enter to her Mary Bracegirdle for the purpose of discussing the dangers of sexual repression.) Sometimes the portrait is of a group each member of which is caught in characteristic pose. This is so at the opening of Chapter Three when Denis arrives to his host and fellow-guests who are having tea on the lawn. At this moment Henry Wimbush is dignifiedly pouring out tea; Jenny Mullion is smiling to herself; Scogan is sitting gauntly erect; Gombauld is vivaciously gesturing, and Anne is lolling amusedly in a deck-chair.

The detached observation of such descriptive passages is often to be found even when Huxley is presenting states of mind. A natural result is the reader's disengagement from any emotions which are being described. But this is not always the case, or not always so to the same extent, for specially interesting about this aspect of the language of *Crome Yellow* are the fine gradations of emotional involvement which it invites. Here are two passages for comparison.

'Denis did not dance, but when ragtime came squirting out of the pianola in gushes of treacle and hot perfume, in jets of Bengal light, then things began to dance inside him. Little black nigger corpuscles jigged and drummed in his arteries. He became a cage of movement, a walking *palais de danse*. It was very uncomfortable, like the preliminary symptoms of a disease. He sat in one of the window-seats, glumly pretending to read.' (p. 63)

'Why had he climbed to this high, desolate place? Was it to look at the moon? Was it to commit suicide? As yet he hardly knew. Death —the tears came into his eyes when he thought of it. His misery assumed a certain solemnity; he was lifted up on the wings of a kind of exaltation. It was a mood in which he might have done almost anything, however foolish. He advanced towards the farther parapet; the drop there was sheer and uninterrupted. A good leap, and perhaps one might clear the narrow terrace and so crash down yet another thirty feet to the sun-baked ground below. He paused at the corner of the tower, looking now down into the shadowy gulf below, now up towards the rare stars and the waning moon. He made a gesture with his hand, muttered something, he could not afterwards remember what; but the fact that he had said it aloud gave the utterance a peculiarly terrible significance. Then he looked down once more into the depths.' (p. 210)

The effects of the ragtime music are amusingly labelled by metaphors, which, since they indicate rather than reproduce nature and value, should not be savoured. Admittedly the phrase, 'jigged and drummed', is straightforwardly apt to the subject, and 'cage of movement' is an accurately useful image, but the main effect is one of definition, excluding sympathy. The second passage comprises one of the least ironic accounts of a state of mind to be found in the novel. The language cursorily read seems uniform in tone, yet there is a subtle variation, for at times Huxley borders on solemnity and at other moments stops just short of an encouragement to smile. But at no time (if the passage is come upon rightly, in context) is the reader much agitated by Denis's plight. There is an interplay of great nicety between on the one hand diction which is both rather beautiful and rather plain (there is only one figure of speech), and on the other hand the absurdity, which is not laughable, of Denis's mood. The illogicality in such a situation of the tears and the exaltation is only implied, as is the falsity of assuming that the muttering bears a 'peculiarly terrible significance'. By employing such diction (consider especially, 'the rare stars and the waning moon') a lyric quality is given to Denis's egotism and self-dramatization. The result is that the hero's mood is understood to be absurd not so much on the ordinary fictional plane of personal psychology and social relations but rather *sub specie aeternitatis*—the scale of reference to which Huxley's mind frequently turns.

I have considered the means by which Huxley presents the appearance of his characters, and one element in his rendering of their thoughts. We have noticed how some detachment is maintained even when the subject is an emotional crisis on the part of the hero, so it is scarcely necessary to comment that on other occasions the language will cause us to view the people of Crome with the coldness proper to critical comedy. This effect is frequently achieved by a certain blandness in the author's remarks about a character or in his representation of a character's thought. The technique is practised at length when in Chapter Nine the sermon which Mr

Bodiham delivered in 1916 is reproduced in its hilariously malicious entirety.[21] After reading the sermon we learn of Mr Bodiham's present thoughts on the subject.

'The Chinese boycott of Japan, and the rivalries of that country and America in the Pacific, might be breeding a great new war in the East. The prospect, Mr Bodiham tried to assure himself, was hopeful; the real, the genuine Armageddon might soon begin, and then, like a thief in the night . . .' (p. 60)

These few lines represent Huxley's commonest practice (in all his fiction) whenever he wishes to convey the workings of a mind : he uses indirect speech, a usage limited in scope but most apt for hostile criticism.

It is also apt for presenting reflections of the connected sort that a certain character may be expected to have, as for instance those of Denis when, at the beginning of Chapter Two, he wanders through the ground floor rooms of Crome (though here, it seems, Huxley rapidly drops all pretence of seeing with Denis's eyes and gives simply a narrator's description). But on other occasions the effect is a loss of immediacy. In 1921 all the pre-Joycean techniques for rendering states of consciousness were to hand, but Huxley, quite clearly, had no use for them, preferring devices consonant with his own modes of thought. A result is that Huxley's evenness of manner is sustained, and ironic ambiguity of the sort which I am considering diminishes or disappears only when a thought which occurs to a character is intelligent enough to be approved of by the author.

So regularly is the bland manner present in this novel that vigilance is required in the reader to ensure that he avoids not so much the solemn perusing of jokes as the amused reading of something perfectly serious. It is interesting to compare in this respect the account in Chapter Twelve of Gombauld's artistic development and ambitions with the descriptive characterization of Ivor Lombard which occurs near the beginning of Chapter Seventeen. There is no irony present in those paragraphs (the second to the fifth of Chapter Twelve) devoted to Gombauld, though by this time there will probably be in the mind of an entranced reader a lingering, latent assumption that all human aspiration is suspect. On the other hand, the fourth paragraph of Chapter Seventeen in which Ivor's gifts are catalogued seems to begin quite seriously, and it is not until we are told that 'He was a good amateur medium and telepathist, and had a considerable first-hand knowledge of the next world' (p. 113) that we can be sure of Huxley's own estimate of his character.

Huxley's use of dialogue is a further means of characterization which is also used as a device for projecting the attitude of the author. *Crome Yellow* has been called a 'radiant conversation-piece', and in this respect, among others perhaps, reminiscent of the novels of Peacock.[22] But, unlike Peacock, Huxley usually attempts to individualize the speech-mannerisms of all his characters. Thus, Priscilla Wimbush speaks in short sentences, or a succession of spasmodic phrases and clauses, conveying rather mannish jollity, while the speech of Henry Wimbush is always as dignified as his person. The language of Mr Scogan's deliverances reinforces his attitudes, since its high degree of rational and grammatical organization expresses a conceptualizing mind which subordinates sensuous and emotive experience, so providing a bulwark against the chaos of nature, and, no doubt, against the expressions on the faces of his audience.

The highly intelligent Scogan, being aware—aggressively aware—of the discrepancy between his rationalism and the existing state of mankind, is not conspicuously a victim of Huxley's irony, but Scogan is diminished by the author (on the whole implicitly) precisely because of his confidence in the limited, dismissive, and—in Scogan's case—uncaring faculty of reason. It is as if Huxley were to agree with his creation that man's antics are absurd in the light of reason, but then to proceed where a Scogan could not or would not follow him in allowing that reasoning itself, in many contexts, is yet another antic.

The various fools of the novel are of course people who are not aware even on an elementary level of the differences which exist between their own attitudes and verifiable facts. This is true also of Sir Hercules Lapith, who is not a fool, but his good sense is assailed by emotional pressures of such strength and unavoidability that sympathy is demanded and tacitly given. Anne Wimbush and Gombauld seem complete, the first accepting and herself an ironist, the second with a reach possibly exceeding his grasp but under no illusions. Since our small glimpses into Anne's mind do not reassure us that her paganism is invulnerable, only Gombauld, a sensible artist, emerges unscathed.

From this point it is convenient to move into a definition of the 'stance' represented by *Crome Yellow*. The book is not in attitude especially Peacockian, however accurately some of its other features

38

may be so described. Contemporary reviewers showed no signs of finding anything other than light-hearted comedy in the novel; and so recent a critic as Angus Wilson, while sensing more in *Crome Yellow* than straightforward comedy, writes:

'... yet there is in these two books [*Crome Yellow* and *Those Barren Leaves*] an exultation, a sense of material pleasure in the natural world that irradiates the scene. They are, in a unique manner, idyllic, pastoral, bucolic.'[23]

I hope the truth of the first of these sentences has been sufficiently demonstrated, but the epithets in the second sentence do not seem very precise.

At the other extreme, D. S. Savage, in an attempt to prove the consistency of Huxley's response to human affairs, presents *Crome Yellow* not as a happy book to be contrasted with later 'gloomy' ones, but as displaying two unhappy themes: the first, 'the disparity of the ideal and the actual', and the second, 'a deliberate hedonism coupled with an underlying sense of personal futility'.[24]

These phrases, while pointing to qualities which are present in the novel, are not adequate. There certainly is in *Crome Yellow* an implication that man's activities are everywhere partial, discordant, unsusceptible to any unifying principle outside the realm of art. The pervasive irony with which this vision is expressed is absent from only one tiny portion of the novel, and that portion is about Gombauld's unfinished painting. It is the artistic product (for example, Caravaggio's 'Conversion of St Paul') that impresses, rather than its creator. As much later as *Eyeless in Gaza* Huxley writes: 'The fact that the Matthew Passion, for example, the Hammerklavier Sonata, had had human authors was a source of hope' (p. 311). The remark conveys the attitude of Mark Staithes, a cynic, but it is an attitude which Huxley himself seems once to have held. Art alone can be, and sometimes actually is, flawless, with its internal contradictions resolved in the pattern of the whole.

In writing *Crome Yellow* Huxley must have aimed at aesthetic perfection on a small scale. The book itself, so to speak, rather than anything in it (except for Gombauld's aspiration) is the positive answer. The mere absence of positive recommendations within the novel must have contributed to its liberating effect upon contemporary readers. It was possible, it seemed, to make perfection out of things themselves imperfect. The fact that Denis Stone is not a

'Little Percy', as Mr Scogan puts it in his scornful description of the usual novel of sensitive youth, is not, that is to say, an Ernest Pontifex, a Stephen Dedalus, a Paul Morel (to select just three names from the many variants who appeared in the twenty or thirty years before the publication of Huxley's novel), probably helped many people to feel that there was no further need to put such a high heroic construction upon exceptional sensibility.[25]

So far I have described what seems to be the fundamental position, but the final quality of the novel lies in the fact that the position is maintained precariously. The brand of pyrrhonism which, in *Point Counter Point*, Huxley attributes to Philip Quarles, is, in *Crome Yellow*, held by a kind of delicate strength against forces which are pulling in the direction of sympathy and partisanship—for Denis, for Sir Hercules.

'If there was any single way of life he could lastingly believe in, it was that mixture of pyrrhonism and stoicism which had struck him, an enquiring schoolboy among the philosophers, as the height of human wisdom and into whose mould of sceptical indifference he had poured his unimpassioned adolescence. Against the pyrrhonian suspense of judgment and the stoical imperturbability he had often rebelled. But had the rebellion ever been serious?' (p. 269f)

These remarks made about Philip Quarles may be used as a basis for comment on Huxley's attitude in *Crome Yellow*. The 'pyrrhonian suspense of judgment and the stoical imperturbability' are notably present, but so also is a kind of rebellion. Not indeed a rebellion in favour of some rival philosophy (as is the case with Philip Quarles), but rather a rebellion of temperament. A strain of melancholy is repressed by the intellectual high spirits; the summer mood is unbreached by forces to which, in its tenuousness, it nevertheless responds.

2

Antic Hay (1923)

The shape of *Antic Hay* suggests a diagram of futility, a wheel at whose still centre the hero cannot stay. Gumbril begins on the circumference, and the wheel is moving very slowly, a treadmill—for him—of teaching.[1] He is moved to a point near the centre from which he can glimpse, even shadowly experience, absolute serenity. And then he is sped back to the circumference of the wheel, which has now become a whirligig. But there is no intimation that Gumbril will ever return to the centre, for, as the novel ends, the taxi which he and Mrs Viveash have hired is about to continue its fruitless journey. It can be no accident that the chapters (Eleven to Thirteen) which are about ideals and the quiet places of the mind occupy almost the exact centre of the novel. Likewise the unexpectedness of the coming and going of these quiet places was presumably not due to an oversight on the author's part, since the chapters are surely intended to represent the arrival to Gumbril of a sort of grace. By formal means Huxley has imitated (though perhaps not deliberately) a characteristic of moments of spiritual illumination, which have often been described in literature (and in theological and psychological studies) as occurring unexpectedly.[2] Quite suddenly the reader, like Gumbril himself, is removed from the usual company and the usual environment. The actual streets of London give way to the ordered beauty of Gumbril Senior's model; Myra Viveash and Rosie Shearwater are replaced by Emily; harsh city noises are no longer heard while we are treated instead to description of Mozart's G minor Quintet and of the quiet of Kew Gardens, and, later, of Gumbril's rooms in Great Russell Street.

The model city depicts what might have been, and Gumbril's father prefaces his commentary on the model by asserting that Wren was not allowed to build a new, incomparably finer London simply because people prefer the familiar even if it is manifestly rotten. Habit, it seems, and lethargy rather than a wholehearted preference for moral and physical squalor are what perpetuate the squalor. The words of Gumbril's father are significant ones, for the entire novel demonstrates the conquest of reason, not by evil passions, but by trivial, unenjoyable habits. In particular, Gumbril is shortly to meet Emily and then weakly to lose her and remain with Myra Viveash. He will be the counterpart of an influential citizen of seventeenth-century London who, having been apprised of Wren's plans, lacked the controlled energy to ensure that the plans were carried out.[3] What Huxley through Gumbril Senior, is desiderating is not on the face of it an extravagant ideal. It does not entail asceticism; it involves not the abandonment of pleasure, but rather the fostering of enjoyment and the loss of joyless addictions. This is suggested by the fact that the model city includes a great variety of styles and shapes. The master-plan embraces the flow of fountains, the sharpness of spires and the square symmetry of official buildings. The colour and quality of the stone varies as do the shapes into which it is fashioned—black and marble elephants as well as the silver Portland stone of the Royal Exchange. The implication is that there is room in the model city for the varieties of true psychological need and healthful activity; excluded are only those qualities which everyone dislikes : staleness, ugliness, inconvenience.

The significance of the model lies paramountly in its expression of spiritual freedom, its celebration of the end of the mind's enslavement by the body. Gumbril Senior states :

'He [Wren] offered to build for the imagination and the ambitious spirit of man, so that even the most bestial, vaguely and remotely, as they walked those streets, might feel that they were of the same race— or very nearly—as Michelangelo; that they too might feel themselves, in spirit at least, magnificent, strong and free.' (p. 135)

But the citizens preferred 'the wretched human scale, the scale of the sickly body, not of the mind' (p. 135).

The bearing of the model city upon much of the rest of the novel is clear : we shall observe the 'wretched human scale' in action and shall see it triumphant. Even Gumbril Senior's gloss upon the happenings of the 1660s constitutes a counterpart to the story of his son, for the pattern of enslavement followed by promise of spiritual liberty followed by descent into further and final enslavement is the same in both instances. The account of the model city arises and remains in the middle of the novel, just as St Paul's itself arose and has remained (in the centre of the model and of Wren's own plans) while 'ugliness and pettiness and dirt' (p. 135) are seen by the author to surround both the historical moment and the 'grace' vouchsafed to his hero. It becomes increasingly clear that for thorough understanding the shape of *Antic Hay* must be taken into account.

The entire point of the model city is endorsed by the style of the prose in which it is described, for Gumbril Senior's words (they seem hardly to be his, and there are no inverted commas) are in marked contrast to the style of almost all the rest of the novel. Order, clarity, elegance : these are the qualities of the exposition, which is yet delivered not coldly but with reasonable enthusiasm.

'Spire out of dome; octagon on octagon diminishing upwards; cylinder on cylinder; round lanterns, lanterns of many sides; towers with airy pinnacles; clusters of pillars linked by incurving cornices; and above them, four more clusters and above once more; square towers pierced with pointed windows; spires uplifted on flying buttresses; spires bulbous at the base—the multitude of them beckons, familiar and friendly, on the sky. From the other shore, or sliding along the quiet river, you see them all, you tell over their names; and the great dome swells up in the midst over-topping them all.

'The dome of St Paul's.' (p. 137f)

Prose of this symmetrical nature is, as we have seen, a not uncommon feature of Huxley's first novel, but in *Antic Hay* the style of the passage represented by this quotation emerges from its surroundings to match the import of the subject matter. The virtues of the prose of *Antic Hay* are elsewhere less elegant than in this series of phrases each immediately juxtaposed with the next to represent the sensation of a glance sweeping delightedly over such a broken, varied but ultimately unified vista as the one described. And then, in the penultimate sentence, the rhythm steadies : one is moving gently on the river, or alternatively, allowing the gaze from the south bank to pause on each tower of the City. The final brief phrase is one of climax and rest, for the eye has been led upwards and stayed on the surmounting dome.

Here, then, in the description of the model city, we have been concerned with an ideal. Mozart's G minor Quintet, on the other hand, represents the real, but faced ideally. If Gumbril Senior's model signifies what might have been, Mozart's music signifies what is, and how to avoid despair. Huxley found no need to describe the entire quintet: for his purpose all that was required was the minuetto, the slow movement and the last movement. Accordingly, Gumbril and Emily arrive late at the Albert Hall, as the minuetto is about to begin. It suggests charming play: 'Ladies and precious gentlemen, fresh from the wit and gallantry of Crebillon-haunted sofas, stepping gracefully to a pattern of airy notes' (p. 150). Gumbril characteristically wonders how such a mood would face the challenge of tragic passion, and Mozart in fact represents in the next, the slow movement, a pure, undistracted sadness that mounts in the end to affirming the existence of God. Again, Gumbril, a complex man, preserves enough detachment to remind himself that his nature is not passionate, and that the sufferings of an artist can be fashioned into something delicious and publicly effective. Gumbril's reflections on the slow movement conclude: 'Blessed are the pure in heart, for they shall see God; they shall make God visible, too, to other eyes' (p. 151). Thus Gumbril accepts gratefully the experience while recalling the impurity of his own heart. And yet lurking behind these words is a conviction that as the experience cannot be sustained so it cannot be sustaining. The music soon confirms these doubts.

Blood beats in the ears. Beat, beat, beat. A slow drum in the darkness, beating in the ears of one who lies wakeful with fever, with the sickness of too much misery. It beats unceasingly, in the ears, in the mind itself. Body and mind are indivisible, and in the spirit blood painfully throbs. Sad thoughts droop through the mind. A small, pure light comes swaying down through the darkness, comes to rest, resigning itself to the obscurity of its misfortune. There is resignation, but blood still beats in the ears. Blood still painfully beats, though the mind has acquiesced. And then, suddenly, the mind exerts itself, throws off the fever of too much suffering and laughing, commands the body to dance. The introduction to the last movement comes to its suspended, throbbing close. There is an instant of expectation, and then, with a series of mounting trochees and a downward hurrying, step after tiny step, in triple time, the dance begins. Irrelevant, irreverent, out of key with all that has gone before. But man's greatest strength lies in his capacity for irrelevance. In the midst of pestilences, wars and famine, he builds cathedrals; and a slave, he can think the irrelevant and unsuitable thoughts of a free man. The spirit is slave to fever and beating blood, at the mercy of an obscure and tyrannous misfortune. But irrelevantly, it elects to dance in triple measure—a mounting skip, a patter of descending feet.' (p. 151)

Throughout the representation of Mozart's quintet there is a scarcely perceptible movement away from Gumbril's reflections, and in this, the final paragraph we seem almost to be responding without an intermediary to the music itself. We might compare another, more famous, literary account of a piece of music, that by E. M. Forster in *Howards End*. Forster, it will be recalled, makes no pretence of occupying the mind of Helen Schlegel (whose reactions interest him more than those of the other hearers), but comments openly in his own voice upon both the Fifth Symphony and Helen's response to it.[4] In contrast, Huxley, by earlier mingling—sometimes without comment—snatches of Gumbril's thoughts with the description of the music, is aided smoothly to conclude with this passage which constitutes a fine attempt to reproduce the feelings and sensations of a listener. That detachment which was so regular a feature of *Crome Yellow* has departed. The effect here is produced by a 'musical' use of language, most notably by the deft repetition of onomatopoeic terms, but also by an order of words which strongly suggests the pulsing rhythm of the music. The repeated onomatopoeic words are 'blood', 'beat' and 'throb', but the effect is enhanced by other words and phrases: 'ear', 'mind', 'fever', 'obscure', 'too much suffering', 'too much misery', 'obscure misfortune', the repetition of which (sometimes with slight variations) helps to consolidate the sense of a frayed and depressed nervous system.

The meaning which we should extract from this passage and remember is that the initial misery is a product of the mind's dancing to the body's tune, and that amelioration occurs when the mind comes to accept the yoke, acknowledges the 'subtle knot', and thereby, like one who has learned to love his fate, is calmed and restored to healthful dominance. If we now review Huxley's interpretation of the quintet we see that the sequence is one of, first, a formal dance (the minuetto) which constitutes a happy, occasionally necessary, unmindfulness of the human condition; secondly, a sadness whose purity, seeking to exclude the body, cannot last, and, finally, a rendering of the true state of humanity in which mind and body are indissolubly linked. What this interpretation of the music summarizes for us is the attitude of Huxley towards his material: the 'dance', of the novel is unquestionably antic, or grotesque, but there is a sort of rejoicing through mere acceptance.

So far, then, we have noticed two aspects of the centre of the novel, the first illustrating architecturally an ideal, in which the 'sickly human body', is subordinated, and the second culminating in a gay acceptance of the fact that the ideal has not been realized. But these two aspects are joined with a third, and the combined whole of the centre formally governs the novel as the axle governs the wheel, or, since we should think also in terms of dancing, a maypole controls and completes the pattern formed by the revolving dancers.

Midway between model city and Mozart quintet, Gumbril and Emily stroll in Kew Gardens, and Gumbril speaks wistfully of quiet places in the mind where one is afraid of lingering. Daily distractions, he asserts, are sought in order to put an end to the quietness which is both desired and dreaded. It is dreaded because absolute attainment entails a kind of death.

' "There are quiet places also in the mind," he said meditatively. "But we build bandstands and factories on them. Deliberately —to put a stop to the quietness. We don't like the quietness. All the thoughts, all the preoccupations in my head—round and round, continually." He made a circular motion with his hand. "And the jazz bands, the music-hall songs, the boys shouting the news. What's it for? what's it all for? To put an end to the quiet, to break it up and disperse it, to pretend at any cost it isn't there. Ah, but it is; it is there, in spite of everything, at the back of everything. Lying awake at night, sometimes—not restlessly, but serenely, waiting for sleep—the quiet re-establishes itself, piece by piece; all the broken bits, all the fragments of it we've been so busily dispersing all day long . . . It fills one, it grows—a crystal quiet, a growing, expanding crystal . . . And at last you are conscious of something approaching; it is almost a faint sound of footsteps. Something inexpressibly lovely and wonderful advances through the crystal, nearer, nearer. And, oh, inexpressibly terrifying. For if it were to touch you, if it were to seize and engulf you, you'd die; all the regular, habitual, daily part of you would die." ' (pp. 146f)[5]

Gumbril seems to be formulating these thoughts for the first time, though perhaps we might imagine that they have vaguely occurred to him before. As he has strayed from the West End to Kew Gardens, wandered without volition away from his regular companions, so he has been brought to the full acknowledgement of a paradox which the entire novel is shaped to illustrate. The crystal of which Gumbril speaks, meaning by that a mental state which (he maintains) is constantly present but normally ignored, resembles these central chapters (Eleven to Thirteen), and in particular the very passage under consideration, surrounded by almost all the features of every other chapter which represent in effect bandstands, factories, jazz-bands, music-hall songs, and boys shouting the news; that is, daily life, antic but necessary. This ancient conception, chiefly through T. S. Eliot, has become a commonplace ('Except for the point, the still point/There would be no dance, and there is only the dance').[6]

Antic Hay is about Gumbril to a greater extent than *Crome Yellow* is about Denis Stone, since not only is Gumbril actively present in all but four of the twenty-two chapters but also his mind is more elaborately explored than is the mind of the earlier protagonist. Interested though Huxley undoubtedly was in the other members of his cast, he nevertheless caused them to revolve around or collide with the hero, thus serving mainly to illustrate the hero's quest, and this is why the function of the first chapter is to characterize him in relation to a particular psychological and moral problem of which, though he is a specific personality, he is also the conscious embodiment.

Briefly the question—and it is one which will preoccupy Huxley for the rest of his life—is about the degree of compatibility between goodness and the probing intellect. How should one bridge the gap, not solely between 'God as a sense of warmth about the heart' and 'God as $2 + 2 = 4$', but also between the 'active radiance' of goodness in such people as Gumbril's mother and the other reality of two plus two? Gumbril seeks a unity which will enfold the pompous, zestful certainty of the Reverend Pelvey, the atheism of Gumbril Senior, the simple goodness of his mother, and the fact of her dying young from a painful disease.[7] Communicated in Chapter One are both the facts of Gumbril's nature and how that nature illustrates a problem which it will be the theme of the novel to investigate. The problem will be continually explored in the novels from now on and, for all the apparent certainties of the works published after 1936, it is only in the closing chapters of *Island* that an answer which carries the conviction of experience rather than mere argument is presented.

The matter is dealt with skilfully in the first chapter by means which Huxley scarcely attempted in *Crome Yellow*. In that novel, it will be recalled, states of mind are observed 'from the outside', being rendered in orthodox syntax and with an ordered clarity that gives the effect of *aperçus* rather than detailed reproductions of experience. In Chapter One of *Antic Hay* the reader seems to have ease of access to Gumbril's mind, to follow without obtrusive mediation on the author's part the swift speculations and the associations, sometimes bitter, sometimes farcical. While learning about Gumbril's past we participate in the fragmentariness of his mind, and at the same time become dimly aware that such fragmentariness—as a general condition—is what the novel is largely about. It is only Gumbril who could pass in a second from recalling with pain the death of his mother to conceiving the possibility of pneumatic trousers, but the inconsistency and the ignobility of such contiguities we all now recognize to be universal.

Thus the novel begins in a natural and traditional manner. We may say that from now on the sequence is roughly as follows: false solution sought amid false milieu; correct solution glimpsed but not grasped; then a spiralling down into a limbo of knowledge without will. In this way, after Chapter Two (which through Gumbril Senior and Mr Porteous briefly announces the theme of positive value) there comes first the group of chapters (Three to Ten) which portrays the grotesquerie of the town and Gumbril's mistaken expedients of disguise and money-making; then the central 'quiet' chapters, and finally Chapters Fifteen to Twenty-two in which characters circle about, meeting, intertwining, farcically and fruitlessly. I shall examine the more important aspects of this sequence.

Chapter Two is in deliberate contrast both with what precedes it (the announcement of the major theme through the medium of Gumbril's broken reflections) and with what is to follow (the pursuit of false solutions). It is a 'quiet' chapter whose function is to anticipate, chiefly in a thematic sense but on a narrative plane also, the central chapters. Old Mr Gumbril and his friend Porteous represent values which Gumbril's own generation have discarded, a point which will be emphasized in Chapter Sixteen when a drunken youth turns out to be Mr Porteous's son. Gumbril Senior is a survivor and he is given the appurtenances of survival. He lives in a decaying square, yet he is an architect. His present commission is to design model cottages for workmen at Bletchley, but his vision, expressed through his models, and especially through the plan which he has drawn of a delightful house, is of buildings that defy rather than imitate Nature. Clearly the notion, which is an elaboration of that put forward by Mr Scogan in *Crome Yellow*, is that the man-made city ought not to imitate God's own handiwork of Nature, but ought rather to express the best qualities in man and thus complement Nature.[8] That Gumbril Senior is an architect whose reasonable aspirations cannot be achieved is important in a novel which is emphatically of the town, a town spiritually and physically in decay. In *Antic Hay* Huxley joins the ranks of those writers (Ruskin, Morris and D. H. Lawrence, to give but three examples) who stress the close relationship between physical environment and quality of living.

As important as these matters in a thematic sense is old Mr Gumbril's evening habit of watching the starlings return to roost in the plane trees of the square. The action of the birds is to be contrasted with the actions of all the human characters (except for these two ageing men and Emily), since the birds circle around the city every day only to return to their 'still centre' in the evenings. The circular movements of the starlings therefore should be compared favourably with the circular movements of the people, who have either an illusion of linear progress (Shearwater and Lypiatt) or the damning awareness that they cannot return to the centre (Myra Viveash and, subsequently, Gumbril).

The next stage in the pattern of the novel consists of a batch of chapters—the third to the tenth—which portrays Gumbril's misguided progress in a milieu most of whose members illustrate responses to certain problems which are by no means confined to the milieu. The technique, which in later novels, notably *Point Counter Point*, Huxley uses more elaborately and more conspicuously, is to present characters whose conversation and styles of living betoken mistaken modes of responding to experience.[9] One obvious purpose of this section of the novel is to cause the reader to meet and become thoroughly familiar with the nihilism of Myra Viveash, the willed heroics of Lypiatt, the triviality of Mercaptan, the satanism of Coleman, the bovarism of Rosie Shearwater, and the obtuseness in emotional matters of her husband.

It is worth while to note in passing some features of these people. Each, with the possible exception of Rosie Shearwater, has an appearance which matches his or her views and behaviour. The names, as usual, are most carefully chosen. 'Viveash' combines an attractive sound with the meaning 'ashes of life'; 'Casimir Lypiatt' suggests operatic heroism; 'Mercaptan', again, though sounding pleasant means something repellent, namely an evil-smelling sulphur compound, and 'Shearwater' conveys—appropriately for the husband—a picture of the sea-bird and the bleak seas which are its habitat. (The name Gumbril, of course, in its hints of glum, gum, gums, gumboil, tumbril, is comically lugubrious, and therefore right for this hero, and as an indication of the author's attitude towards his material.) Several characters have natures variants of which occur in other works. It is unnecessary to comment in this connection on Gumbril himself or on Myra Viveash, but it is perhaps worth remarking that Shearwater is the first of the emotionally obtuse or naïve scientists, the last of whom is Henry Maartens of *The Genius and the Goddess*; that Rosie Shearwater's tendency to adopt roles is repeated, with modifications, by Grace Peddley of 'Two or Three Graces', by Mary Thriplow of *Those Barren Leaves*, and by Ruth Maartens of *The Genius and the Goddess*; and that Coleman is the earliest of a line which includes Spandrell (*Point Counter Point*) and Dr Obispo (*After Many a Summer*).

It is interesting also to note various direct comments by Huxley which further illuminate some of these natures. Mercaptan's view— a mistaken one—of the eighteenth century in France can be understood more fully by reference to the essay 'Crébillon the Younger' in *The Olive Tree*. There is in the essay 'Baudelaire' (*Do What You Will*) an analysis of a nature which is a sombre version of Coleman's. Huxley's views on bovarism are expounded in Chapter Four of *The Devils of Loudun* and Chapter Five of *Island*.

In a way which is reminiscent of *Crome Yellow* but in terms of the novelist's art is a considerable advance on the earlier book, these early chapters present a series of scenes several of which make their own, almost separable points while forming part of a connected narrative. In order we observe, Gumbril and Mr Bojanus; Lypiatt at the Albemarle Galleries; the restaurant scene; the scene at the coffee-stall; Mrs Viveash sitting for Lypiatt; the exhibition; Mr Bojanus on the subject of leader and herd; Gumbril as the Complete Man, and Mr Boldero on the techniques of advertising.

It is permissible to label the contents of the chapters in this manner since Huxley is still using an episodic mode of construction, but most of the episodes are less clearly bounded than are those of *Crome Yellow*. Only three of the scenes mentioned above are in the strictest sense superfluous to the narrative, for while Gumbril is obliged in the course of furthering his new career to visit his tailor and to have at least one important conversation with his business manager, it is not necessary for the former to be a sound amateur sociologist and the latter to analyse with such skill the duplicities of advertising. The two monologues by Mr Bojanus (in Chapters

Three and Eight) and the one by Mr Boldero (in Chapter Ten) are worthy of a Mr Scogan in content, though not of course in the manner of their delivery. The purpose of these conversations is formal and thematic, by which I do not mean solely that some antic ways are expounded by Bojanus and Boldero, but also that the very meetings between Gumbril and these two men are minor features in a design of collisions between incongruous persons.

The author repeatedly brings together personalities so strikingly at variance with one another that an effect of incongruity is gained well beyond that which is to be expected of any comic production. For this there is a clear reason : while we cannot suppose that Huxley had in mind the actual movements of the Hay (of which no very clear description exists), it is likely that he thought in terms of a dance whose actions and participants are, at least from the point of view of a spectator, comically distorted. (Marlowe's Gaveston desired that his dancers should also be goat-footed, but plain lasciviousness is only an aspect of the general animalism—the enslavement of the mind by the body—to which Huxley, in choosing his title, presumably referred.) An important feature of the 'dance' of this novel is the repeated linking of ill-suited partners. In this respect the meetings between Gumbril and Bojanus and those between Gumbril and Boldero are less notable than several other confrontations. There is total opposition, for instance, between Mrs Viveash and her two chief admirers, between her ennui and both the bravura of Lypiatt and the emotional naïvety of Shearwater. Likewise, Huxley impels Lypiatt in all his gauntness against the plump and placid Mr Albemarle, and, in the second part of the novel, causes Lypiatt to come raging and hurt into the *dix-huitième* parlour of Mr Mercaptan. Similarly, among those who, in the fourth chapter, make up the party at the restaurant there is a high degree of incompatibility, to emphasize which Huxley opens the scene with the declamation by Lypiatt of his sentimental poem, 'The Conquistador', so that the sophistication of Gumbril and Mercaptan (in particular the belittling cleverness of the latter) is immediately opposed to the aspirations of the artist. Shearwater in all his stolidity is then introduced and offset against the blasphemous high spirits of Coleman, who has with him, to complete the extraordinary variety, the illiterate Zoe.[10]

In the next chapter, when the party repairs to Hyde Park Corner, there is also incongruity of place, for a coffee-stall is almost the least accordant of backcloths before which to discover Myra Viveash and her escort, Bruin Opps. There follows at this point what is surely one of the best-contrived scenes in the novel. The yellow light of the coffee-stall reveals a number of ill-clad people but emerging from them 'a tall tubed hat and a silk-faced overcoat, a cloak of flame-coloured satin, and in bright, coppery hair a great Spanish comb of carved tortoiseshell' (p. 57). The description and dialogue which follow exemplify an important feature of the structure of *Antic Hay* by composing a perfect *concordia discors*. There are marked divergencies among the members of Gumbril's own party and between that party and the plebeians behind them. While, for example, the arrogance of Opps is being opposed to the frivolity of Coleman, the conversation of Gumbril's entire group is balanced against the conversation of the surrounding workfolk. The parallels and contrasts are deliberate but not, in their detail, crudely emphasized. Myra's account of a dreary evening in the vicinity of Hampton Court is the first part of a sequence which is completed when the poor man tells his tale of a walk to Portsmouth and back in a vain search for work. Each part of the sequence is concerned with a fruitless, unpleasant journey and with hunger.[11] This much is plain though unobtrusive. But with more subtlety, throughout the whole scene Huxley is showing contrasting attitudes towards the flesh. To Myra the flesh signifies beauty and pleasure; to Shearwater it is material for dissection and study; to Coleman it is a means of damnation, and to the poor couple (the wife is pregnant) the flesh is that which, sickeningly and exhaustingly, dominates mind and spirit. Despite clear sympathy for the poor couple (Gumbril alone of his group strains to overhear the tale, is perturbed, and thus initiates a collection of money), the attitude here of the author towards his material is one of observing, with a mixture of humour and disgust, clownish activities in which, repeatedly, one sort of irrationality is made doubly absurd by being matched with another sort.

It is unnecessary to emphasize the structural principle of contrast in numerous other scenes of *Antic Hay*, and indeed now that we have sufficiently considered both this principle and the main form of the novel (the 'wheel' with its 'still centre') it is time briefly to recall the thread of the narrative. The story of Gumbril flows through and sometimes around the episodes, for periods in conjunction with the subsidiary stories of the loves of Lypiatt and Shearwater for Myra Viveash. It is as if we are onlookers at a dance who notice a few of the dancers once or twice only, while the movements of some others we follow, though intermittently, for a longer time, and those of Gumbril himself we see almost without interruption from beginning to end. Thus, Zoe and Bruin Opps are each glimpsed once as they pass by, but we watch the execution of two separate movements by the assistant at the Albemarle Galleries, and we study entire sequences performed by Rosie Shearwater and Lypiatt, the first of these characters being, for a time, in partnership with Gumbril, and the second being chiefly controlled, as it were, by Myra Viveash. On a plan such as this the narrative is sustained.

It is pertinent also to notice while we are still thinking in terms of a dance that a theme of seeming or masking emerges towards the end of the first half of the novel, so that on reflection, after reading about the actual disguising of Gumbril and the adoption by Rosie Shearwater of the role of *grande amoureuse*, we can see that other characters too have strongly marked styles rather than personalities. One aspect of the absurdity which (in the light of Reason, not necessarily by conventional standards) invests Mercaptan, Coleman, Lypiatt, Mrs Viveash, and Shearwater—and to a lesser extent other figures—is the mere coherence and vividness of their personal styles. Mercaptan and Coleman we know almost entirely through their conversation, supported by the comments of the author as a spectator, and only fractionally do we enter the minds of Shearwater, Lypiatt, and Myra, so that all these people largely remain as masked and capering dancers. This is made more apparent by the comparative variegatedness of Gumbril's experience. Indeed Gumbril wishes to become the Complete Man only partly to fulfil a sort of modern dream of the Renaissance (the hero as compound of flamboyant wit, virility and learning) but also presumably to subdue his own painful contradictoriness.

In the main, then, the first part of *Antic Hay* expresses with a variety of means the problem embodied by Gumbril, and on the plane of narrative, causes Gumbril to pursue a totally unsatisfactory solution amid people whose own responses to experience are mistaken. The hero has been detained in a grotesque dance. There follows the vouchsafement to Gumbril of a grace the promise of which he fails, through velleity, to seize. It is fitting, therefore, though also melancholy, that he should return to the line of dancers, but now he is aware that he can never more break away. 'Never more', croaks Gumbril, after Poe's raven, in response to the conjecture by Mrs Viveash that joy is unlikely to return.

The relapse is stressed by the contrast between Emily, with whom Gumbril spends a night of innocent enchantment, and Myra who immediately afterwards involves Gumbril in her own boredom. Emily is associated with a governess cart, wild flowers and a cottage; Myra's typical conveyance is a taxi, her scent is of Italian jasmine and her drawing-room is 'tastefully in the movement' (p. 165). For Mrs Viveash 'Only time kills' (p. 166), but with Emily time is abolished. Most importantly, however, each lady has been the victim of an outrage upon the emotions, but whereas Emily has responded to early, unconsummated marriage to a drunken boor with nothing worse than wariness, Myra has allowed the death in France of her lover to destroy her capacity for affection.

One object of the cabaret which Myra and Gumbril at this stage attend is to display the full consequences of Gumbril's drift away from serenity and Reason. The band plays a 'Shakespeherian rag' the words of which are nonsensical but, in the context, full of meaning, since the important line of the refrain, 'What's he to Hecuba?', is used by Huxley to imply a general indifference of people to one another. Most of the patrons are in fancy dress, that is, in flight from themselves and from consideration of consequences and responsibilities, even as Gumbril is trying to convince himself that it is not he but the clown within him who is acting thus foolishly.[12] The significance of the dance-tune enters Myra's thoughts in this manner.

'Nil, omnipresent nil, world-soul, spiritual informer of all matter. Nil in the shape of a black-breeched moon-basined Toreador. Nil, the man with the greyhound's nose. Nil, as four blackamoors. Nil in the form of a divine tune. Nil, the faces, the faces one ought to know by sight, reflected in the mirrors of the hall. Nil this Gumbril whose arm is round one's waist, whose feet step in and out among one's own. Nothing at all.' (p. 170)

Nil is not omnipresent to the reader who is, on the contrary, sharing the author's own vivaciously ambiguous response in which an intellectual and aesthetic delight merges into and mitigates the vision of nullity which he is representing. And a similar though keener ambiguity permeates the playlet which now follows. The Monster 'begotten in a night of immaculate pleasure' or, alternatively, 'conceived in lust and darkness' (p. 172) is reared phthisically in the squalor of London merely to love a lady whose beauty masks a nature of total triviality, to be humiliated by a prostitute, and then to die in consequence of his aspiration to love and Reason. The playlet manifests, I believe, not a truly Swiftian disgust with the body, but rather an abhorrence of the diseased or ugly body.[18] An underlying assumption of the entire novel which has earlier reached the surface in the description of the model city now emerges again. The assumption is that only the life of Reason will produce minds and bodies harmonious in themselves and with each other. This ideal condition can hardly be brought about in any environment other than a splendidly Michelangelesque *urbs*, but, embitteringly, a large measure of the condition must be present in a people before they build fine cities. The ideal condition is also one in which a 'night of immaculate pleasure' could never be conversely termed 'lust and darkness' because body and spirit would then be one, a state which prevailed, the Monster supposes, among the young people of Sparta. But under existing conditions the aspirant to Reason will fail. The playlet proclaims this view, and nothing in the novel contradicts it. The pessimism in Chapters Fifteen and Sixteen of *Antic Hay* is like the pessimism earlier expressed through description of part of the last movement of Mozart's G minor Quintet, because the context in both instances is one of sprightly acceptance. The mode of acceptance now is ironic. The playlet itself, for instance, expresses all that I have tried to expound, and more, but is at the same time a burlesque of solemnly pretentious drama. Furthermore, while Gumbril fully understands—indeed, explains—the implications of the song, 'What's he to Hecuba?', he is himself deluded in supposing that a quintessential self remains untarnished by his activities and free to hover away over memories of childhood pantomimes or anticipations of Emily. Gumbril's present ignorance of the loss of Emily adds point to his delusion, and in particular to his allowing his rooms to be desecrated (for that is what it amounts to) by Myra, Coleman, and Porteous Junior.

A vision of aridity comes to Gumbril only the following day after he has received Emily's letter. At this point Huxley properly refuses to turn his comedy into a quasi-tragedy by dwelling on Gumbril's belated self-knowledge : instead he contrives through Gumbril's railway journey a pause in the main action. Such a pause is needed at this stage because a sort of last movement is about to begin. At the same time the railway trip foreshadows the chief structural feature of the last movement which is to consist mainly of a series of vain or humiliating journeys. Light, anticipatory hints of a journeying motif have been heard before—in the wanderings of Myra

Viveash and the poor couple, in the movements of Gumbril Senior's starlings, and, more vaguely, in the abandonment of a job or the tramping of city streets. (*Antic Hay* is thus to be contrasted with *Crome Yellow*, which is, in one sense, a static book.)

Chapters Eighteen to Twenty are principally about the movements of Rosie Shearwater and Lypiatt. The first of these characters has been set in motion, as it were, by Gumbril who has not only fostered her vanity and self-delusion, but has also given her his address as 213 Sloane Street, the home of Mr Mercaptan. Her progress is one of passing, or being passed, from Gumbril to Mercaptan, and then to Coleman. She sees the passage from Gumbril ('Toto') to Mercaptan as a promotion to which she is by nature fully entitled. In reality she who thought to use others is herself used, and her translation from bored wife to exposed odalisque in Coleman's bedroom is a degradation. The suggestion is that Rosie's culmination, to be reached in the closing chapters of the novel, will be, like all the culminations, the beginning or consolidation of a sterile life.

Lypiatt, too, now begins the movement towards his nadir, from which there is no hint that he will rise. He has been set in motion by Myra whom he loves and who originated the comparison between his paintings and advertisements for vermouth. Consequently Lypiatt arrives to Mercaptan, and after the brief, rather painfully farcical scene at Sloane Street, returns in suicidal mood to his lonely rooms, there to be visited by Mr Boldero who is seeking to commission him to design pictures advertising pneumatic trousers. Since Gumbril suggested this proposal, he is jointly responsible with Myra for leading the artist to his nadir.

It is natural that Gumbril and Mrs Viveash should be absent from Chapters Eighteen to Twenty partly because they, being for the moment somewhat in the position of puppet-masters, should be out of sight, but principally as they must be reserved for the last two chapters which comprise what Myra calls their 'Last Ride Together'. The closing section of the novel includes the observation in turn of all the main persons of the drama, and the observation is largely achieved, realistically and conveniently, by the visits which Gumbril and Myra pay to each of them merely for lack of anything better to do. The impression given by the taxi-journey is certainly not that of a 'Last Ride Together' in the sense of Browning's poem, but rather (in spite of the fact that Gumbril is going abroad on business) of a never-ending rotation. The other characters are last glimpsed in comparatively static poses, but in each instance (with the possible exception of Gumbril Senior, but he, too, is a victim of his environment) it is the stasis, not of fulfilment, but of pointlessness. Thus Myra and Gumbril without knowing it leave Lypiatt uncharacteristically detached from his own experience, and one cannot be certain whether he will proceed to suicide or not. Mercaptan has fled for safety from his flat, and we last see him recounting to a Mrs Speagle his experiences in the Isles of Greece. Coleman and Rosie Shearwater are last seen in tableau, as it might be, he blood-bespattered and blasphemous, and she the embarrassed odalisque. Gumbril Senior we leave more or less as we found him—exhibiting the starlings to Myra—but he has sold his model city to pay for debts incurred by Porteous's son. Finally, Shearwater, in precise parody of all the other vain movements in the book, is observed exerting himself upon a stationary bicycle, and imagining as he does so that he is making a tremendous journey of escape.

The design of *Antic Hay* is much more complex than that of *Crome Yellow*, but the second novel can be seen, in the end, to be as unified as the first. This has not always been apparent. For instance, an early critic, one of the very few to comment upon the design of *Antic Hay*, notes 'its cheerful promiscuity, its vivid contrasts, and unexpected juxtapositions', but then proceeds to assert that 'the effect of his alterations of mood is bound to be centrifugal and disintegrating'.[14] I hope it has been sufficiently demonstrated that, on the contrary, everything is held very firmly to the centre.

The language in *Antic Hay* is likewise more varied than the language in *Crome Yellow*. Now the patent harmony of style has all but departed and we meet instead something harsher and more varied, but the verbal structures of *Antic Hay* fall together producing a *concordia discors* of their own. In this novel Huxley has often tried to follow, at least in outline, the movements of his characters' thoughts, to render plausible conversations, and to contrast by syntax such opposed states of mind as that of Shearwater feverishly cycling and that of Gumbril responding sensitively to the slow movement of Mozart's G minor Quintet. The manner generally is less urbane and less ironic than the manner of *Crome Yellow*, and it is worth remarking in passing that Huxley, in satirical vein or not, is the reverse of the kind of author (Evelyn Waugh, for example) who produces a large part of his effect by describing disastrous events in polite and casual terms. The main point of these remarks will be sufficiently illustrated by examining a piece of the conversation which takes place, in Chapter Five, before the coffee-stall at Hyde Park Corner.

' "$x^2 - y^2$," Shearwater was saying, "$= (x+y)(x-y)$. And the equation holds good whatever the values of x and y . . . It's the same with your love business, Mrs Viveash. The relation is still fundamentally the same, whatever the value of the unknown personal quantities concerned. Little individual tics and peculiarities—after all, what do they matter?"
' "What indeed!" said Coleman. "Tics, mere tics. Sheep ticks, horse ticks, bed bugs, tape worms, taint worms, guinea worms, liver flukes . . ."
' " 'The 'orse must be destroyed,' says the beak. ' 'E's too old for work.' 'But I'm not.' I says. 'I can't get a old age pension at thirty-two, can I? 'Ow am I to earn my living if you take away what I earns my living by?' "
'Mrs Viveash smiled agonizingly. "Here's a man who thinks personal peculiarities are trivial and unimportant," she said. "You're not even interested in people, then?"
' " 'I don't know what you can do,' 'e says. 'I'm only 'ere to administer the law.' 'Seems a queer sort of law,' I says. 'What law is it?' "
'Shearwater scratched his head. Under his formidable black moustache he smiled at last his ingenuous, childish smile. "No," he said, "No, I suppose I'm not. It hadn't occurred to me, until you said it. But I suppose I'm not. No." He laughed, quite delighted, it seemed, by this discovery about himself.
' " 'What law is it?' 'e says. 'The Croolty to Animals law. That's what it is,' 'e says." ' (p. 64f)

Huxley here makes a satirical point without undue heightening or distortion of the probable. The conversation at the coffee-stall is neither unlikely to have occurred nor implausible in its details. Shearwater is a man who readily formulates his views when it seems necessary, and he has just been teasingly drawn into doing so by Mrs Viveash. It has earlier been shown that Coleman, the second speaker, practises swift, irreverent verbal associations; therefore he is likely to seize upon the word, 'tics'. His development of this word associates directly and naturally with the theme of the poor man whose horse may well have suffered from some of the ailments gleefully catalogued by Coleman. In addition, the principal topics of the two conversations make precise comments upon each other, since Shearwater's lack of interest in people, especially in individual peculiarities, is related to the application of a humane law, the 'Croolty to Animals law', to a specific case in which individual circumstances should have been taken into account. And, of course, it is harshly amusing that the one topic should be academically pursued within earshot of the other.

This medley of attitudes and styles exemplifies the fragmentariness which is Huxley's chief concern. The art of the passage that has just been examined represents in little the art of the entire novel which predominantly consists of the placing side by side of apparently incongruous elements in such a way that a common theme emerges. I have now sufficiently remarked on these matters and it remains to stress that whereas in *Crome Yellow* the style was itself a conspicuous agent of cohesion, in *Antic Hay* the language varies so much that it takes on, in relation to the novel which it composes, a function like that of the varied buildings of the model city, or the movements, equally diverse, of Mozart's G minor Quintet. As always, unity lies mainly in the attitude of the author, but in *Antic Hay*, as compared with *Crome Yellow*, greater responsibility for achieving unity rests with the whole design.

Although the novel, like the model city and Mozart's music, is unified by art, one cannot assume that to Huxley at this stage art was comfortable enough. *Antic Hay* is the first of Huxley's novels to offer positive moral values, and—except for *Brave New World*— it is the last in which such values are wholly defeated. This would invite the conclusion that the book is decidedly pessimistic if it were not for a ubiquitous vivacity which modifies, though it may not absolutely belie, such a conclusion. It is possible to be mainly impressed by the vivacity as Evelyn Waugh seems to be when he writes:

'There is an insistent undertone, audible through the carnival music, saying all the time, not in Mrs Viveash's "expiring" voice, that happiness is a reality.'[15]

Such a reading is a corrective to that view of the novel which, overlooking the gaiety, takes in almost exclusively the portrait of post-war malaise.

The real tension, however, is between a keen veneration, even a need, for purity, and a thorough-going scepticism. Purity, of course, means wholeness as well as innocence, so that the quality is manifested in the dome of St Paul's, in Brunelleschi's dome and in the variations on Diabelli, as well as in Emily, Gumbril's mother and the young girls of Sparta. (The concomitant is distaste for the impure, which includes not only divided or corrupt personalities but also 'tetters, poxes, blood-spitting, rotting of bones.'—p. 181) But Huxley's scepticism leads him not only to observe that purity is generally overwhelmed or evaded but also to detect no avenue of change. The achievement of the novel is to hold in balance these two awarenesses, by art, laughter and intellectual exuberance.

3

Those Barren Leaves (1925)

One of Huxley's minor skills was that of choosing titles. Most of the books are felicitously named, and so are many of the lesser-known essays, articles and stories. Presumably the title of the third novel, in its allusion to Wordsworth's poem, 'The Tables Turned', has the usual aptness, so that Huxley in 1925 meant to announce—though with Gumbrilesque humour and self-deprecation rather than the Wordsworthian solemnity—that he had produced another four hundred pages which, whatever their merits, might justifiably be regarded as conveying an inferior mode of understanding.

> 'Enough of Science and of Art;
> Close up those barren leaves;
> Come forth, and bring with you a heart
> That watches and receives.'

It is true also that Calamy's departure for the mountains, there to watch and perhaps to receive, and Francis Chelifer's belief that art is 'the last and silliest of the idols' (p. 84), combine to demote mediate knowledge. Chelifer puts reading on a par with playing halma, and Calamy regards books as things to be left behind, but how far are we to trust either of these two characters? I shall suggest that Huxley himself was not certain. It is as well to imagine a faintly questioning note, as well as humour, in the title.

There is surely an additional point in the title. Huxley is concerned with decay and the transience of human life, with people as leaves that inevitably fall. But what if the leaves are barren, the lives, that is to say, spiritually infertile and therefore (to the author) a source both of regret and humour?

A few rather heterogeneous elements are yoked together in *Those Barren Leaves* so that, although the yoking is adroitly managed,

61

the reader receives a flavour somewhat less unified than the flavours offered by the other novels before *After Many a Summer*. The plainest element is that of comedy which varies from the completely light-hearted (for instance, the wooing of Irene by Lord Hovenden, which is reminiscent of P. G. Wodehouse) to the sardonic, as in the death by food-poisoning of Grace Elver. A principal vehicle of the comedy is self-deception, or deception of others, in love. Another component is the working-out of personal problems through, not one, but three characters. Features of the author's nature are presented for his own appraisal in the persons of Calamy, Francis Chelifer, and Mary Thriplow.[1] This strand of the novel is the one which culminates in Calamy's retreat. A third distinguishable element comprises much depiction of the Italian scene after the manner of a travel-book, and in fact resembling some of the essays in *Along the Road*, which was first published later in the same year (1925). Clearly the travel-book element provides background for many of the episodes, but that is not its only function.

These, then, are the three main elements of the novel, and we may guess that it was partly for the purpose of accommodating them all smoothly that Huxley decided to divide the book into five parts. The first notable characteristic of the structure of *Those Barren Leaves* is the division into parts, a device which helps to put together features which on the plane of narrative have little consistency. What, for instance, has sightseeing in Italy to do with the autobiography of Francis Chelifer? To consider Chelifer and all that he implies, especially in relationship with the concluding aspirations of Calamy, was evidently most important to Huxley at this (and later) stages of his intellectual progress, but there remained presumably the technical problem of how to attach the beliefs and life-story of Chelifer to a comedy set in Italy. It seems likely that no manœuvrings or reasonable expansions of the Italian narrative could adequately supply the details of childhood in Oxford, of Gog's Court, and of Barbara Waters; and that when the expedient of the autobiography was hit upon, it was seen that it could be included only as a separate part. Even so, it would have been possible to include Chelifer's past as a lengthy 'digression', but for the fact that other material, too, is by the strictest standards extraneous. Much of the sight-seeing in Part IV, 'The Journey', neither pushes forward the narrative nor, in any substantial way, develops a theme, but no one, presumably, regrets its presence. Part IV is a happy contrivance by which Huxley simultaneously put to use material which might otherwise have been lost (he still had plenty to spare for *Along the Road*) and, principally for the sake of refreshing the reader, got most of his characters away from the palace of the Cybo Malaspina. Similarly, there is much to be said for placing the entirely serious arguments of Calamy in a final distinct section away from the comedy.

The first of the three elements which I have mentioned, the element of comedy, is preponderantly present in Part I, 'An Evening at Mrs Aldwinkle's', Part III, 'The Loves of the Parallels', and Part IV, 'The Journey'. Part II, 'Fragments from the Autobiography of Francis Chelifer', and Part V, 'Conclusions', are the sections most concentratedly concerned with self-appraisal by the author. The travel-book element is not confined to 'The Journey' but it is more prominent there than anywhere else. That it is possible without distortion to make this cursory analysis reveals a difference between *Those Barren Leaves* and the other early novels. Up to *Eyeless in Gaza* there is in each of the other novels such a thorough fusion of mixed attitudes that separation of the elements can only be made after careful thought; but in *Those Barren Leaves* Huxley quietly indicates the differences. The reader is aware by the time he reaches Part II that he is involved with something akin to a symphony, with breaks and changes of mood, rhythm, and melody (though the changes here are not heavily stressed). *Those Barren Leaves*, unlike *Point Counter Point*, is not intricately 'musicalized', but Huxley may well have been influenced by his exceptional awareness of the art of musical composition.

Again, *Those Barren Leaves* differs from every one of the other novels in having no hero whose viewpoint the reader tends, though with detachment, to occupy.[2] Neither Chelifer nor Calamy has a function of this kind so that instead of presenting one basic narrative thread (such as the thread provided even by the relative inactivity of Jeremy Pordage in *After Many a Summer*) Huxley gives us four stories of roughly equal structural importance. They are all love-stories in an extended sense of the term, and all are more or less comic. It is easy to imagine each one appearing in quite separate form, the slightest being about the capture of Irene Aldwinkle by Lord Hovenden, the least conclusive relating the pursuit of Chelifer by Lilian Aldwinkle, the most caustic concerning the relationship of Mr Cardan and Grace Elver, and the most serious recounting the abandonment of Mary Thriplow by Calamy. Although Calamy's final resolution is the most solemn event in the novel, the story of his brief *affaire* with Mary Thriplow is no more important in itself than any of the other stories since the resolution does not follow at all compulsorily from the *affaire*. Calamy, though not the hero of the novel, is an heroic conception of a sort commonly encountered in the popular fiction of the nineteen-twenties. One is probably right to suspect that Huxley chose a character who is handsome, physically brave, virile and distinctly upper class simply to allay readers' doubts and his own. It is obviously more persuasive that a man with every social advantage rather than one with some social deficiency should opt for the contemplative life, and in fact all Huxley's admired characters from now on are given, if not good looks, at least robust common sense and practical efficiency.

The plan on which the four stories are presented indicates an element in the genesis of the complex technique of *Point Counter Point*. The later novel is a network of parallels and contrasts, some of the principal 'ribs' of which are made up of several love-relationships. In *Those Barren Leaves*, as in *Point Counter Point*, the stories are introduced and concluded one by one so that the reader's interest shall be sustained; and all but one of the stories in each of the novels is about a discrepancy between expectations and results, thus giving the impression that love must generally be disappointed. (In the present novel it is only the simple souls, Hovenden and Irene, who escape disappointment, and in *Point Counter Point* the relationship of Mark and Mary Rampion is the only satisfactory one.)

Mary Thriplow and Calamy meet in the first chapter, and in Chapter Four we become vaguely aware of Hovenden's love for Irene Aldwinkle. It is in Part III, after the long 'digression' of Chelifer's autobiographical fragments, that Mrs Aldwinkle begins to pursue Chelifer, and Cardan abducts Grace Elver. In the first chapter of Part IV Hovenden and Irene agree to marry; in the seventh chapter, through the medium of Chelifer's jottings, we note finally his opinion of Lilian Aldwinkle, and in Chapter Nine takes place the funeral of Grace Elver. In the course of the first three chapters of Part V the relationship of Calamy and Mary Thriplow is gradually ended. In this way are spaced out the beginnings and endings of four narratives, three of which concern illusions, for while Mary Thriplow and Lilian Aldwinkle delude themselves about their partners, Grace Elver is the victim of Mr Cardan's pretences.

These stories, however, provide, as do the stories in *Point Counter*

Point, only the ribs of the novel and much of the material is barely connected with them. Apart from the whole of Part II, 'Fragments from the Autobiography of Francis Chelifer', there are about ten other chapters scattered throughout the length of the novel which are generally or entirely about other matters. As in *Crome Yellow*, there are several minor stories or anecdotes, such as the episode of Mr Cardan and the grocer's brother's statue or the small episode of Mrs Chelifer and the starving cats. In addition there are the writings in Miss Thriplow's diary. There is also, for the first and last time in Huxley's fiction, much overt comment by the author, and, more important, there are the lengthy portraits of Cardan, Lilian Aldwinkle and the summer palace of the Cybo Malaspina. When we have also taken into account other characters (Mr Falx and the various persons in Chelifer's past), the incidental verse, and the discussions of such matters as the Etruscan language and the quality of Roman civilization, we realize fully that part of the charm of this novel lies in its variety. I shall next consider how the variety is managed.

The first fact to be noted is that each part of the novel has its own characteristic mood as well as its own clearly defined subject-matter. Part I is like the opening scenes of countless plays in which, while stories are got under way, the audience is mainly delighted by mere exposition. (The first twelve chapters of *Point Counter Point* are similarly, though much more intricately, conducted.) This part begins and ends with Mary Thriplow in self-deceiving solitude. Early in Chapter One she prepares a face to meet the face that she expects to meet, and in Chapter Nine, alone with her diary, she does her best to evoke in herself pure emotion. The seven intervening chapters comprise a leisurely portrait of a group of people and a place on one summer evening. The method is a simple chronological one by which, after the initial description in Chapter Two of Lilian Aldwinkle (a central feature of her make-up links her with the type of superannuated belle so common in Restoration Comedy) and the remarks in Chapters Two and Three about the palace (whose grandeur now, as in the past, fails to disguise the mere humanity of the inhabitants), the characters are presented in turn as they contribute to the conversation at the dinner-table, and afterwards discuss a variety of topics on the terrace or in the saloon. Cardan's monologues alternate with more sporadic conversation during which the author tells us of some of the characters' pre-occupations. Thus, a high proportion of the third chapter consists of Mr Cardan's words, but Chapter Four is more concerned with the private thoughts of Irene, Hovenden, Calamy, and Mary Thriplow. The light-hearted mood of Part I is scarcely broken by Calamy's account in Chapter Seven of his dissatisfaction, from which the reader absorbs at most a hint of gravity to come, and in general the opening of the novel constitutes a genial attack on affectation and stupidity.

I have referred to Part II, 'Fragments from the Autobiography of Francis Chelifer', as a 'digression', and in a purely descriptive rather than a pejorative sense it is that. Most of the details of Chelifer's childhood and of his youthful disillusionments, even the account of his present way of life in England, are superfluous if he needs just to be established as a realist who will have no truck with romantic shadows; if, in other words, he is to serve simply as a comical foil for Lilian Aldwinkle. The truth is that the account of Chelifer's past is somewhat digressive only on the level of plot; thematically, and in terms of tone and mood (we should have a musical analogy in mind) Part II comprises a very important part of what Huxley wishes to say. I shall later examine Chelifer's attitudes in some detail, but for the moment it is perhaps sufficient to say that Chelifer, a considerable and very funny ironist, represents a part of the author which the author chooses to diminish by parody.

The tone of this second part is sharper than the tone of the first, and the targets of the humour more comprehensive. No longer are various sillinesses being shown up, with the implication that this particular group of people (and perhaps the milieu that they represent) are deficient in qualities of reasonableness and decency which may be found elsewhere, for Chelifer finds nothing admirable under the sun. And Huxley, who must be presumed to agree with a good deal of Chelifer's diagnosis, does not find Chelifer admirable. Since Wittgenstein, Bach, Shelley, La Rochefoucald, the game of halma, conversation at a London salon or at Miss Carruthers's boarding house are all means of passing the time; since love, art, humanism, and liberal politics are all demonstrably ineffective substitutes for religion, and since mankind displays only the 'jungle virtues' (erratic and undependable impulses to kindness, for instance), we are, in Part II, being faced with a denial of all the commonly held values. But the predicament is treated humorously, even exhilaratingly, because Huxley is rejoicing through having to construct something upon which to rejoice. This fact is as yet unknown to the reader.

After Chelifer has been brought to the palace by means of his bathing accident, Huxley can proceed smoothly with Part III, 'The Loves of the Parallels', a title which is reminiscent of Marvell's simile in 'The Definition of Love' of lovers as parallel lines stretching to infinity and never meeting.[3] At first the technique in this section perfectly bears out the title since Huxley passes from the problem afflicting one couple to the problem afflicting the next. When the three established couples have been dealt with in this way during Chapters One to Four, we follow Cardan on his trip into the Maremma for five diverting chapters, by the end of which he, too, has a partner. After Cardan's return with Grace Elver to the palace there is a chapter about the impression made upon everyone by Mrs Chelifer, and then for the last three chapters we return to the subject of love. Part III contains a good deal of theorizing, in conversation, in private thoughts, in confidences to a diary, about love, and if there is an overriding satiric point it is at the expense of those who attempt in accordance with fashionable ideas to intensify their emotions. Hovenden, Irene, and Grace Elver are each in different ways naturally in love, but Mary Thriplow and Lilian Aldwinkle (the former with some deliberateness, the latter unconsciously) cultivate what they assume to be appropriate feelings, while the sophisticated men, Calamy, Chelifer and Cardan, frankly acknowledge to themselves their indifference. Huxley is illustrating amusingly and at length certain reflections which, though they are without modification his own, he gives to Miss Thriplow.

'In the eighteenth century [Mary Thriplow writes in her diary] people tried to make out that they were rational and polished. The cult of the emotions began in the nineteenth. It has had a new turn given to it by Bergsonism and Romain-Rollandism in the twentieth century. It is fashionable now to be exactly the opposite of what it was fashionable to be in the eighteenth century. So that you get emotionally impotent people simulating passion with their minds.' (p. 263)

It would be easy to qualify some of the historical detail in Miss Thriplow's remarks (to point out, for example, that the 'cult of the emotions' really began in the middle of the eighteenth century[4]), but the author's chief point, which is based on immediate, contemporary observation, is not in doubt. For much of the novel Huxley is saying humorously or solemnly that sensibility is the current fetish. To be precise, it is one of the current fetishes, the other principal one being art, and both in *Those Barren Leaves* are under attack.

To some extent Part III is a return to a lighter vein because much of the comedy is on an ordinary social plane. Thus, Lilian Aldwinkle solicits Chelifer, her captive poet, and Hovenden bewilderedly pursues Irene. Nevertheless, towards the end of this part, Cardan's meeting the Elvers seems to foreshadow some fiercer business.

The fourth part begins at least in the same vein, with the slight difference that one target, art, is increasingly aimed at. What Huxley, through the comments of Chelifer and Cardan, is demolishing, is not only art-snobbery but also the supposition that the past (exemplified by surviving Roman and Etruscan art) must have been spiritually better than the present. One way in which Huxley differs from some of his contemporaries is in his conviction that the twentieth century is no less favourable to spiritual development than previous periods: it is merely unfavourable in different ways. I have in mind simply that T. S. Eliot, for example, apparently regarded the secularism of the present age as a peculiarly strong obstacle on the path towards spirituality. When in his essay, 'Religion and Literature', Eliot writes that 'modern literature . . . is simply unaware of, simply cannot understand the meaning of, the primacy of the supernatural over the natural life',[5] his regretful attitude has no exact parallel in Huxley's works. Lawrence, too, inveighs against the absence in modern times of a sense of the mystery of human existence and of a desire to preserve the mystery. But Huxley, while dwelling on the bad effects of secularism (in *Ape and Essence* more forcefully than anywhere else), seems to assume that the chances of attaining non-attachment in a non-secular time—say the seventeenth century, so convincingly portrayed in *Grey Eminence* and *The Devils of Loudun*—were no greater than they are today, and that nothing else finally matters.

It is towards the end of Part IV that Huxley presents the crucial problem of the book. Grace Elver has died accidentally and in great pain.

'The tragedy of bodily suffering and extinction has no catharsis. Punctually it runs its dull, degrading course, act by act to the conclusion. It ennobles neither the sufferer nor the contemplator. Only the tragedy of the spirit can liberate and uplift. But the greatest tragedy of the spirit is that sooner or later it succumbs to the flesh. Sooner or later every soul is stifled by the sick body; sooner or later there are no more thoughts, but only pain and vomiting and stupor. The tragedies of the spirit are mere struttings and posturings on the margin of life, and the spirit itself is only an accidental exuberance, the products of spare vital energy, like the feathers on the head of a hoopoo or the innumerable populations of useless and foredoomed spermatozoa. The spirit has no significance; there is only the body. When it is young, the body is beautiful and strong. It grows old, its joints creak, it becomes dry and smelly; it breaks down, the life goes out of it and it rots away. However lovely the feather's on a bird's head, they perish with it; and the spirit, which is a lovelier ornament than any, perishes too. The farce is hideous, thought Mr Cardan, and in the worst of bad taste.' (p. 334)

It is hard to think of any other modern English writer so much possessed by death as Huxley. Death in his novels is often not so much a finale or a departure which produces its effect upon other characters; it is also a fact and a process to be contemplated in itself. Even in *Crome Yellow* Denis climactically thinks of suicide, while Sir Hercules and his wife actually kill themselves. Not many authors, one imagines, would in such a context include the business of severing the artery with a razor. In *Antic Hay* the Monster dies on the same evening that Lypiatt considers killing himself. Frequently the death is a climax and a turning-point. In *Point Counter Point* the deaths of little Phil and Webley occur, as does the death of Grace Elver in the present novel, just before the close, thus modifying all that has gone before and casting a shadow forward over the conclusion. By the time we close the novel old John Bidlake is about to die and Spandrell has been shot. In *Eyeless in Gaza* the details of the death of Brian Foxe (there are, of course others) are withheld until nearly the end; in *Time Must Have a Stop* the early farcical death of Eustace Barnack—followed by his revelations of life beyond the grave—is balanced by the later saintly death of Bruno Rontini. *After Many a Summer* reflects Huxley's preoccupation more concentratedly and obviously than any of the other novels. Just as characteristically Huxleyan is the car-accident and the mutilation of Katy Maartens in *The Genius and the Goddess*. In *Brave New World* the death of the Savage is the denouement, while earlier the act of dying has, for serious satirical purposes, been transformed into a painless event. In *Island*, too, the death of Lakshmi takes place with a minimum of pain, but this time a straightforwardly serious recommendation is being made. It is hardly necessary to comment upon the malformations of *Ape and Essence* or the descriptions of decrepitude, torture and death in two non-fictional works, *Grey Eminence* and *The Devils of Loudun*.

The passage quoted above about the death of Grace Elver is a very important one. It represents a peculiar feature of *Those Barren Leaves* in being a direct address by the author to the reader,[6] but its subject-matter is a clear definition of something which tacitly imbues a wide range of the writing. The remarks include no doubt or compensatory equivocation, and are not answered—are not intended to be answered—by Calamy's final conjectures.

In one sense of the title Grace Elver is one of the barren leaves, a woman whose life has been unproductive and whose death does not fructify in the lives of others. It is true that Miss Elver gives exercise to Mrs Chelifer's charity, as do the starving cats in Rome, but one cannot be sure how seriously to take this. Her death affects Mr Cardan, but not, it seems, in any specially valuable way. Her character and fate perhaps constitute a kind of test-case : if meaning and value can be assigned to them, all will be well.

As a structural device the death acts as a pivot, a means of modulating from the varying degrees of humour up to now (the end of 'The Journey') to the solemnity of the last chapter of 'Conclusions'.[7] We had thought that we were engaged with a social comedy, and that even Chelifer with his sweeping criticisms of all the usual notions of value was a part of the comedy. But something both exceedingly nasty and farcical succeeds the cheerful fun, and is succeeded in turn (though not immediately) by quiet reflections. It is natural to recall *Candide*, the ghastliness of some of the incidents and then the quiet concluding sentence : ' "Cela est bien dit," répondit Candide, "mais il faut cultiver notre jardin." ' In a sense which may not be opposed to Voltaire's, Calamy is beginning to cultivate his garden when he retires to the mountains, for he says to Cardan, 'I begin to find in myself a certain aptitude for meditation which seems to me worth cultivating' (p. 374).[8]

There is not an abrupt movement from the funeral of Grace Elver to Calamy in his mountain retreat. The first three chapters of 'Conclusions' are a judicious winding down, and there is mild humour in the last glimpses of some of the characters. The suggestion here, as well as the formal arrangement, is precisely right. People remain as they are, unregenerate, absurd; and when one man embarks on an unusual course which may lead to self-improvement there is no sense of a grand finale. All is tentative, diffident, reasonable. To judge from his practice Huxley tended to distrust the glorious ending—the glory of tragedy or of promise—because most of his novels end with some kind of bathos or defeat, whatever positive recommendations may have been made within them.

It is time now that we have considered in outline the structure of the novel to pay closer attention to one revealing part of the structure: the 'Fragments from the Autobiography of Francis Chelifer'.

Part II is an interlude in the narrative of a special and important kind, for in it actions which take place elsewhere are mirrored and their implications writ large. If the novel generally aims to undermine the contemporary cult of the emotions, then the story of Chelifer's love for Barbara Waters is the main exemplary tale. The essence of Chelifer's youthful mistake is his compelling desire that all quotidian life should be aesthetically perfect. Long after Chelifer has discovered the gulf between the boring inanity of Miss Waters and the image of beauty which she presents to him he is still enthralled, so that only she can break off the relationship.[9] However, the 'Fragments from the Autobiography of Francis Chelifer' have a wider purpose: while seeming to mount an attack only on romanticism they also, and more importantly, assault the scepticism of the mature Chelifer.

Chelifer has certain things in common with his creator: a Wordsworthian father, an exceptionally charitable mother, and some similar qualities of mind. Leonard Huxley has recently been depicted by Mr Ronald W. Clark as follows:

'And there were the days, as some of the children later remembered, when Leonard would stand and speculate, gazing at the mountains with reminiscent eye and thinking aloud of things past.'[10]

This picture resembles the picture of Chelifer Senior taking his son to the top of Snowdon ('as the equivalent of Church-going'—p. 120) and there quoting from 'Tintern Abbey'. Mrs Chelifer, too, with her parties for Oxford undergraduates—parties that in recollection seem faintly ridiculous as well as intensely happy—may be compared with the real-life mother, Julia Huxley, as she is portrayed in the sixth chapter of Mr Clark's book.

With these comparisons in mind, and provisionally accepting Part II as a cautionary tale, let us consider some of Chelifer's characteristic remarks.

'This game of art strangely resembles conjuring. The quickness of the tongue deceives the brain. It has happened, after all, often enough. Old Shakespeare, for example. How many critical brains have been deceived by the quickness of *his* tongue! Because he can say "Shoughs, water-rugs and demi-wolves" and "defunctive music" and "the expense of spirit in a waste of shame" and all the rest of it, we credit him with philosophy, a moral purpose and the most penetrating psychology. Whereas his thoughts are incredibly confused, his only purpose is to entertain and he has created only three characters.' (p. 99)

' "A sense of something far more deeply interfused." Ever since that day those words, pronounced in my father's cavernous voice, have rumbled through my mind. It took me a long time to discover that they were as meaningless as so many hiccoughs. Such is the nefarious influence of early training.' (p. 122)

Both passages proclaim Chelifer's usual determination to believe that a yellow primrose is neither more nor less than a yellow primrose. But in spite of the fact that Chelifer is finally defeated by Calamy (for that is a good part of what the conclusion amounts to) we should not make the mistake of assuming that in passages such as these Chelifer is expressing the exact opposite of Huxley's own thoughts. Christopher Isherwood has said of Huxley that,

'He would often hold forth on the futility of literature in general. The great masters expressed themselves marvellously, of course—but what was the point of it all? What was it all *about*?' [11]

Chelifer's remarks about Shakespeare are therefore akin to Huxley's own views; akin, but at the same time, subtly different. The difference lies in Chelifer's cocksure, dismissive manner. We may be sure that when Huxley used to hold forth on the 'futility of literature in general' he did so, however impishly, with an underlying concern, so that Chelifer's attitude to Shakespeare is a caricature of the author's attitude. The dismissal of Shakespeare is designed as a corrective to the idolatry of art, or to the attempt to impose upon life the exclusive order of art. Huxley always had a vigilant sense of the limitations of language and never failed to regard literature as only roughly related either to daily experience or to spiritual reality. Mr Isherwood reports Huxley as saying that,

'. . . "the world of knowing-about-things is unsatisfactory. It's no good knowing about the taste of strawberries out of a book. The more I think of art I realize that, though artists do establish some contact with spiritual reality, they establish it unconsciously." [12]

All this has a clear bearing on the use of Wordsworth's 'The Tables Turned' to provide a title for the novel, and a more direct reference still is offered by Francis Chelifer's contemptuous treatment of 'Tintern Abbey'. This character's refusal to believe that there is a 'something far more deeply interfused' is of course not Huxley's refusal, but there is through Chelifer's remarks a rejection of the tendency to identify words with whatever they are supposed to refer to. Chelifer Senior's knowledge of the something far more deeply interfused is like the knowledge of strawberries out of a book.

I have previously suggested that a proper way to see Chelifer is as a parody of one strand in the author's make-up. He is one who adopts a false remedy after making a correct diagnosis. Having observed that the aesthetic qualities of a thing are not the measure of its other qualities, he comes to treat beauty as a snare. I think it likely that a temptation to do this presented itself to Huxley at some stage. In addition, Chelifer is the perfect sceptic against whom to test one's penchant for mysticism, for he, in addition to delivering the usual arguments (that mysticism is both false and an evasion of social responsibilities), carries these arguments to their logical conclusion. Chelifer is exceptional in the degree of his alert antagonism to the most minute hint that an experience may have some spiritual value. If he is right (and Huxley wishes to examine the possibility) then life is fairly represented as he represents Miss Carruthers's boarding house and Gog's Court.

The function of Francis Chelifer, therefore, in addition to providing the reader with much amusement, and, after his arrival at the palace, becoming part of a narrative pattern of couples, is that of devil's advocate. The style of writing given to him is fairly close to Huxley's own but at the same time revealingly different. The cynical element, the playfulness beneath the elegance which one often finds in the early Huxley, itself becomes the object of parody. Chelifer, who seems exceptionally aware, is unobtrusively placed on a lower level of awareness than the author by being given a certain dandified pomposity and too much conviction. What happens is that a feature of the author's own mind is distanced and abjured.

In contrast, the manner given to Calamy seems to be exactly that of Huxley himself in conversation.

'But even if it is impossible to get at reality, the fact that reality exists and is manifestly very different from what we ordinarily suppose it to be, surely throws some light on this horrible death business. Certainly, as things seem to happen, it's as if the body did get hold of the soul and kill it. But the real facts of the case may be entirely different. The body as we know it is an invention of the mind. What is the reality on which the abstracting, symbolizing mind does its work of abstraction and symbolism? It is possible that, at death, we may find out. And in any case, what is death, *really*?' (p. 369)

The style of these remarks may be compared with the style of that small sample of Huxley's conversation reported by Mr Isherwood, and for fuller reference we have Huxley's answers to questions put to him by interviewers for the *Paris Review*.[13] We find that the same features are present. In both the reality and the fiction there is a combination of self-assurance, intellectual curiosity, and unconcern with self arising from sheer interest in the subject-matter. The arguments are always presented with the utmost clarity, and often take the form of questions. For all the fluency no trouble is taken to achieve the syntactical perfection of a speech by Mr Scogan, and the colloquialism of 'this horrible death business' is perfectly Huxleyan. Calamy, we must conclude, is as much like the author in speech as he is unlike him in being rich, conventionally handsome, and an amorist. He too represents a strand of Huxley's nature, perhaps the strand which, in opposition to the Cheliferian traits, Huxley had come to regard as worthy of respect and cultivation.

So far I have spoken as if Francis Chelifer alone were the opposition to Calamy, and all that Calamy represents, but in fact Mr Cardan too has a function of this kind. There is no need to dwell on Cardan as the entertainer : the brilliance, though not the profundity, of his conversation surpasses that of any other of Huxley's accomplished talkers. A good deal of the fascination of the novel is due to the presentation of this character, and it is possible that for some readers an image of Cardan remains when all else is forgotten. His physical appearance, as well as his talk, is amply established; and unlike Scogan, his predecessor, he does more than talk. So detailed is the description of Tom Cardan's appearance when he is introduced in Chapter Three that, as with Mr Scogan, one immediately senses the portrait of a real-life person. In this instance it is probably Norman Douglas.[14]

Cardan's conversation at the dinner-table in the third chapter is, in addition to its value as amusement a means of smoothly presenting Mr Falx and Lord Hovenden, since both of them are bound to dissent from Cardan's views. Mr Falx's role is that of obtusely puritanical foil to Cardan, the shrewd cavalier. Again, as in the presentation of Lilian Aldwinkle, there is something of the tradition of Restoration Comedy in this opposition. And the same humour through incongruity which we noticed in *Antic Hay* is present here, though to a lesser degree.

When all this has been said, however, Mr Cardan is not in the novel solely for amusement. He, like all his counterparts from Mr Scogan to Mr Bahu, represents an intelligent response to life of a sort which it seems likely that Huxley felt a continuing need to reckon with. Cardan's views are so clearly right, up to a point. For example, it is he who in Chapter Three argues in disagreement with Mr Falx's social optimism that tyrants will in the future (the novel was published in 1925) as in the past bolster their power with public show. More importantly, it is Cardan rather than Chelifer who in 'Conclusions' has the power to discomfort Calamy. He brings the arguments for mysticism up against the fact of death (the conquest, as it would seem, of the soul by the body) thus causing Calamy to focus his attention upon the one truly formidable difficulty. Beside this Chelifer's 'inverted sentimentalism' is easily brushed aside. Cardan, like Chelifer, is a sceptic, but superior to Chelifer in not making a fetish of his disbelief. And Cardan, unlike Calamy or Chelifer, is ageing, has imagined vividly what might be the circumstances of his own death, and has been impressed by the last hours of Miss Elver.

These remarks may seem to treat too seriously an obviously comic creation, but the recurrence in Huxley's fiction of the type of mature or ageing cavalier hedonist is due, I think, as much to serious curiosity as to never-failing amusement. The observations made by Cardan as so lacking in all the usual varieties of self-deception that he demands either capitulation or confutation of an especially rigorous sort. Gradually, from *Those Barren Leaves* onwards, Huxley became more certain that while the intelligent cynic is right about human nature as it is and always has been, he is wrong to suppose that individual self-change is impossible.

Miss Thriplow, too, is both an amusing study and a representation of something important to the author. Her tendency to misuse her natural gift of sympathy by play-acting resembles a trait which is present not only in two fictional characters with whose personality Huxley's own personality is not likely to be confused—Grace Peddley and Ruth Maartens—but also Gumbril and Philip Quarles, who are in different ways self-projections on the author's part. Through Gumbril's activities arising from his feeling that he belongs to 'all the herds' (p. 93) there is caricature of Quarles's, that is, the author's 'amoeboid' mind, whose 'choice of moulds depended at any given moment on the books he was reading, the people he was associating with' (p. 268f).[15] Likewise, Mary Thriplow constitutes self-parody. Huxley is at this stage still concerned about his apparent lack of rigid selfhood and not sufficiently sure that his chameleon capacity can be an asset.

There may be further self-caricature in Miss Thriplow's readiness to find in all the situations of her life material for her stories. Huxley (like Chekhov in his invention of Trigorin) is well aware of the ridiculous element in an author's leap for his note-book. In addition, there is the emotional impotence with which Miss Thriplow credits her friends, and her high regard for keen sensibilities. This, as we have seen, is the subject of what amounts to a short essay by the author delivered as a commentary upon Miss Thriplow and her type, an essay which anticipates the treatment in *Point Counter Point* of Philip Quarles's lack of emotion.

But as being more immediately relevant to the theme of *Those Barren Leaves* we should notice Mary Thriplow's attempt to meditate in Chapter Three of 'Conclusions'. Huxley may well be making fun of his own early attempts. But certainly he is, with his usual intellectual caution and alertness to the possibility of ridicule by sophisticated people, disarming criticism by incorporating his own piece of burlesque.[16]

In an episode such as this the humour of *Those Barren Leaves* and its serious purposes are at one. There are places in the novel, however, where either pure comedy or pure gravity holds sway, and this may be the reason why critics have tended to stress one quality or the other. For the most part, later critics have dwelt upon the seriousness of *Those Barren Leaves*. D. S. Savage, for example, refers to this novel as 'the first to be written from a serious questioning of life'[17], and proceeds to write of it in relation to that one aspect. Peter Bowering asserts that the book 'is, in spite of the Peacockian elements, a morality on love, age and death.'[18] He, too, is chiefly concerned with features other than the 'Peacockian elements'. I have not made much of the humour, although it may well be argued that *Those Barren Leaves* is richer in comic material than any of the other novels, and, certainly, much of the language has primarily a comic function. The quiet tones and the blandness of *Crome Yellow* have here given way to something more emphatic, more glittering, and perhaps more confident. We can laugh with a minimum of reflection at many passages in this novel, which is often careless and gay—the only one of Huxley's novels in which, symptomatically, he buttonholes the reader from time to time and introduces so preposterous a name as Lady Giblet. This 'morality on love, age and death' is presented to a large extent in the manner of an expansive humorist.

Another way of putting the matter is to say that alongside, or merging into, the serious tones there are the tones of three distinct humorists : Cardan, Chelifer, and Huxley himself. It is Huxley who describes for us the busts of the lords of Massa Carrara and relates the story of Hovenden's proposal to Irene; it is Chelifer who, in his noticeably different manner, reproduces a sample of life at the offices of 'The Rabbit Fancier's Gazette'; and it is Cardan who characteristically holds forth on the decline in the art of flattery. This amalgam of comic styles and of comic styles with serious ones is an extraordinary feat.

One early critic, Leonard Woolf, assumed, in contrast to the later critics whom I have mentioned, that Huxley had tacked on a 'philosophy of life' in order to give his amusing novel direction and purpose. Having stated that '*Those Barren Leaves* is the best novel by Mr Huxley that I have read', Leonard Woolf continues :

'Where Mr Huxley fails, he fails in company with practically all novelists who are now writing. They do not know exactly what they are after. Is it to tell a story, 'delineate character', or give a cross-section of life? None of these things, by themselves, are going to produce a first-rate novel, and clever writers like Mr Huxley recognize this, and attempt to overcome the difficulty by superimposing on the typical novel, with its characters and story, a philosophy of life. But superimposition is always fatal in art.'[19]

We have no need to demonstrate that these words show a misreading of Huxley's intentions, but the words do indicate a defining feature of *Those Barren Leaves*. There is some discrepancy between what for convenience might be called the 'subject-matter' and the author's way of viewing the subject-matter. It is a 'morality on love, age and death' but it is also a cheerful work. Not surprisingly, therefore, some critics feel that they have read a comedy to which a bit of unwonted solemnity has been finally added, while other critics, reading back from 'Conclusions' and from the subsequent development of Huxley's thought, minimize the gaiety of the book. But there is no strain of sadness, as in *Crome Yellow*, and no harshness as in *Antic Hay* or *Point Counter Point*. The fun is purer than the fun of *After Many a Summer*. The author seems to be holding in check neither sharp condemnation nor dismay. For some reason, which may have been connected with a dawning hope that the absurdities and pains of life can be transcended, Huxley's laughter generally lacks the usual component of pessimism.

4

Point Counter Point (1928)

Philip Quarles writes in his notebook :

'Put a novelist into the novel. He justifies aesthetic generalizations, which may be interesting—at least to me. He also justifies experiment.' (p. 409)

To justify experiment is plainly a part of Philip's own function, so that analysis of the structure of *Point Counter Point* might advisedly begin with a consideration of Philip's remarks in Chapter Twenty-two. We shall be asking how and to what effect the material of this novel has a musical form.

'The changes of moods, the abrupt transitions' (p. 408) which Philip notes in Beethoven also in a manner occur in *Point Counter Point*, and for the moment I shall select only one of many possible examples. In the thirty-second chapter, immediately after the murder of Everard Webley, comes the scene in which Sidney Quarles appoints Philip as his literary executor; that is, a killing described with gravity (though its context is ironic and its aftermath includes farcical elements) is followed by the preparations for his own death of a Molièresque personage anxious to ensure the immortality of his reflections on life.

The next observations in Philip Quarles's notebook are about the retention in music of an original theme. Beethoven states then distorts a theme which nonetheless remains perceptibly the same, and Diabelli moves through the 'whole range of thought and feeling, yet [contriving] all in organic relation to a ridiculous little waltz tune' (p. 408). This process too takes place in *Point Counter Point*. There are several themes in the novel and we are presented with a considerable variety of thoughts and feelings in relation to each of them. For instance, death is presented not only in the ways which I have mentioned but also through the terror and poignancy of little Phil's illness, the suicides of Spandrell and Miss Cobbett, and the self-absorption (somewhat ironically treated) of John Bidlake in his last weeks. The words of Lord Edward Tantamount to Illidge on the most economical means of disposing of corpses comprise one of several other, minor examples.

'A novelist,' Philip goes on to say, 'modulates by reduplicating situations and characters.' He shows 'dissimilars solving the same problem' or 'similar people confronted with dissimilar problems' (p. 408). These phrases bring to mind the subtle parallelism of *Middlemarch* or *Anna Karenina*, but whereas George Eliot and Tolstoy, being 'congenital novelists', reproduce the blur and density of life, Huxley in his markedly different way wishes the reader consciously to reflect upon, for example, the varied reactions to infidelity of Marjorie Carling, her husband, Walter Bidlake, Rachel Quarles, and Janet Bidlake. These people are 'dissimilars solving the same problem'; and the phrase may perhaps be used in an extended sense to describe the rival doctrines or attitudes which Huxley, through particular appropriate characters, examines.

There is, it seems, yet another way of modulating upon a theme : the novelist can choose to consider the events which transmit his theme in terms of various aspects—'emotional, scientific, economic, religious, metaphysical, etc' (p. 409). In a rough, unsystematic way Huxley does this too. Over and above the inevitable movements from, say, the emotional to the economic aspects of a situation which may be found in any novel, there are in *Point Counter Point* occasional, deliberate and emphasized shifts, as, for instance, when Marjorie Carling's feelings about her pregnancy (in the first chapter) are contrasted with the physiological facts.

These are the chief techniques of musicalization which can be gathered from Philip Quarles's notebook, but many more are used in the novel. As a preliminary to examining the structure in detail it will be as well to offer some broad clarification of this very complex work.

The epigraphic use of a quotation from Fulke Greville tells us clearly that a main theme is 'Passion and reason, self-division's cause'[1], but it is less clear whether the novel was intended to answer the problem stated by Fulke Greville or merely to bear him out. It is possible to see *Point Counter Point* simply in terms of Rampion versus the rest, but if we do our disappointment in the presentation of Rampion is all the keener. Most critics, from Lawrence himself onwards,[2] have found Rampion unsatisfactory as a piece of characterization, and it must be true that he is not so impressive a figure as Huxley hoped he would be, but I am now concerned with the author's intention rather than the quality of the result. It is reasonable to assume that Huxley, for all his enthusiasm at this time for Lawrence, deliberately wrote a book in which a version of Lawrence's views would form a melody of great relative sanity, but not a melody of absolute and final triumph. Rampion, after hearing the close of the *heilige Dankgesang* of Beethoven's A minor Quartet, says to Spandrell, 'Almost thou persuadest me' (p. 598), and the remark may be used, I suggest, to convey Huxley's own response to the views of Rampion–Lawrence. The gaze of the reader when he is balancing Rampion against the opinions and behaviour of other characters is often focused through Philip Quarles, who admires only Rampion but knows that he cannot emulate Rampion's style of life. The novel is probably best regarded as a rounded presentation of metaphysical inconclusiveness, for on the one hand is the blatant self-division of most of the characters and on the other hand are either the unsatisfactory certainties of such persons as Lucy Tantamount, Webley, and Rachel Quarles, or else a philosophy of life (Rampion's) which Philip Quarles cannot live by.

Huxley's own remarks indicate that this is the right way to view the novel. In the essay, 'The Rest is Silence', he writes:

'From the abbreviated play [a dramatization of *Point Counter Point*] it was necessary to omit almost all the implied or specified counter which, in the novel, tempered, or at least was intended to temper, the harshness of the "points". The play, as a whole, was curiously hard and brutal.'[3]

The word, 'temper', suggests that Rampion's marriage, the *heilige Dankgesang*, and the rest of the positive elements were never calculated even to cancel out, still less to overwhelm, the negative elements.

Certainly, almost all the characters are either victims of some form of division between passion and reason or act as depraved agents of the division in others. The behaviour of these personages constitutes the 'points', as Huxley puts it, but the points are not a mere miscellany, for they fall into clearly definable categories and thus make up themes or variations upon themes.

There is, first, self-division in love. The principal embodiment of this theme is Walter Bidlake whose regard for Lucy Tantamount is, as he realizes, 'mad and shameful'—an accurate but common-place phrase which it is convenient for the moment to extract from its context of intricate analysis. Variations upon this theme, ranging in tone from the serious in relation to Walter to the farcical in relation to Sidney Quarles, and embracing the past or present activities of a good proportion of the characters, contribute more in quantity to the 'weave' of the novel than any other element.

Next there is what may be described as the 'philosophical' theme which subsumes all those social, political, and religious attitudes which in the course of the novel are clearly formulated by the characters and, either by implication or in the words of Mark Rampion, are found wanting. The one common fault of all the 'philosophies' except Rampion's is that they are partial in over-looking or specifically denying the needs of some features of human nature. This partiality may or may not give rise to a painful sense of self-division in the character (the communism of Illidge, for example, does promote discord in his make-up, whereas Everard Webley's fascism seems to leave him psychologically unscathed), but it is, to use Rampion's words, 'always away from the central norm, always away from humanity' (p. 564). Huxley's non-fictional deliverance of this message is, principally, in the essay, 'One and Many'. Here is the concluding paragraph of that essay:

'If men are ever to rise again from the depths into which they are now descending, it will be with the aid of a new religion of life. And since life is diverse, the new religion will have to have many Gods. Many; but since the individual man is an unity in his various multiplicity, also one. It will have to be Dionysian and Panic as well as Apollonian; Orphic as well as rational; not only Christian, but Martial and Venerean too; Phallic as well as Minervan or Jehovahistic. It will have to be all, in a word, that human life actually is, not merely the symbolical expression of one of its aspects. Meanwhile, however, the Gadarene descent continues.'[4]

The 'points' of *Point Counter Point*, the negative aspects of the novel, constitute a portrait of the 'Gadarene descent'. So far in my descriptive list of the 'points' I have mentioned two which are countered by Mark Rampion (whose marriage is healthy and whose opinions are in a sense 'correct'), but there are two more categories of harshness to which Rampion provides no answer. The first and more nebulous category may be termed 'filial'; the second concerns death.

Huxley's novels show a persistent, though often slightly muted preoccupation with the relationships between parents and children. (The most intensive treatment of the subject is in *Eyeless in Gaza*.) In *Point Counter Point* the matter is scarcely obtrusive, but enough interest is taken in filial or parental attitudes for these attitudes to form a theme of their own. The theme constitutes one of the 'points', for it embraces different forms of misunderstanding, perversity, and irrationality, and—to take examples—it moves between the mild absurdity of Lord Edward Tantamount's innocence as against his daughter's amorality, to the sombre ironies in the story of the Quarles family.

None of the positive elements in the novel effectively answers the questions which Huxley by implication raises through the filial theme. Rampion simply leaves these matters untouched; the *heilige Dankgesang* is presented as ineffable but not necessarily relevant, and the intelligent, dogmatic Christianity of Rachel Quarles is given no weight. These remarks apply with even greater force to the conspicuous theme of death, which Huxley—and it is an important part of his total meaning—accommodates only in a formal sense.

It is time, since the ground has now been cleared, to see how this unusually complicated novel is put together : after that it will be possible to grasp it, undistortedly, as a whole.

The opening chapter is rather more serious than the opening chapter of any of Huxley's earlier novels. Its principal topic, the expense of spirit in a waste of shame, is a fresh one for Huxley in so far as this is the first time that a lover at the height of his infatuation recognizes the ignobility of his mistress. Denis, Lypiatt, the Monster, and Chelifer all at some stage confuse beauty with truth, but Walter Bidlake knows from the outset that he is in love with a 'refined and perfumed imitation of a savage or an animal' (p. 75), as Illidge later calls Lucy. The analysis of the condition of Walter (and Marjorie) is conducted in a tone that is almost matter-of-fact : only faint impulses to smile, to pity, to scrutinize superiorly, are encouraged in the reader. He is chiefly invited to care and not to care, to partake of an attitude which is common from now on in the novels.

At the end of the first chapter, Tantamount House is mentioned so that, in accordance with a technique of linkage which is repeatedly used in *Point Counter Point*, the topic of the next chapter is anticipated. The notes, therefore, continue into Chapter Two, but the key changes. At present what is happening in the splendid hall of Tantamount House constitutes a tribute paid by philistinism to art. The performance of Bach's Suite in B minor for flute and strings given in a household whose only truly appreciative occupant is engaged, two flights up, in amputating the limbs of a newt, provides a framework in which the author can bring forward in two short chapters a large proportion of the *dramatis personae*, and can do this in tones which are appropriate to these particular characters and to this stage of the novel. For the persons now present at Tantamount House are the less serious characters, the characters, that is, whose ways of life and destinies excite little sympathy in the author; and the novel grows more consistently serious towards the close.

The term, 'fugal allegro', which could be used to characterize roughly the entire novel, may be more strictly applied to these opening chapters. The technique is chiefly one of presenting pieces of dialogue between persons present at the Tantamounts' party accompanied by brief descriptions and—wherever it is desirable—summarized biographies. Thus, initially in Chapter Two we read snatches of the conversation between Lady Edward Tantamount and John Bidlake interspersed with sufficient details of Lady Edward's background. Since it would be clumsy and boring to present abbreviated biographies of both characters in this one chapter, we are now told mainly about Hilda Tantamount, and most of the details (which are more important) of John Bidlake's past life are held in reserve. Similarly, in the third chapter, the scene of which is Lord Edward's laboratory, we are plunged immediately into three pages recounting facts of Lord Edward's past (his relationship with his wife has been dealt with in passing in the previous chapter, so now it is his discovery of a vocation which concerns us), followed by conversation between Lord Edward and his assistant, Illidge. Again, the more important personage, Illidge, is merely introduced so that his character and attitudes can be developed in a more leisurely way as the novel progresses.

Proceeding for the most part in this manner, Huxley is able to introduce fifteen highly distinctive characters in the course of the first eleven chapters. Having dealt with a good proportion of the backgrounds of Marjorie Carling and Walter Bidlake in Chapter One, and having disposed of the past lives of the Tantamounts in

Chapters Two and Three, the author can now present, one after another, nearly all the numerous personages. For the sake of variety the past lives of only one more couple, the Rampions, are included at this early stage. (And, of course, the shifting of the scene to Bombay in Chapter Six also helps to achieve variety.)

Lord and Lady Tantamount are little more than figures in the comparatively light-hearted comedy which is one element in the ambiguous tone of the novel, so that the excursions into their past lives are made partly for the sake of humour and partly as first steps in the recurring practice of 'flashback'. Moving about in time gives depth, perspective to what is mainly (despite the memorable events, most of which occur towards the close) a crowded picture of people and attitudes rather than a thoroughgoing narrative.[5]

The first prolonged and serious treatment of the past is the story of the Rampions which takes up Chapter Nine. But before that the comedy at Tantamount House has been expanded by the introduction of a number of guests who have little in common but the assumption that one's own peep-hole to the universe is the correct one. Each peep-hole is naturally the result of disposition and personal circumstances. Thus, to take examples, in Chapter Four there is a meeting between Hilda Tantamount and Everard Webley (charm, malice, and vagueness versus open bullying), and a meeting between Illidge, the communist of proletarian origins, and Major Knoyle who is typically military. In Chapter Five Illidge's moralizing hatred of the upper classes is placed beside Walter Bidlake's obsession with Lucy, and Lord Edward's indifference to politics is brought into conflict with Webley's preoccupation with 'saving England'. The aim is not solely or mainly to produce laughter, since the author is implying that the only right vision must be one that unifies and transcends these narrow personal visions.

When Huxley wishes to make a certain kind of point he will bring about sudden, jarring changes of mood, but in the first section of the novel there are no such effects. On the contrary, the changes are gradual. Towards the end of the fifth chapter, therefore, we return to Marjorie Carling. Her present feelings are perhaps 'comic' in one sense of the word, but they are scarcely funny; and when after that we are briefly returned to Tantamount House it is to find John Bidlake suffering from what he supposes to be indigestion, yet there is already a faint hint of some more serious illness. He is asked about his daughter, Elinor, and her husband, Philip Quarles, so that when the first complete break comes (Chapter

Six) the reader has been prepared for it, in terms of both mood and subject-matter.

Chapter Six, is, of course, wholly serious, since the characters introduced in it are wrestling with a problem which is the author's own and share the author's own reasoning self-awareness. What has to be brought out is the quality of Philip Quarles's mind, and this is achieved by incidents (the car's running over a pariah dog), description (Philip wears a surgical boot), appropriate dialogue, interior monologue, and authorial remarks. In these ways we learn of Philip's 'Pyrrhonian indifference, tempered by a consistent gentleness and kindness' (p. 106), of his anxiety to conceal what little emotional life he has, and—most important in one way—of his 'quick, comprehensive, ubiquitous intelligence that could understand everything, including the emotions it could not feel and the instincts it took care not to be moved by' (p. 107). The inclusion of Philip as a dramatization of the author's problem is different from other fictional self-projections that come to mind in that authors usually cast themselves as heroes, and in doing so either recount problems which they have solved before writing the book (for example, *A Portrait of the Artist as a Young Man*), or try to solve problems in the act of writing (as Lawrence does in most of his novels). *Point Counter Point*, on the other hand, is best seen as a novel without a hero—unless anyone should wish to propose Mark Rampion—and a statement rather than a solution of the problem is what the novel is, quite deliberately, all about. This then is the use made by Huxley of a device he found in André Gide's *Les Faux Monnayeurs* : the novelist within the novel. But Gide's Édouard is is not Gide even to the limited extent that Philip is Huxley,[6] and what the two uses have in common is the theorizing about the art of writing. In the course of the novel Philip's problem will be fully dramatized, but, to speak summarily, his presence is the result of the author's concern over his own emotional indifference (a concern which may well have been foisted on him by others, and notably by Lawrence[7]).

When, in Chapter Seven, we are returned to Tantamount House it is partly for the purpose of continuing the story of Walter and Lucy, partly (through snatches of conversation, as at a play) to herald Spandrell and the Rampions, who are shortly to appear, and partly to introduce Molly d'Exergillod.

In the five pages of the eighth chapter there is conveyed in vivid outline a picture of a trio at a café table. Indeed the representation reminds one of an allegoric painting. On one side of the table, well illuminated, are Mark Rampion and his wife, a 'thin, fierce, indomitable little man' and a 'big golden woman' (p. 130); while on the other side, his head in shadow or else lit pinkly by the table-lamp, is Spandrell, bitter, cadaverous. Love of life, in other words, is opposed to hatred of life. At the close of the chapter as Spandrell begins his remarks about his 'regular technique' with young women, Mary Rampion starts to reminisce, and thus we are transported back for the whole of Chapter Nine to the meeting and early married life of the Rampions. Here, then, is the second and last wholly unironic chapter in the novel. It is long—twenty-nine pages—and well placed. The length of the chapter is acceptable because it tells a story which is both interesting and vital to an understanding of the example which the Rampions are in the novel to convey. It is well placed partly for the minor reason that it is enclosed by Spandrell's anecdote of his own corruption, and thus corresponds in little to the placing of the Rampions in the novel as a whole, but mainly because this first swelling of the 'counter' theme comes neither too soon nor too late. The story of the Rampions is certainly a softened version of the relationship between Lawrence and Frieda (in particular it moderates the tensions between the Lawrences[8]) but it does bring out the Lawrentian ideal of a prickly, creative partnership in which individualities are not blunted.

The return to the present, to Sbisa's restaurant, in the tenth chapter gives us, first, a brief indication of Rampion's message—and this will be repeated in other terms and will eventually reach a crescendo in Chapter Thirty-four—and, secondly, a realization of where the truly serious arguments of the novel are going to lie: they will be apportioned between Spandrell and Mark Rampion. In *Those Barren Leaves* Huxley looked first to Chelifer's 'realism' and then to Calamy; in *Point Counter Point*, while the decision is emphatically in favour of Rampion's 'life-worship', the arguments for looking beyond the muddle of life have still to be accommodated, and this need is satisfied through the oddly impressive figure of Spandrell. In what is very largely a *roman à clef*[9] Spandrell seems to be one of the very few characters to have been invented, though he is formed partly from literary-historical ingredients. His appearance, some of his sentiments, and some of the circumstances of his life are taken from Baudelaire, while his nature probably also owes something to Dostoevsky's Stavrogin.[10] But, in forming these skeletal features is the author's profound interest in the degradations to which spiritual people are susceptible, an interest which is given full rein in *The Devils of Loudun* but which is here held in check—necessarily so, since other characters, and especially Rampion, must not be over-shadowed.

It is Chapter Eleven, the penultimate chapter of what may be seen as the opening section of the novel (the 'overture' or 'first movement'), that brings together, rapidly and exhilaratingly, all of the four principal themes, thus consolidating what has gone before and foreshadowing things to come. This chapter is perhaps the best example of the method and the effect of the entire novel. Its considerable length—thirty-one pages—is divided into thirteen sections (one consisting of only five lines) in the course of which the reader is whirled from one locale to another. The chapter seems to cover a period of an hour or two, but some of the conversations in different places which necessarily follow one another in the novel are to be understood as taking place simultaneously. The technique is that of having each section make its implicit comment upon the neighbouring sections. How often a method of roughly this nature is used in Huxley's novels! The root-principle of one of his structural techniques is that of comment—not always ironic—by contiguity. To look forward, the time-scheme of *Eyeless in Gaza* sometimes produces this effect (among others), and so does the 'cutting' of *Brave New World*; to look back, the scene at the coffee-stall in *Antic Hay* is in the same category. In *Point Counter Point*, as we might expect, a 'musical' effect is achieved. Thus, the flippant conversation at Sbisa's in the opening section, being mainly about Grundyism and sexual inhibition, prefaces the topic of the second section—Beatrice Gilroy's pseudo-maternal relationship with her lodger, Burlap. Meanwhile the rather dowdy chatter at Sbisa's continues but soon moves into a serious denunciation by Rampion of the effects of science and industrialism. At the same moment in time, apparently, in the laboratory at Tantamount House, Lord Everard and Illidge are enthusiastically discussing man's tendency to consume overmuch the fruits of the earth. Since those fruits are sometimes, as Illidge puts it, 'fossilized carrion', it is entirely apt that at Sbisa's Spandrell should now be quoting Baudelaire : ' "Et pourtant vous serez semblable à cette ordure" '.[11] In this way two forms of hatred of life, Illidge's and Spandrell's, are contrasted with each other (both men, in entirely different ways, would revel in the thought of 'decay bacteria') and are together contrasted with Rampion's wholesomeness. After the party at Sbisa's has broken up we first hear comments by Rampion upon Spandrell, and then, as Walter, Lucy and Spandrell are left alone, the conversation turns to the subject of old age. The 'filial' theme, as I have called it, now dominates, for we move between Lord Edward's conversation on the telephone with his father, the Marquis of Gattenden, and Lucy's describing with unaffectionate mockery the naïveties of her father. From this we proceed to observation of old John Bidlake who, at about the time that Lucy is calling him the 'only possible old man', is exhaustedly climbing his stairs and recalling his past life. Finally, a sharp but artless girl, Polly Logan, delivers her views on the older people she has met during the course of the evening. The pattern is perfect. The four themes of self-division in love, 'philosophic' differences, conflict between age and youth, and death, are woven together, and every important character (except Philip and Elinor Quarles) so far introduced is included. The chapter is at once a summary, a development, an omen, and an indication of the diversity which has to be unified.

The 'first movement' (for musical analogies are apt, if they are not pressed too hard) should be imagined to end with Chapter Twelve. By this time Walter has returned to Marjorie and promised a fresh start. Following that in the order of presentation, though taking place at the same time, is the conversation between Spandrell and Lucy. This conversation is something in the nature of a coda containing 'phrases' the significance of which will not be fully revealed until the end of the novel. Spandrell and Lucy each feel a need to press beyond common experience, to indulge in what Huxley later in his life called 'downward self-transcendence'.[12] 'But the deathly sort of liveliness is the most lively really,' says Lucy (p. 214), and her words are representative of the notes upon which we reach the end of the beginning.

The new impetus which starts with the opening words of the thirteenth chapter goes forward until the end of Chapter Twenty-one. It is now convenient to include elements of the past lives of Burlap and Spandrell, and these elements are interwoven with pictures of their present ways of life and with the continuing story of Walter Bidlake. At the same time Huxley includes at an early stage in this section of the novel (Chapter Fourteen) a depiction of the country home of Philip and Elinor, thus anticipating the close of the section which is chiefly about the return to England of the Quarleses. The thematic parallels and contrasts are not stressed but we should notice the common unsatisfactoriness of both the love-affairs and the filial relationships. The love-affairs (and I include those of Philip and Elinor which are at present only foreshadowed) are ultimately alike in that they reduce or deflect rather than enlarge the personalities of the partners. The marriage of Mark and Mary Rampion is held up as a model of mutual enrichment, and in contrast with this Walter, Burlap, Sidney Quarles, Philip and Elinor all accomplish through love a degree of self-impoverishment.

The most interesting of the other features of the chapters now being considered is the welling-up in Chapter Thirteen of a theme which has previously run an inconspicuous course and afterwards twists its way through diverse moods and personalities. We read about the nature of the feelings which Burlap had for his wife before she died.

'His ardours were those of a child for its mother (a rather incestuous child, it is true; but how tactfully and delicately the little Oedipus!); his love was at once babyish and maternal; his passion was a kind of passive snuggling.' (p. 232)

Shortly afterwards Spandrell recalls childhood felicities when he and his widowed mother travelled in Europe together. The Oedipal nature of their relationship (Spandrell, a tardy Hamlet, denounces her even now for marrying again) is the explanation of Spandrell's impulse to self-destruction. From these 'abnormal' matters we pass to the healthily-developing little Phil (the refreshing picture of whom is clouded, but momentarily, by his fear of lying down in the dark), and from little Phil back to several specimens of the persistence into maturity, or even into old age, of infantile attitudes. Burlap, for instance, is put to bed like a sick child by Beatrice Gilroy. Likewise, Sidney Quarles is a man who plays with machines and puzzles, Carling is a self-pitying drunkard, and Spandrell's behaviour is interpreted as a refusal to grow up. The remarks in these and other instances are too specific to be ignored. The play of reference is between old age (Sidney Quarles, John Bidlake, and the Marquis of Gattenden), real childhood, and childhood-in-maturity. Only Rampion has true maturity, for even Philip Quarles (who was, we learn, a 'withdrawn', unaffectionate child) is censured by his wife—and probably by the author himself—for lacking 'natural piety', in Wordsworth's sense.[13] A form of growth is advocated, though not very explicitly, in which all the human faculties move upwards, as it were, while real childhood is not forgotten but remembered forever as part of the enlarging pattern. Philip has virtually forgotten his own childhood and has developed lopsidedly. Particular persons and events are deliberately related to the general subjects of evolution and heredity, for Rampion has drawn a picture in which men of the future are a 'company of little gargoyles and foetuses with heads too large for their squelchy bodies', while Elinor, contemplating her son, reflects that a 'whole population of strangers inhabited and shaped that little body, lived in that mind and controlled its wishes, dictated its thoughts, and would go on dictating and controlling' (p. 337f). *Point Counter Point* is a novel of familial ramifications because the author wished to define the individual not only by considering him in various aspects—'emotional, scientific, economic, religious, metaphysical, etc' (p. 409)—but also by indicating the things, people, events which have contributed to his present make-up.

The extracts from Philip Quarles's notebook which occupy Chapter Twenty-two, in serving as a reader's guide to the purpose and methods of the novel, are not crude intrusions, for they further characterize Philip and in a rhythmic sense match the other 'codas' which conclude stages of the book. And from now on Philip's jottings are used to convey the significance to a rationally enquiring mind of some of the events.

From the chapters that follow (Chapters Twenty-three to Thirty-one) Burlap, who has lately been prominent, is for the sake of variety completely dropped. This, one might say, is Webley's phase of the novel. His friendship with Elinor Quarles temporarily replaces in interest the movement towards each other of Burlap and Beatrice, and it begins to blossom just as the love-affair of Walter and Lucy is fading and the liaison of Sidney Quarles and Gladys wobbles to its collapse. This is one feature of the pattern. Seen in another light, Webley illustrates the evil results of industrialism which Rampion expounds and Philip Quarles privately reflects upon. Webley's love of power (which attracts Elinor) is an assertion of the human will against the rest of the natural order. This, and more, is exemplified in the twenty-ninth chapter in which we first observe Webley addressing the British Freeman in Hyde Park and then learn of various reactions to his speech. Illidge wishes to kill him, Elinor is further attracted to him, and Philip detachedly criticizes him. Here by the standards of the novel is a false action followed by three false reactions. Not merely Webley but also Illidge, Elinor, and Philip are involved in the fragmentation which Rampion repeatedly holds forth about, for Philip's intellectualism, though it yields a correct diagnosis, is as partial and distorted as Illidge's hatred and Elinor's love. All are implicated in the general rot.

When immediately after this, two men, Webley and Spandrell, act against nature in a wood the point is emphasized. Webley, wandering in the wood with Elinor, arrogates to himself the beauty of the flowers, while Spandrell walking in the same wood with a prostitute knocks off the heads of flowers. Also against nature in quite a different sense is the tumour discovered in John Bidlake's stomach. Not all of the allusions made in this part of the novel are explicit, so it is worth remarking on the comparisons being drawn between the embryo within John Bidlake and the embryo within Marjorie Carling; between Bidlake as a painter of voluptuous flesh and Bidlake now corrupted in the flesh, and—most disquieting of all—between the ageing, childlike artist and little Phil, who is also falling ill and is also doomed.

Of the four sub-themes which can be discerned moving together, and sometimes merging, throughout the novel, two predominate in the closing chapters. These chapters are overwhelmingly about how to live (the philosophical theme) and about death. Filial matters are absorbed into the theme of death, and only one love-story, the story of Beatrice and Burlap, derisively remains. The ironies now are intensified in pace and grimness. Elinor is hastening home to her sick child as her lover, Webley, in gay and vibrant mood, is killed. The details cluster on the pages. There is, for instance, the wording of Mrs Quarles's telegram: 'Philip rather souffrant and though unalarmingly should advise prompt home-coming Mother' (p. 508). There is the fact that Elinor leaves the keys of her flat with Spandrell. There is also the exuberance, even greater than usual, which fills Webley as he drives to meet Elinor. Later, while Elinor sobs over little Phil, Spandrell and Illidge are engaged in the farce of trussing the body of Webley; while his child elsewhere is moaning in pain, Philip Quarles is copying down in his notebook the gibberish of a paraphasia patient, and Lord Edward Tantamount talks of the more efficient distribution of the phosphorous from corpses.

It is in Chapter Thirty-four that the 'philosophic' theme reaches its climax, at least on the level of explicit (and memorable) discussion. Here three leading 'perverts' of the novel—Burlap, 'a pure little Jesus pervert'; Philip 'an intellectual-aesthetic pervert'; Spandrell, 'a morality-philosophy pervert' (p. 564)—are rounded on by Rampion who utters at length the positive argument of the novel (though

Rampion's words, as I have suggested, should not be taken as having behind them the full force of the author's convictions).

There are theatrical elements in the closing pages, but Spandrell is a theatrical person, and, though the killings themselves are as little realized as killings in many a detective story, no commonplace writer would contrive such remarkable contiguities. Spandrell is killed after failing to convince Rampion of the greater realities of the spirit and while the music from the gramophone is asserting those realities. Immediately afterwards, and as a final coda of triviality, Burlap is found 'accepting the universe' and romping with his new mistress in the bath.

In writing *Point Counter Point*, Huxley, one imagines, found an excellent vehicle for the expression of his state of mind in the late nineteen-twenties. The elaborate design, far from being superfluous, is at one with the vision. This vision consists in the first instance of a pressing awareness of the connectedness of things. Lord Edward reads a translation of the words of Claude Bernard: 'The life of the animal, for example, is only a fragment of the total life of the universe' (p. 39) and Philip Quarles writes in his notebook, 'The whole story of the universe is implicit in any part of it' (p. 341). What emerges very clearly from the novel is Huxley's understanding of remarks such as these, an understanding which is more than theoretical. A novel can be only a fragment but it can indicate or fail to indicate the lines of extension which run from it. Huxley's evident need at this time was to find a way of writing which would show a multiplicity of relationships and would strongly suggest countless more. This is the first reason for the musicalized form of the novel. But things are not merely connected; they are also modified by their connections. The vast assemblage of ironic parallels and contrasts composes a satire directed against the assumption that any one phenomenon can validly be appreciated without knowledge of all its relationships to other phenomena. Since such knowledge is humanly impossible, we can at least strive for consistent awareness of partiality, and, of course, for increased knowledge. One of the most peculiar and constant features of Huxley's vision is his ability to see every thing, every form of behaviour, in the light of many other things, and the keenest irony is always directed towards the person who sees the fewest connections. Thus a Burlap has few angles of vision whereas a Philip Quarles has many. Again, music, with its rapid changes of mood and theme, is the perfect model for a mind such as Huxley's.

A further point arises from these considerations. Huxley is now more urgently than before dealing with three ways of reconciling contradictions. The three ways, which were adumbrated even in *Crome Yellow*, are those of the spirit, the 'pagan' response, and art. In the first novel, Denis had a moment of spiritual vision, Gombauld and the author himself were artists, and Anne was a pagan. In *Antic Hay* the purely pagan response was seen as a thing of the past (the young girls of Sparta), and the ideal of body and spirit becoming one can be achieved only through art. In *Those Barren Leaves* a version of the pagan response is the 'realism' of Chelifer : this realism and the spiritual aspirations of Calamy are again fused within a work of art. But they are still not fused in life. Yeats said that you can have either 'perfection of the life, or of the work'; Huxley never ceased looking for both. In *Point Counter Point* the three ways are represented by the music, by Rampion, and by the vision of the novel as a whole. By using a musical form Huxley found a way of presenting the three ways without giving to any one of them a prominence he could not accept.

Rampion–Lawrence is the most impressive 'pagan' that Huxley has so far come across. Rampion simply accepts the multifariousness and regards all ways of trying to unify it as perversions. Philip Quarles writes in his notebook :

'You've got to go further than the nineteenth-century fellows, for example; as far at least as Protagoras and Pyrrho, before you get back to the obvious in which the non-intellectuals have always remained.' (p. 441)

This is the latest version of the aspiration first represented by Denis Stone's envy of Anne Wimbush.

The music, however, strongly suggests a different (though ultimately related) view. Huxley's interpretation in Chapter Two of Bach's Suite in B minor, which in some respects anticipates the climactic use of Beethoven's A minor Quartet, offers the clearest statement. In the allegro each instrument asserts its individuality.

'Each is always alone and separate and individual. "I am I," asserts the violin; "the world revolves around me." "Round me," calls the 'cello. "Round me," the flute insists. And all are equally right and equally wrong; and none of them will listen to the others.' (p. 32)

These words can serve to indicate one of the chief things that Huxley does in *Point Counter Point* : he gives distinct form to his distaste for the ordinary egotism which most of us take for granted. (Rampion's ideas perhaps constitute a sort of 'egotistical sublime'.) The novel, is, as we have seen, very largely a fugal allegro in which we jump, so to speak, from the 'cello to the violin, from one political philosophy to another, from one view of love to another, from one self-bound individual to another; and it takes this form for no idle reason.

The Sarabande that follows the Rondeau of Bach's Suite, in suggesting the vision that a loss of self-centredness brings, is used to foreshadow the playing of the *heilige Dankgesgang* in Chapter Thirty-seven.

'It is a beauty, a goodness, a unity that no intellectual research can discover, that analysis dispels, but of whose reality the spirit is from time to time suddenly and overwhelmingly convinced. A girl singing to herself under the clouds suffices to create the certitude. Even a fine morning is enough. Is it illusion or the revelation of profoundest truth? Who knows?' (p. 32f)

Presented in this manner the experiences to which Bach's music points may be no more conclusive than any other experiences, but later Huxley causes even the cocksure Mark Rampion to be *almost* persuaded by Beethoven's Lydian harmonies. And yet Rampion's 'paganism', which seems narrowly to win the day, is itself, along with the music, contained and therefore defeated by the vision of the novel as a whole. It would have been simple to end the novel with Beethoven triumphant, or Rampion, but instead it ends with Burlap. The two pieces of music, the Bach and the Beethoven, the first coming just after the beginning of the novel and the second coming just before the end, fail to enclose the disunity, and thus imply, not pessimism exactly, but a refusal to be optimistic.

Rampion's views, like the views expressed directly by Huxley in the essay, 'One and Many', are, I believe, an adaptation of a leading feature of Lawrence's 'doctrine' in the direction of notions to which Huxley was struggling at this stage of his career. A. E. Dyson, in the course of puzzling out the reasons for the failure of Rampion as a character, makes the following remarks:

'The pivotal question in this novel, and indeed in Huxley's whole career as a novelist, turns out to be simply this: is Rampion big enough to contain the whole novel, or is he not? As it turns out, he is not; mainly, one senses, because Huxley's emotional prejudice in his favour cannot finally overcome the weight of creative intuition that works against him. We are not convinced in the end that Rampion is talking about realities; and this is because Huxley himself is unconvinced, despite the very best will in the world . . . Rampion hasn't explained, for all his good sense, the complexities of sexual depravity which Lucy Tantamount, Walter and Burlap in their different ways exemplify. He has analysed but not saved Spandrell, whose nihilism plays a terrifying part in the novel's climax. Above all, he has been unable to exorcize certain *facts*, which haunt Huxley's imagination in all that he writes.'[14]

It seems very likely that Huxley himself was unconvinced by the attitudes he put into Rampion's mouth; and yet to readers of Huxley's later writings these attitudes are not unfamiliar, for basically they have to do with the acceptance of diversity. Such acceptance is exactly what Anthony Beavis achieves at the close of *Eyeless in Gaza* and—to omit the intervening heroes—it is what Will Farnaby achieves at the end of *Island*. But these two protagonists also discern that the totality of the many must be a One. As the result of meditation, Anthony concludes that, 'beneath all being, beneath the countless identical but separate patterns, beneath the attractions and repulsions, lies peace' (p. 618f), while Will, as the aftermath of a drug, sees the indivisibility of good and evil. At the time of *Point Counter Point* Huxley must have sensed the usefulness of something in Lawrence to his own search. But the something was, I suggest, obscurely felt to be unsatisfactory : hence, partly, the scene in which Rampion fails to meet the challenge of Beethoven's music, hence the areas of the book (notably the deaths) which leave one with the impression that Rampion's talk is merely talk. By 1936 Huxley had found the answer, for in Chapter Twenty-six of *Eyeless in Gaza* he has Anthony conclude from a reading of 'The Man Who Died' that Lawrence wanted to 'work up' the primal material of life only to a certain arbitrary point, the point of animal (rather than cerebral) awarenesses, but that the most logical endeavour would be to drive through both animalism and cerebration to spirituality. Nevertheless, in 1928 Huxley plainly felt that Lawrence's rejection of intellectualism, indeed of any premature conceptualizing, was somehow on the right, 'pagan' lines. In this way, *Point Counter Point* represents not so much a by-way from Huxley's path in the direction of Lawrentianism, as a species of thicket, for which the musicalized form is an excellent expression.

Both the musicalized form of the novel and its harshness require no further defence except to say, first, that a search must include every relevant thing, and secondly that in order to include everything without false emphasis some means of total grasp must be offered to the reader. Although remarkable things happen in *Point Counter Point* it does not present a development in the usual sense. It is designed to be remembered somewhat as music is remembered. This cannot be done with perfect success, as Alexander Henderson has pointed out.

'It is not easy to see how fiction could imitate the abrupt transitions of music. The use of a multitude of characters and parallel plots would not really do it, because the reader would separate out in his mind the stories which the author had been at such pains to weave together . . . The reasons are, I think, that fiction is too diffuse, and does not move as swiftly as music. Huxley, questioned on this point, agreed that the novelist can never really achieve the striking, abrupt transitions of music, partly for the reasons given, and also, he suggested, because fiction is not so symbolic as music.'[15]

Towards the end of his life Huxley made some similar observations.

'We can see more than one thing at a time, and we can hear more than one thing at a time. But unfortunately we cannot read more than one thing at a time. In any good metaphor, it is true, there is a blending, almost at a point and almost in one instant, of differences harmonized into a single expressive whole. But metaphors cannot be drawn out, and there is no equivalent in literature of sustained counterpoint or the spatial unity of diverse elements brought together so that they can be perceived at one glance as a significant whole.'[16]

However, these two sets of remarks fail to amount to a good reason why a novel should not in such a way aspire towards the condition of music. I think it likely that the reader of *Point Counter Point* does not to any marked degree 'separate out in his mind the stories which the author has been at such pains to weave together': on the contrary he holds in his mind, as nearly as is possible with prose fiction, a cross-woven thing.

5

Brave New World (1932)

One of the fundamental technical problems in writing *Brave New World* must have been how to present a clear portrait of the imaginary society while also developing actions and characters. A similar problem presumably arises whenever a writer sets out to produce a work of this kind.

The general category to which I am referring is that of fiction which describes an imaginary commonwealth in order to comment critically upon an existing commonwealth. The bulk of such fiction produced up to the end of the nineteenth century was utopian, while the bulk produced in the present century has been 'anti-utopian' or 'dystopian'.[1] In regard to the writer's methods of handling his material it surely does not greatly matter if the fictional society is better or worse than the society in which the work was written. In either case we are told which prevailing tendencies to foster and which to avoid, so that an author of a utopia proper and an author of a 'dystopia' both have a similar object as well as similar artistic difficulties.

The criticism of an existing commonwealth may, of course, take the form of direct satire as for example in *Erewhon*, or may be exemplary, as in *News from Nowhere*. A work of this nature may or may not also be a piece of science-fiction as that genre, or sub-genre, is defined by Mr Kingsley Amis.

'Science fiction is that class of prose narrative treating of a situation that could not arise in the world we know, but which is hypothesised on the basis of some innovation in science or technology, or pseudo-science or pseudo-technology.'[2]

While the majority of Mr Amis's numerous examples are adventure stories, he does include utopian works and, clearly, *Brave New*

World is emphatically science-fiction under this definition. *Gulliver's Travels*, on the other hand, is not (in spite of the techniques shown to Gulliver at the Grand Academy of Lagado), but Swift's work and Huxley's have elements in common. Taking account of the main sub-categories we should call *Brave New World* satirical utopian (or 'dystopian') science-fiction.

Producers of utopian works, as opposed to writers of adventure stories set in imaginary worlds, must often have to calculate how feeble they can allow the narrative to be. Sometimes they allow it to become very feeble indeed on the assumption that little more is required than a sort of route along which to display features of the imaginary society. Thus, in *Erewhon* the narrator reaches the country in the course of the first six chapters, and from then on there is a minimum of action until, in the penultimate chapter, he makes his escape with Arowhena. In the intervening twenty-two chapters the characteristics of Erewhonian society are recounted as the narrator, on one elementary pretext or another, is brought into contact with them. If Butler wishes to tell us about the musical banks, for instance, he simply has the narrator taken to a bank by lady members of the Nosnibor family. Similarly, when in *News from Nowhere* William Morris has set the dreamer to relate his dream our attention is given to London transfigured rather than to the dreamer's movements in London.

In a strikingly different way H. G. Wells, being an excellent story-teller, cannot but engross the reader in every step of Mr Barnstaple's adventures in *Men Like Gods*. This book combines exceptionally well all the ingredients of good narrative, including memorable characters (consider Rupert Catskill, a satirical portrait of Winston Churchill), with serious recommendations as to what human beings should strive to become. *Men Like Gods* is a leisurely and expansive book so that Wells is able to include both the usual conversations explaining what the perfect society is like and how it came about, and a good deal of physical action (in particular the revolt led by Catskill).

Orwell, too, contrives elements of the thriller in *Nineteen Eighty-four* while giving a detailed picture of life in the future, and a potted history of the preceding half-century. But perhaps it is fair to say that his task was in one respect easier than the tasks of the other authors I have mentioned, since the society of the year, 1984, is an easily recognizable extension of the late nineteen-forties in Europe. Therefore, less needs to be explained to the reader; and in one instance where explanation is demanded, the workings of 'Newspeak', Orwell found it necessary to use an appendix. In *Brave New World* there are equally ingenious things full accounts of which Huxley managed to work into his plot.

Huxley's book is rather short; it is nearer in length to *Erewhon*, or *News from Nowhere* than it is to *Nineteen Eighty-four* or *Men Like Gods*. The first two of Gulliver's voyages occupy almost the same number of pages. But Huxley had a vast amount to say, so that if he had chosen to dilate, after the manner of Swift or Butler, upon the characteristics of his society, the book would have been a large one. This is all the more interesting because Huxley's usual tendency is to expand rather than to compress. In other novels he generally devotes many pages to kinds of matter that in *Brave New World* sometimes occupy only a few lines.

I suggest that the compressed quality of *Brave New World*, among its other functions, constitutes Huxley's solution to the problem which I am considering. He was confronted on the one hand with a great array of pseudo-facts and on the other hand with a narrative. The facts were of primary importance and somehow all had to be included, but for aesthetic reasons the narrative had to match the expository material in length and scope. One alternative would have been to swell out the narrative either by lengthier disquisitions upon the characters and incidents or by the addition of more incidents. What we have instead is concise presentation of a great many ideas and fantasies skilfully woven into a plot of roughly the size and degree of complication that we find in some of Huxley's other shorter novels.

Though the plot is fairly substantial and at no point a mere device for sustaining interest, the most impressive aspect of the novel is the wealth of imagined social, political, and technological detail. Bokanovsky's Process, the technique whereby one ovary can in exceptional cases be made to yield over sixteen thousand persons, is described with such pseudo-scientific elaboration that this process alone is sufficient testimony to the author's ingenuity. And yet while the techniques of incubation and Bokanovskification constitute the basis of the new society, they form only one of numerous similar feats of inventiveness on Huxley's part. We have also the neo-Pavlovian infant-conditioning methods (books and flowers are examples of things early associated with unpleasant shocks); the sleep-teaching process by which infants acquire, among other things, elementary class-consciousness; and the encouragement in young children of erotic play. For adults, in addition to the drug, *soma*, there are the many mechanized amusements such as Riemann-surface tennis, Escalator Fives, the Feelies, and Obstacle Golf. There is, moreover, the apparatus of sexual activity : the pregnancy substitute, the bandolier-containers for contraceptives, the Malthusian belts. And more importantly there is the entire mental attitude in which polygamy is the socially-accepted norm and monogamy the social disgrace; in which ideas of family, of mother and father, have grown obsolete and even obscene. Huxley creates for us not only the scientific and technological differences between the society of the early nineteen-thirties and the society of the seventh century After Ford, but also the accompanying changes in modes of thought. For instance, it has become improper and unwholesome to wish to spend time alone, to fall in love, or to read old books for pleasure (though for an enterprising person they are accessible). The Headmistress of Eton—inevitably a co-educational school—denies with blushing indignation that she ever reads Shakespeare. Huxley contrives likewise to present both the manifestations of secularization and the modes of consciousness which the total defeat of religion has brought into being. In fact religion is travestied in the Solidarity Services, and the office of Archbishop of Canterbury has dwindled into the position of Arch-Community-Songster, while the Christian cross has had its head cut off to form a T (after the model T Ford) and a normal expression of conventional veneration is 'Our Ford'.

Naturally Huxley also had to include the main historical happenings which have helped to produce the new world, and (as a most important feature) the rationale of the new social order. These are normal and almost obligatory elements in any utopian work. There was, it seems, a Nine-Years War which began in AF 141, and brought about, by means of Anthrax bombs and other biological weapons, such a likelihood of total destruction that world-wide federation and foolproof control of the people were the only acceptable alternatives. And so we learn about not only the war but also its immediate aftermath, which included economic collapse and the wiping-out of pockets of resistance, as, for instance, when two-thousand 'culture-fans' were gassed in the British Museum Massacre.

I have recalled these familiar features of *Brave New World* as a means of indicating now, at the outset, the scope and complexity of Huxley's material. The next step is to show how, and how skilfully, the material is organized.

Huxley begins with exposition thinly disguised as story; not, as is common in works of this kind, with 'pure' story. Very often a traveller in space or time (or space-time), who is recounting his experiences to the reader or to a group of listeners, is first brought to the new world, and his manner of getting there may be an adventure in itself. Thus Wells's Mr Barnstaple in *Men Like Gods* has his car-accident; Butler's narrator journeys with Chowbok to the distant mountain ranges, and, most famously, Gulliver is shipwrecked. Orwell, on the other hand, plunges straight into the world of 1984 and the doings of his hero, Winston Smith. In the same way, Huxley dispenses with preliminaries, but, unlike Orwell, he holds his main characters and main actions in reserve. There are good reasons for this. Huxley's new society is so strange that an oblique presentation of it would not have been adequate. Exposition was necessary, but Huxley evidently wished to avoid the clumsinesses which are so common even in the most impressive utopian works. Consequently, while a small amount of action is taking place from the very beginning, and is doing so within the society of AF 632, what is more importantly being achieved is communication to the reader of the main scientific element in the foundation of the society. Only on such a basis as this (the reliable 'manufacture' of human beings rather than their fallible gestation, birth, and upbringing) is such a society conceivable. Since the processes involved and indeed the whole conception of mass-producing people are sufficiently startling (or were sufficiently startling in 1932) Huxley scarcely risks boring his readers by such an opening. Later on, perhaps, when people have become concerned with the activities of Bernard, John, and other interesting characters, even a few pages of pseudo-scientific explanation might have been a shade less welcome. But at the beginning or elsewhere such explanations in a novel should be as brief as is compatible with an effect of verisimilitude.

'Still leaning against the incubators he gave them, while the pencils scurried illegibly across the pages, a brief description of the modern fertilizing process; spoke first, of course, of its surgical introduction— "the operation undergone voluntarily for the good of Society, not to mention the fact that it carries a bonus amounting to six months' salary"; continued with some account of the technique for preserving the excised ovary alive and actively developing; passed on to a consideration of optimum temperature, salinity, viscosity; referred to the liquor in which the detached and ripened eggs were kept; and, leading his charges to the work tables, actually showed them how this liquor was drawn off from the test-tubes; how it was let out drop by drop on to the specially warmed slides of the microscopes; how the eggs which it contained were inspected for abnormalities, counted and transferred to a porous receptacle; how (and he now took them to watch the operation) this receptacle was immersed in a warm bouillon containing free-swimming spermatozoa—at a minimum concentration of one hundred thousand per cubic centimetre, he insisted; and how, after ten minutes, the container was lifted out of the liquor and its contents re-examined; how, if any of the eggs remained unfertilized, it was again immersed, and, if necessary, yet again; how the fertilized ova went back to the incubators; where the Alphas and Betas remained until definitely bottled; while the Gammas, Deltas and Epsilons were brought out again, after only thirty-six hours, to undergo Bokanovsky's Process.' (p. 2f)

This nicely constructed sentence with its rather hurried succession of noun clauses governed by one subject, 'he', and—for well over half its length—by one verb, 'showed', achieves just the right effects of casual knowledgeability and surreptitious humour. The students now listening to what amounts to a peripatetic lecture naturally understand the general idea of incubation but need to be told some of the chemical and technical details. Huxley's manner of repeating the Director's words suggests that he, the author, and we, the readers, share familiarity with these details to which the young trainees are being introduced, as well as a sophisticated rapport which excludes both Director and trainees. This is an excellent way of passing off the most startling of innovations as if it were common-place (thus anchoring us in the world of AF 632), while at the same time keeping the characters in the sphere of satire. The method also preserves Huxley from having to dwell at tedious length upon the techniques of incubation and having to invent the uninventable. For instance, the 'technique for preserving the excised ovary alive and actively developing' can be referred to in passing, with the implication that we either are thoroughly acquainted with these matters or would not now want to bother our heads with them.

Huxley's attitude in the passage which I have quoted is, broadly speaking, the attitude of much of the book. Most aspects of the novel are treated coolly and sometimes with seeming offhandedness, however alien or shocking they might be. A tone of mockery governs the presentation both of innovations and of characters' behaviour. (The tone is absent, as I shall presently note, from only a few special parts of the novel.) Since the new techniques have not im-proved human nature, both the techniques and human nature can be mocked. In so far as *Brave New World* is a parody of *Men Like Gods*, the parody consists not only in a portrait of a spiritual decline from the standards of the twentieth century but also, and perhaps mainly, in the fact that people, in spite of momentous changes in environment, often behave in thoroughly familiar ways.[3] Whereas in Wells's imagination the distant future, or a contemporary world in a different dimension from ours, always belongs to radically different beings (god-like Utopians, bestial Morlocks, ennervated Eloi), Huxley's characters manifest all the usual vanities and selfishnesses. Such a remarkable change as the disappearance of family life is principally shown as having altered the objects of taboo or scatology. The scientifically-determined caste system has not abolished snobbery in the upper classes: for instance, a pretty girl is prouder to be the sexual partner of an Alpha-Plus than of a mere Alpha.

The opening chapter illustrates this point quite clearly, because in it the exposition of Bokanovsky's Process and accompanying techniques proceeds via a piece of social comedy of the usual Huxleyan sort. The Director is a pompous administrator; Henry Foster is the regular naïvely clever scientist, and the students unquestioningly take notes in a time-honoured manner. Sycophancy, gullibility, and various comic trappings of any hierarchical institution at any period are all still in evidence.

But these attributes are conveyed with the brevity which I have previously mentioned. For once, and very suitably, Huxley does not contemplate at length the qualities he is describing. The tone of dispatch is present even in the opening sentences.

'A squat grey building of only thirty-four stories. Over the main entrance the words, CENTRAL LONDON HATCHERY AND CONDITIONING CENTRE, and, in a shield, the World State's motto, COMMUNITY, IDENTITY, STABILITY.' (p. 1)

The promptitude here, the businesslike absence of verbs, is calculated to reduce the sense of something wonderful being described. It is part of Huxley's purpose throughout the book to offer the marvellous as though it were commonplace, and so one almost misses the information (which in most of his other novels he would typically have stressed) that the building has 'only' thirty-four stories, and almost accepts without question the function of the building, the fact that there is a World State, the nature of the motto, and, perhaps, its not being in Latin.

Similarly, for all the proper length of the second paragraph Huxley makes no fuss over the symbolic mortuary quality with which he invests, of all places, the Fertilizing Room.

'The enormous room on the ground floor faced towards the north. Cold for all the summer beyond the panes, for all the tropical heat of the room itself, a harsh thin light glared through the windows, hungrily seeking some draped lay figure, some pallid shape of academic goose-flesh, but finding only the glass and nickel and bleakly shining porcelain of a laboratory. Wintriness responded to wintriness. The overalls of the workers were white, their hands gloved with a pale corpse-coloured rubber. The light was frozen, dead, a ghost. Only from the yellow barrels of the microscopes did it borrow a certain rich and living substance, lying along the polished tubes like butter, streak after luscious streak in long recession down the work tables.' (p. 1)

Thus the scene of the first chapter is set: a dead and frozen light, corpse-coloured workers each performing his part to bring into the world new life which, if all goes well, will be spiritually dead, or at least debased. But almost immediately a small comedy is played against the incubators and gleaming microscopes, and the comedy continues when, in the second chapter, the party moves to the sunny nurseries in which takes place a systematic removal of any budding love of nature to ensure that shades of the prison-house close earlier and more irreversibly than they otherwise would. The chief scientist under attack in *Brave New World* is Pavlov, and the chief scientific doctrine, behaviourism.[4]

At this stage Huxley is still as obliquely and entertainingly as possible telling the reader what he needs to know about the society. The shocks continue (as babies are terrorized and hurt by electricity; as small children repeat in their sleep the hypnopaedic slogans), and so does the minor story of the Director's showing students around his establishment. The tone of the first chapter likewise continues to prevail in the second; a tone which by ridiculing the people and the environment mitigates shock but produces its own—and, it may be, more lasting—kind of effectiveness.

However, the method of the first two chapters cannot be pursued for long. Though Huxley is conveying information in a concise way he clearly cannot by this means expound almost every important feature of his society before the main plot begins. Consequently, in Chapter Three he adopts a fresh and exhilarating technique which may as well be called 'cutting'.

As we have noted in earlier chapters, in particular the chapters dealing with *Antic Hay* and *Point Counter Point*, Huxley often makes implicit points (for all his general explicitness) by arranging meaningful contiguities. It seems likely that this procedure was not simply a tactic, but a product of his very cast of mind. In the third chapter of *Brave New World* a method of this kind is used more blatantly than elsewhere, and is used not solely to offer ironic contrasts but also to tell the reader a great deal in a short time.

The manœuvres are very smooth. At the opening of the chapter the minor story continues as the Director leads his party of students into the garden of the Central London Hatchery and Conditioning Centre. All is proceeding as we have come to expect when the students observe children at play and even when they come face to face with Mustapha Mond, the Resident Controller for Western Europe. Then abruptly the scene changes and for a few short paragraphs we are told about workers coming off duty. This is the first mention of Bernard Marx and Lenina Crowne whose story is now unobtrusively beginning. The camera, as it were, now moves back again to the garden where Mustapha Mond is starting to explain *ex cathedra* why the past was bad. History, though bunk, serves to remind the higher castes, who alone know anything about it, of the felicities of the present.

The chapter now proceeds by a succession of separated paragraphs which alternately consist of Mustapha Mond's remarks (or the author's gloss upon them) and conversations taking place in the men's and women's changing rooms. While Henry Foster and a colleague, overheard by a resentful Bernard Marx, are discussing the sexual desirability of Lenina Crowne, Lenina herself is disclosing her frame of mind to a friend, and outside in the garden the Controller is discoursing on the bygone evils of family and parenthood. As the chapter unfolds we learn through the Controller's words nearly all we need to know about present customs and attitudes and the history of the past seven hundred years. Meanwhile, present attitudes are being exemplified by the other two conversations, and attention is being paid to two leading characters.

The method of the third chapter is an extension of methods used before by Huxley, notably in the coffee-stall scene of *Antic Hay* and in several parts of *Point Counter Point*. It is an overtly humorous and stylized extension. The pace of change accelerates as the chapter progresses, so that at the beginning the paragraphs devoted to each locale are fairly long and they gradually become shorter, until for about the last third of the chapter we are being whirled between one locale and another in a succession of tiny paragraphs, often consisting of only one line. Thus, by causing snatches of three conversations to interpenetrate one another Huxley achieves his two objectives, the first to conclude rapidly but adequately all the necessary exposition and the second to commence the narrative proper. At the same time the method of cutting contributes by its rhythm to the tone of mockery which characterizes this and most other parts of the novel.

At this point (a little under a quarter of the way through the book) the stage is set for the main actions to move forward. From now on social and environmental characteristics, however impressive they may be in themselves, will generally not push narrative and characterization away from the foreground. Nevertheless, for aesthetic reasons as well as for convenience, a modified version of the method of Chapter III is continued for the next two chapters, and, indeed, is used very often throughout the length of the book.

Chapters IV and V are thus each divided into two parts which describe the separate doings of Bernard and Lenina on the evening of the day on which the novel begins. (To pursue individuals along their different paths over the same period of time is a device which Huxley repeatedly uses, the most complex example being the presentation of the first evening of *Point Counter Point*.) The first part of each chapter is devoted to Lenina and the second part to Bernard. Clearly, one object of this procedure is to compare the two characters, the perfectly-adjusted girl who wholeheartedly enjoys her helicopter trip followed by a visit to a cabaret, and the miserably peculiar man who first pours out his grievances to a friend, Helmholtz Watson, and then feels alone at a Solidarity Service. Here once more, in Bernard and Lenina, is the root of the opposition between Denis Stone and Anne Wimbush, between Walter Bidlake and Lucy Tantamount (and variants of these opposed types appear in later novels).

The next major step in the narrative of *Brave New World* is the introduction of the Savage and his mother. Indeed this is a true turning-point in the novel for it is here, in Chapters Seven and Eight, that the problem which the novel was written to explore (but not to solve) first becomes apparent. Up to now, admittedly, no responsive reader could have supposed that Huxley was recommending his republic. The irony has not been heavily disguised. And yet, as part of the author's design, such a reader would have been puzzled. Here is a society which fulfils what many have regarded as their best hopes for the future of mankind : war, want, and disease are things of the past; personal and social conflicts scarcely exist. But since the author chooses to make this state of affairs seem absurd, what kind of resolution is he going to provide? Is Bernard Marx, who seems unsatisfactory to other characters, intended to seem unsatisfactory to us?

The presentation of the Reservation and of Linda and John does nothing to settle the reader's doubts, for those are what might be described as 'creative doubts'. Huxley's own dilemma is thus being shared. The dilemma might best be defined in contrast to H. G. Wells's certainties in *Men Like Gods*. In that novel (of which *Brave New World* started out by being a parody) the Utopians are shown as being unquestionably right, vastly superior to the pathetic, muddled Earthlings. The most formidable Earthling, Rupert Catskill, is also the most ridiculous in his Churchillian assertions that strife is the necessity and glory of fully human existence. Huxley, on the other hand, while having uncommonly strong yearnings for peace, beauty, and wholeness (as we have repeatedly noted in earlier chapters) and consequent feelings of repugnance for the opposite qualities, is not persuaded that the Catskill doctrine is entirely wrong. Through the character of the Savage we can see Huxley brooding over the question of the necessity for personal struggle and suffering. He finds the idea that there may be no end to this necessity both appalling and probably true. In *Island*, as a result of thirty more years of concern with this problem, he presents a society in which avoidable suffering is avoided and the pains remaining (including personal conflict) are at least treated in the most efficient and practically compassionate ways. But now, in 1932, he can only ridicule Wells's optimism and reveal in his description of the Reservation and of John's upbringing how dismayed he is by the usual human squalor. In a foreword written in 1946 to the Collected Edition of *Brave New World* Huxley makes the following remarks :

'If I were now to rewrite the book, I would offer the Savage a third alternative. Between the utopian and the primitive horns of his dilemma would lie the possibility of sanity—a possibility already actualized, to some extent, in a community of exiles and refugees from the Brave New World, living within the borders of the Reservation. In this community economics would be decentralist and Henry-Georgian, politics Kropotkinesque and co-operative. Science and technology would be used as though, like the Sabbath, they had been made for man, not (as at present and still more so in the Brave New World) as though man were to be adapted and enslaved to them. Religion would be the conscious and intelligent pursuit of man's Final End, the unitive knowledge of the immanent Tao or Logos, the transcendent Godhead or Brahman. And the prevailing philosophy of life would be a kind of Higher Utilitarianism, in which the Greatest Happiness principle would be secondary to the Final End principle— the first question to be asked and answered in every contingency of life being: "How will this thought or action contribute to, or interfere with, the achievement, by me and the greatest possible number of other individuals, of man's Final End?"' (p. ix)

These remarks, apart from their general interest and the foretaste which they offer of Huxley's later utopia, indicate that *Brave New World* is a portrait of a dilemma. They suggest also that the Savage, whose place in the novel I am now examining, was regarded by the author as the true hero. As a matter of fact Huxley has here done again what he has done conspicuously since *Those Barren Leaves* and will continue regularly to do in the future: he has divided presentation of his problem among several characters rather than focusing it through one character alone. If Bernard represents an ineffectual and ignoble response to the problem of pain, the Savage is capable of tragic heroism (or would be seen in that light in another sort of book), and Helmholtz Watson is the sensible man who will think the problem out.

But it is through the Savage that Huxley concentrates some of his sharpest feelings. If the utopian horn of the dilemma is unacceptable to the author, he also finds the primitive horn very hard to accept.

'The coyote-man raised his whip; there was a long moment of expectancy, then a swift movement, the whistle of the lash and its loud flat-sounding impact on the flesh. The boy's body quivered; but he made no sound, he walked on at the same slow, steady pace. The coyote struck again, again; and at every blow at first a gasp and then a deep groan went up from the crowd. The boy walked on. Twice, thrice, four times round he went. The blood was streaming.' (p. 94)

In Chapters Seven and Eight Huxley achieves effects which are diametrically the opposite of the effects produced in most of the rest of the book. Partly in this way he arranges a perfect aesthetic and philosophical balance between the utopian and the primitive horns of the dilemma; between the minimization of suffering and the positive search for suffering. Hence the inclusion of this scene of penitential torture, which of course foreshadows John's self-flagellation and suicide in the final chapter. These central scenes are not unnecessary pieces of self-indulgence on the author's part, for Huxley, as so often, is seeking to reconcile opposites. Consequently, in the words that I have quoted, there is contemplation, restrained not loosely relished, of the scene : the man clad as an animal; the loneliness of the boy; the sympathetic but unnerving noises from the onlookers; the sound of the whip; the sight of the blood. Although this is a portrait of what Huxley in the foreword of 1946 calls 'lunacy', a 'life . . . hardly less queer and abnormal' than the Brave-New-Worldian life, it is not a comic portrait. One form of lunacy is funny but the other form is not. In these central chapters of *Brave New World*, as in the equivalent chapters of *Antic Hay*, there is a reversal of mood and tone. The eye moving along the frieze takes in a series of rather alarmingly humorous scenes and then without warning is confronted with grotesqueness of a different and unfunny kind. From now on the reader's response to the book will be more ambiguous than it has been, and in this way his 'creative doubts', as I have called them, will grow to match those of the author.[5] Sooner or later in most of the novels there are moments, sometimes (as in the present novel) whole chapters, in which a reversal of roughly this sort takes place. Sooner or later there is a hinging-point, though it may, oddly enough, come near the beginning (the dog on the roof in *Eyeless in Gaza*) or near the end (the death of Miss Elver in *Those Barren Leaves*).

Here, then, in the portrait of the Reservation : its ceremonies, superstitions, diseases, the repellent features of its aged folk, the smells, lice, dead dogs, snakes, the lastingness of the brightly-coloured but often filthy clothes, the murderous sexual possessiveness, there is a contrived polar opposite to conditions in civilized society. And John, whose history is told in the eighth chapter, is so completely the antithesis of the scientifically-conditioned members of society as to have had inflicted upon him what seems to be almost every category of psycho-pathological experience. Fatherless, he has been brought up by a drunken, sporadically-loving mother who is hated and has been assaulted before his eyes by her neighbours, whose sexual activities have often taken place within his earshot, and who has filled his head with mythologies which conflict with those of the Reservation. Once, as a child, he tried, oedipally, to kill his mother's lover, but was humiliated in the attempt. He has always been rejected and despised by his fellows.

110

There is no derision in the portrait of the Reservation, but only in the description of Lenina's reactions to it. Likewise, the elations and desperations of John's past are recounted, not stirringly, but with no lack of sympathy.

'His heart seemed to have disappeared and left a hole. He was empty. Empty, and cold, and rather sick, and giddy. He leaned against the wall to steady himself. Remorseless, treacherous, lecherous . . . Like drums, like the men singing for the corn, like magic, the words repeated themselves in his head. From being cold he was suddenly hot. His cheeks burnt with the rush of blood, the room swam and darkened before his eyes. He ground his teeth. "I'll kill him, I'll kill him, I'll kill him," he kept saying.' (p. 109)

John is a warrior to put up against the Brave New World, but this does not mean that he is the author's champion. His tormented yearnings are merely the dramatic reverse of the spiritually debased stability which is the norm. Huxley always treats a lost violent soul (a Spandrell, a Mark Staithes, a Helen Amberley) more seriously than a hollow man, but never with admiration. And, of course, John becomes a part of the comedy through various later incidents, such as his refusal of Lenina's advances, and particularly through his Shakespearean diction. The laughter which he sometimes arouses is never unsympathetic. When he replies to a question on the telephone by saying, 'If I do not usurp myself, I am,' or informs Lenina that she is an 'impudent strumpet', he is funny but not ludicrous or unlikeable. It is not in the least an artistic error that John should be an implausible character, a concoction of antitheses to the sphere in which he is placed, because any serious attempt to make him realistic would have broken the unity of the novel.[6]

That John's self-education should have included Shakespeare and his utterances larded with familiar lines from the plays is, if we leave the humour out of account, principally a way of opposing to the narrow experience (and consequent tawdry vocabulary) of the Brave-New-Worldians a rich and comprehensive experience, incomparably well expressed. Thus we have the emphasized contrasts between a 'feely' called 'Three Weeks in a Helicopter' and *Othello*, between Shakespeare's poetry and Helmholtz Watson's.

The author has so designed this novel that from now on, that is for most of the second half, our response to the events is as uncertain as his own. The new society is meaningless, pointing to nothing outside or beyond itself, but happiness preponderates over misery;

the alternatives are at best a search, in the way of Helmholtz Watson, or the apparently crazy pursuit of misery in the manner of the Savage.

Huxley's method is to propel us rather quickly, but not over-hastily, towards the long climactic scenes. Chapters Eleven and Twelve are thus divided into smallish sections in which, primarily, there is a renewal of social comedy as Bernard ignobly enjoys his brief period of popularity, Linda, the Savage's mother, sinks into a pro-longed *soma*-holiday, and the Savage grows disgusted with civilized society. There is a good deal of Huxley's usual adept portraiture of the snobberies and vanities of social life, and there are also serio-comic pictures of the conflict between two attitudes to concupis-cence. John, loving Lenina more each day, welcomes his emotions but loathes his bodily appetites, while Lenina desiring John more and more, hates her emotions and seeks to lose them in sexual activity. Here again, or rather, as part of the same total problem, Huxley is dramatizing his own doubts, for he has always derided (with varying degrees of sympathy) both the torments of unsatisfied sexual yearnings and unimpeded sexual release. (Thus there is some-thing unsatisfactory about both Denis Stone's attitude to Anne Wim-bush and Ivor Lombard's seduction of Mary Bracegirdle; about Calamy's easy conquest of Mary Thriplow, as well as about Chelifer's pursuit of Barbara Waters.)

The two large episodes towards which this section of the novel drives are the behaviour of the Savage in the Park Lane Hospital for the Dying and the interviews with Mustapha Mond. The first of these brings the entire dilemma to its starkest point, while the second constitutes a discursive analysis of the point. Each episode, to match its importance and intrinsic interest, occupies two chapters.

I have previously commented upon Huxley's preoccupation with death, pointing out, in effect, that none of the novels fails to give evidence of this preoccupation. Although the deaths in *Brave New World* are not treated with that overt or barely concealed horror and fascination that one finds in some of the other novels, they provide clear clues as to the precise nature of Huxley's concern. The farce at the Park Lane Hospital is a means of attending once again to the problem that Calamy was left with at the close of *Those Barren Leaves*, the problem of whether death really is the conquest of the soul by the body. Brave-New-Worldians assume— indeed, think they have proved—that an individual is the sum of the suggestions implanted into him, and, therefore, since he is bound

112

to be reluctant to leave this happy life, it is humane to distract him in his last hours. The Savage, who welcomes suffering, is appalled by this procedure. No better means could be found of exactly opposing the happiness principle to the Final end principle. What Huxley is considering is the possibility that, if this life is all, then happiness may be the most reasonable aim and the Brave-New-Worldians may be right. Immortal longings can and perhaps should be scientifically removed. But if this life is not all (and even Mustapha Mond thinks that 'there quite probably is' a God), the society is undoubtedly as much in error as it appears to be. In its own way, though it seems to lie outside the main trend of the earlier novels, *Brave New World* is as sure a portent as any of the future direction of Huxley's thought.

Artistically and as a means of best illustrating the theme the scenes at the hospital are in their proper place. As comedy they provide the hectic culmination of many preceding absurdities, and thematically they present the crux of the whole matter of the book. Now in place of comparatively sedate antics (I do not include the happenings at the reservation) we are presented with Linda dying as the music from the Super-Vox-Wurlitzeriana rises to a crescendo, as numerous identical children clamber in play over the neighbouring beds, and as the Savage weeps in horror and distress. The immediate aftermath of her death is the knockabout episode when the Savage throws boxes of *soma* pills out of the hospital window and fights with frenzied children and police in gas-masks. Huxley is here using the conventions of farce (for the scene resembles the high moments of a farce both in its situation and in its occurrences) to express ambiguities, because the actions of the Savage are as wrong-headed in their way as are the actions of the scientifically-conditioned participants. One senses from the tone of these episodes that here is no simple matter of one right-minded victim (or three victims, if we include Bernard Marx and Helmholtz Watson) versus many persecutors, but rather of two opposed forms of error, one of which, because it is perpetrated by a brave rebel, enlists our sympathies (but not very keenly). John is right in principle to cling to spiritual values, but he is clinging to the wrong values; the Brave-New-Worldians are right in principle to abolish the pains of death, but they have abolished them in the wrong ways.

At this stage of Huxley's career it is not clear that one of the things he is reaching out for is a valid way of dying happily. Much light is thrown back on Huxley's earlier aspirations both by *Island*

and by Laura Archera Huxley's biographical work, *This Timeless Moment*. In it she writes:

'There are two diametrically opposite views about dying. One is that the best way is to go without knowing it, to slip away—hopefully when sleeping. The other view—less prevalent but more spiritually enlightened—is that one should die as aware and clear-minded as possible; that death is one of the great adventures of life, and one should not miss it or block it by unconsciousness. In this view, it is thought that the future life of the "soul" or "consciousness" or "mind" (whatever word one uses for that which pervades the body and gives it life) is influenced to a great extent by the thoughts and feelings at the moment of death.
'Aldous believed in the latter.'[7]

Laura Huxley also reproduces Huxley's own account of his ministrations to his first wife, Maria, as she was dying.

' "I would urge her to advance into those lights, to open herself to joy, peace, love and being, to permit herself to be irradiated by them and to become one with them." '[8]

The implication of this entire remarkable account (with which Chapter Fourteen of *Island* should be compared) is that death should not be an occasion for sorrow on anyone's part. This is why, thirty years earlier, Huxley produced such a curious scene as the one we are now discussing: behind it, as behind the whole book, lies a rejection of both horns of the dilemma and perhaps a hope that a third way will ultimately be found.

Something similar may be said of the two chapters devoted to the interviews with Mustapha Mond. The comedy diminishes, becoming largely confined to Bernard's pusillanimity and John's Shakespearean locutions. The denouement lies some way ahead, but it is time to begin a quietly thoughtful section of the sort which sooner or later appears in nearly all of Huxley's novels.

The main matter of these interviews lies in Chapter Seventeen in which John is left alone with Mustapha Mond. There is almost no comedy in this chapter: it consists of a straightforward debate the object of which is to enable the author to tell the reader as openly as possible what the alternatives are. The outcome of the argument is not victory for John, except in the sense that he sticks to his guns. Mustapha Mond is not the victor either in spite of the fact that he has a complete answer to all the problems raised by the Savage. This scene, which obviously resembles the meeting of O'Brien and Winston Smith in *Nineteen Eighty-four*, emphasizes an important difference between Orwell's work and Huxley's. Orwell, having no doubt that Winston Smith is right, causes his hero to be wholly broken in spirit by a wrong but all-powerful adversary. Clearly a society like that of *Nineteen Eighty-four* has to be avoided at all costs. Huxley, on the other hand, presents an open case as if to say : 'Here are the facts and the arguments; we must choose one of these alternatives.'

The perfect reasonableness with which Mustapha Mond develops his side of the case suggests strongly that Huxley is dramatizing a conflict of his own. He is opposing happiness to truth and beauty. In effect Mustapha Mond points out that art and science both belong in their 'purer' forms to truth and are, or are capable of being, incompatible with happiness. The same may be said of personal freedom. Religion, too, is as likely to be an agent of misery as of joy. Social justice, in the sense of social equality, is impossible, and so we must accept either the discontents of inequality or a type of conditioning in which nobody feels unjustly treated. To these arguments, so far as Huxley can at present see, there is only one answer, namely that one attaches a low priority to happiness.

' "All right, then," said the Savage defiantly, "I'm claiming the right to be unhappy."
' "Not to mention the right to grow old and ugly and impotent; the right to have syphilis and cancer; the right to have too little to eat; the right to be lousy; the right to live in constant apprehension of what may happen tomorrow; the right to catch typhoid; the right to be tortured by unspeakable pains of every kind."
'There was a long silence.
' "I claim them all," said the Savage at last.
'Mustapha Mond shrugged his shoulders. "You're welcome," he said.' (p. 197)

The perfect balance of these words, like the perfectly balanced debate which they summarize and conclude, is an example of how Huxley's meaning in this novel is aided by structure. Mustapha Mond has the last word probably to counteract in our minds the simple nobility of John's final statement, which must not be given too much weight.

A similar consideration may have partly determined both the

existence and the tone of the concluding chapter. In some fashion Huxley could have caused the words I have just quoted to form the conclusion of the novel. After all, the Savage could have been returned to Malpais, and it would have been easy to mention earlier that this was to be his destiny. But, characteristically, Huxley wanted one more chapter with whose ambiguous note (re-introducing a species of humour) the reader could fitly be left. There are a few moments of simple seriousness. Even Bernard has lost his fears.

'There was a silence. In spite of their sadness—because of it, even; for their sadness was the symptom of their love for one another—the three young men were happy.' (p. 199)

After that there are elements of the splendid and the ludicrous in John's self-flagellation; in the visits to him of various callous journalists; in his faltering attempts to remember his mother and to forget Lenina; in the use of phrases from *Macbeth, King Lear*, and *Hamlet* which are at once accurate and inapposite; in the jeering sightseers, and finally, of course in John's suicide. These are bedlam scenes, for the obtuse cruelty of the spectators is brought to bear upon one who has become quite lunatic, and will shortly kill himself 'while the balance of his mind is disturbed'. This is not in fact a tragic end but an end which recalls Huxley's remark that 'tragedy is the farce that involves our sympathies; farce, the tragedy that happens to outsiders.'[9] In the last chapter of *Brave New World* Huxley has tilted the scales away from the side of tragedy without pushing them down on the side of comedy.

The emphasis of my remarks in this study of Huxley's first piece of science-fiction has been upon aspects other than those for which the book is famous and, perhaps, for which it is commonly read. I have shown little interest in the predictive value of the novel. Not only in a study of the present sort, but also in any general appraisal of Huxley's work, *Brave New World* should be viewed primarily as we view any of the other novels. It is not an oddity, but takes its place in the line of development of Huxley's art and thought. It displays some of the usual preoccupations and variations upon some of the usual types of character. The doubts expressed by *Point Counter Point* have not yet departed and the certainties of *Eyeless in Gaza* lie four years in the future. It is likely that at the time of writing *Brave New World* Huxley did not simply regard himself as delivering dire warnings about the future, so that the reason why so many people have since gone to the book is not the only reason why it was written. In 1932 Huxley was working out his own problems and, consciously or otherwise, constructed an allegory of these as well as a piece of pure prediction. The plight of Bernard, the Savage, and Helmholtz Watson is not merely to do with a possible future but is also a modern plight. Fundamentally indeed, the problems which Huxley through these and other characters was trying to solve are age-old ones.

When, in 1946, Huxley wrote a foreword to the Collected Edition of *Brave New World*, he referred to his former self as 'the amused, Pyrrhonic aesthete who was the author of the fable' (p. viii). A study of the novel bears out this description of the author, but in a somewhat different sense. The phrase, 'amused, Pyrrhonic aesthete', conveys an impression of unconcern and this seems to have been how the older Huxley saw his younger self, that is, as an Anthony Beavis before conversion. Amused he certainly was, and an aesthete too, for it is surely the perfect form of the novel rather than its ideas as such which have ensured its popular survival. The word, 'Pyrrhonic', is also accurate provided that one means—what Huxley himself perhaps did not mean, or was not stressing—a kind of sceptic whose scepticism is a means of energetically showing up illusions rather than a means of resting frivolously. The chief illusion which *Brave New World* shatters has less to do with an unthinking faith in scientific progress than with the assumption that truth, beauty, and happiness are reconcilable goods on the plane of ordinary, unregenerate human activity.

6

Eyeless in Gaza (1936)

More than any other of Huxley's novels, *Eyeless in Gaza* demonstrates the calculated use of form to match and consolidate the meaning of the words. Some of the correspondences that we have noted in previous chapters were, in all probability, only semiintentional : the author's sense of the plastic or the musical may frequently have operated without clear invitation to do so; but about the design of this novel there is nothing fortuitous.

Clearly there is some strategy to detain the reader in the sequences of *Eyeless in Gaza*, but this is the lesser part of the reason for the experiment, because Huxley is chiefly concerned with aspects of the moral psychology of time. The strategic element, however, is the one that it is best to deal with first.

The narrative is largely about three periods in the life of Anthony Beavis : prep. school, early twenties, and early middle age. Of these, the first is disposed of in the early part of the novel, while the second is interspersed with the third almost to the end. But this is to state the matter too roughly because if we wish to get a clear picture of the design it is necessary to note the arrangement of four main blocks of time. The earliest events take place between 1902 and 1904 when Anthony is aged eleven to thirteen and is at Bulstrode School. The main event of these years is the funeral of Mrs Beavis. Next, between 1912 and 1914 Anthony, now twenty-one to twenty-three, becomes friendly with Mary Amberley, kisses Joan Thursley for a bet, and so helps to bring about the suicide of Brian Foxe. During the third period, 1926 to 1928, the narrative is rather more about Mary and Helen Amberley than about Anthony, for it is in these years that Helen steals from shops in the Gloucester Road, marries Hugh Ledwidge and has an *affaire* with Gerry Watchett;

while Mary, her own *affaire* with Gerry having concluded, starts to take morphia. After that, apart from two events which occur in 1931, the narrative moves on to the summer and autumn of 1933 when Helen leaves Anthony after the episode of the dog on the roof, meets Ekki Giesebrecht, and is divorced from Hugh Ledwidge. The happenings of 1933 to 1935 make up half of the book and also include the journey to Central America, the killing of Ekki, and Anthony's decision to speak at the pacifist meeting.

The first thing to be said about the arrangement of these periods is that Huxley begins *in medias res* in terms of the quantity of material, but he begins at a penultimate point in terms of dates. On August 30th 1933, the date of the first chapter, Anthony and Helen are together in a house near Cannes, and the entire narrative ends only about eighteen months later; but into those eighteen months are crowded about half of all the events. Naturally these late events, being the conclusions of various actions, must be described towards the end of the book (the reader never *knows* the full details of a conclusion before he has learned of its antecedents, though he is often allowed to guess), so that Huxley, beginning where he does, is able to strike backwards sporadically while holding the conclusions tantalizingly in reserve.

To see what a great advantage the author gains by this procedure we may imagine a purely chronological sequence. Suppose that the narrative had begun at the beginning, that is, on the day of the funeral of Anthony's mother, and had proceeded through the rest of the events of 1902 to 1904, followed by the events of 1912 to 1914, and so on down to 1935. The first deficiency of such an arrangement would have been the threadbareness of pattern, consisting of chunks of time pushed up against one another. And of course it would have been alien to Huxley's purpose to provide linking material, for it is only with certain isolated episodes in the lives of the characters that the author is concerned. The only alternative to a chronological sequence, namely reminiscence or flashback, perhaps inserted into the events of 1933 to 1935, would not have been a technical improvement because suspense would have been lost.

Moreover, the narration of many of the events in their natural order might easily have produced boredom, especially when it is necessary (as it so often is in this novel) to include much reflection. For example, the scenes in the villa near Cannes occupy Chapters One, Three, Eight, and Twelve. Very little happens until the arrival of the dog in Chapter Twelve, before which occurrence even the love-making is used primarily to evoke Anthony's thoughts and memories (though the physical scene is vivid enough) and there is not a great deal of dialogue. For all the interest of Anthony's re-flections it is better, in a novel, that such material be presented in stages rather than en bloc. It seems, too, that Huxley, as a good raconteur, was anxious to hold off as long as possible the most dramatic moments of his stories. Thus the arrival of the dog is delayed from the first chapter to the twelfth. In a similar way the amputation of Mark Staithes's leg in Chapter Forty-seven comes as the climax (though not the conclusion) of a sequence which has its beginnings in the journey from Colon described in Chapter Forty-one. The most striking instance of this technique is the story of Brian Foxe's suicide which begins in the twenty-seventh chapter and ends with the discovery of his body in Chapter Fifty-two. Here, of course, I am referring only to the chain of immediately causative events and ignoring the glimpses of Brian in childhood and at Oxford all of which bear solely on his suicide and its significance for Anthony Beavis.[1] It is true also that the first hint to the reader of Brian Foxe's fate is given in Chapter Three when the smell of Helen's sun-warmed skin causes Anthony to recall Brian and the manner of his death.

This is perhaps the best example of the chief tactical advantage of Huxley's method. A. E. Dyson puts the matter as follows.

'Now what does Huxley hope to gain by this method? Mainly, I would say, psychological suspense. For much of the time we are wondering *why* the characters are as they are, and the author deliberately holds back key events until we have been able, from their behaviour, almost to deduce what has happened in the past. The extremely important episode surrounding Anthony's relationship with Brian at the time of his death is kept until near the end, when it comes almost with the shock of recognition. Several times Huxley is enabled by his freedom with time to supply vital clues to his characters at moments when these are most useful to our total understanding of them. And we are less disposed to commit ourselves to hasty judgment when certain vital clues from the past are still likely to be revealed. There is, too, something curiously and usefully disturbing about the rapid transitions between (say) Mary Amberley's youthful brilliance, and her squalid degradation in middle age.'[2]

To illustrate some of these remarks let us briefly survey the story of Helen Amberley. When we first meet her in Chapter One she is married to Hugh Ledwidge, living with Anthony, and carrying 'her hell about with her'. Of the nature and causes of this hell we know nothing, but by Chapter Five in which Helen, seven years younger, steals from a butcher's shop, we begin faintly to understand. A little later, in the eighth chapter, there is an obscure reference to some painful episode at a midwife's in the rue de la Tombe-Issoire, but the abortion is not described until Chapter Thirty-nine (at which stage we appreciate fully what has earlier been unclear—the baleful effect of Gerry Watchett upon the lives of Mary Amberley and her daughter). By rather less than half way through the novel we have noticed Helen moving towards marriage with Hugh Ledwidge, but only in Chapter Forty-five do we read of her desperate coming to him in the museum and of his panic at the thought of a real alliance with the girl he has embraced so often in fantasy. There is a fairly early glimpse of Helen as a dedicated communist (Chapter Twenty-three) but the main source of her political attitudes, the relationship with Ekki Giesebrecht, is not thoroughly exposed until much later. Similarly, we learn in the thirty-eighth chapter that Ekki has been killed by the Nazis, although the details are disclosed only a few pages before the end of the book.

The method of recounting Helen's progress achieves the 'psychological suspense' to which Mr Dyson refers. In this novel, more than any of his others, Huxley must have wanted us to be deeply interested in the lines of development which his major characters follow; and since he could not achieve—perhaps did not wish to achieve—full, leisurely, thoroughly-realized portraits of changing characters, he was wise and resourceful to use unusual means of sustaining interest. The result is that the reader is alive with curiosity every time Helen, for example, comes on to the stage; each 'snapshot' of her produces the fascination one feels in life when, having met some remarkable or puzzling person, one afterwards catches glimpses of her career and hears, from time to time, anecdotes of her past.

There are more important things to be said about such matters as the arrangement of Helen's story, but, first, some other tactical devices deserve to be mentioned. One of these is the distribution both in time and in the actual sequence of the novel of the most vivid events or images. For most readers, presumably, after much of the rest of the novel has been forgotten, some, if not all, of the following features are retained : Helen's stealing the kidneys; the ragging of 'Goggler' Ledwidge; the dog's falling on the roof; the discovery of the body of Brian Foxe; the pictures of Mary Amberley as a morphia addict; the amputation of Mark Staithes's leg. For some readers there may of course be additional outstanding events or images, but of those I have mentioned there is at least one for every phase of time in the novel. Each phase carries its own image or images which help considerably to heighten response. Furthermore, Huxley evidently took pains to produce scarcely any considerable batch of chapters without some striking event or image to fascinate the reader. As it happens, if the story or stories had been presented chronologically there would have been a reasonable spacing-out of these striking things, but Huxley, wishing to leave the discovery of Brian's body until nearly the end, probably saw the need to insert some substitute, and this may be one reason for the fairly early arrival (Chapter Twelve) of the dog.

An additional point here is that Huxley apparently wanted a fair number of impressive occurrences to come towards the end thus providing a series of climaxes (as in *Point Counter Point*), but so to contrive matters that the earlier parts of the book were not comparatively dull. This object he achieved, since the first quarter of the novel contains both the ragging of Hugh Ledwidge and the episode of the dog : it is only the second quarter (roughly speaking) which lacks this kind of vividness, but to some extent makes up for it by introducing or continuing threads—Brian's meeting Joan Thursley, Helen's tangled relationships—which we wish to follow.

The novel of course is made up of many threads which can easily be distinguished from one another, though they intertwine or merge and finally move to a single point which is the state of Anthony's mind on February 23rd 1933. It is possible to describe some of these threads as long ones, such as the central history of Anthony himself from the age of eleven to forty-four and the story of Helen (whom we observe in the days before she has a relationship with Anthony) from 1926 to 1935. The most useful way to look at the arrangement, however, is to discern many sequences which are more or less unbroken in time but are broken in narration. The story of the day of the dog, for example, is in this category, and so also are the following : the events from the morning of the funeral of Mrs Beavis to the morning of the ragging of Hugh Ledwidge; the conversation at Mary Amberley's party on December 8th 1926; the happenings on the journey in Central America, and the story of the fatal relations between Joan Thursley, Brian and Anthony, beginning with Joan's confidences to Anthony about Brian's sexual reluctance. Some of the sequences are concentrated, after the manner of *Point Counter Point*, into a day or an evening, while others cover about a month (the trip to Central America) or three months (the antecedents of Brian's suicide). There are clear advantages in separating the chapters which recount such chains of action. The first advantage is suspense (of a different kind from the 'psychological suspense' noted earlier) which is managed without producing irritation or serious impatience in the reader. In fact, as we have noticed, there are occasions in *Eyeless in Gaza* when the case is the exact opposite: the matter being related is so lacking in intrinsic excitement that a straightforward reading, without gaps, might be rather tedious. This is probably true, for instance, of the story of the day of the funeral followed by Anthony's return to Bulstrode School. It is true also that Anthony's diary, which itself forms a sequence, the account of an intellectual and moral growth, could hardly have been presented in successive chapters. The diary is not begun until 1934 but the extracts from it are advisedly spaced out from the beginning to the end of the novel. (There are other reasons for the manner of presentation of the diary.) All these points are related to the fact that the subject-matter consists of a number of 'snapshots' whose significance and whose relevance to one another can be conveyed without detailed and extensive commentary. Indeed such commentary would be positively destructive.

It is convenient now to ponder the other, much more important reason for the experiment with time. Sufficient guidance is given to the reader in the early chapters. The novel opens with Anthony Beavis looking at photographs of his mother, Mary Amberley, and others, and musing about the discrepancy between one's recollections of times past and the bare, detached record of those times provided by photographs. What matters is the quality of a recollection because it is the subjective impression with all its confusion of feeling, blurred moreover and altered by the events of the intervening years, that affects the individual's present conduct and view of himself. The novel is about the moral function of memory.

Shortly afterwards, at the close of Chapter Three, we read these words:

'At the time of the event certain particles happened to be in a favourable position. Click! the event found itself caught, indelibly recorded. For no *reason* whatever. Unless, it now rather disquietingly occurred to him, unless of course the reason were not before the event, but after it, in what had been the future. What if that picture gallery had been recorded and stored away in the cellars of his mind for the sole and express purpose of being brought up into consciousness at this present moment? Brought up, today, when he was forty-two and secure, forty-two and fixed, unchangeably himself, brought up along with those critical years of his adolescence, along with the woman who had been his teacher, his first mistress, and was now a hardly human creature festering to death, alone, in a dirty burrow? And what if that absurd childish game with the flints had had a point, a profound purpose, which was simply to be recollected here on this blazing roof, now as his lips made contact with Helen's sun-warmed flesh? In order that he might be forced, in the midst of this act of detached and irresponsible sensuality, to think of Brian and of the things that Brian had lived for; yes, and had died for—died for, another image suddenly reminded him, at the foot of just such a cliff as that beneath which they had played as children in the chalk pit. Yes, even Brian's suicide, he now realized with horror, even the poor huddled body on the rocks, was mysteriously implicit in this hot skin.' (p. 24)

Here is a theory about the purpose of memory which points to the main explanation of the design of the novel. Anthony has just rejected the Freudian account of the workings of memory and now finds himself disturbed by the apparent sheer pointlessness of memory-by-association. The theory that next occurs to him is start-lingly expressed to Western ears but in fact describes the manner in which everyone to a greater or lesser degree actually uses his recol-lections from time to time, that is, as data upon which a present moral choice can be based.

Huxley's attitude here towards memory might profitably be con-sidered in relation to Proust's attitude.[3] The latter was deeply im-pressed by the disparity between a recollection of an experience and the quality of the experience at the time of its occurrence. Only rarely and fortuitously does the full flavour of an experience return in later years, and this, of course, is what happens when Marcel takes the madeleine and when, at Balbec, he bends to remove his boots. These Proustian moments resemble the moment when the smell of Helen's flesh brings back to Anthony the childhood games with Brian in the chalk-pit, but Huxley's use of this capacity of memory is much more rigidly moralistic than Proust's. Life to Proust, as to the Wordsworth of the 'Immortality Ode', was a pro-gressive deterioration of the ability to be spontaneously absorbed in the beauty of the moment, and Proust thought that memory should be used to cut through the rind of habits and concepts in order to re-create, so far as possible, formative impressions. This was the way to self-knowledge. To Huxley, however, any self-knowledge gained by such means (or any other means) should be used directly for self-improvement: illumination through the memory is simply an aid to virtue. This, certainly, is the didactic burden of the book, and more than once in his later writings Huxley speaks disparagingly of the use of personal recollections for any less stern motives.[4] One suspects, therefore, that when he causes Anthony to regard Proust as a wallower in the filthy water of recollections, he is adversely commenting both on Anthony's reluctance to remember the past and on what is seen as Proust's self-indulgent eagerness to do so.

Anthony is one who up to now (August 30th 1933) has employed his memory for moral purposes as little as possible. Indeed he has preferred to try to cut himself off from his own past. 'I would wish,' he says to Helen Ledwidge, 'my days to be separated each from each by unnatural impiety' (p. 9).[5] Many details support the characterization of Anthony as a man to whom the past is a burden and whose memory for the quality of his own experiences is weak. For instance, he too readily pushes out of his mind the death of his mother, and, at the age of thirty-five he has to be told that a man at a party is the 'Goggler' Ledwidge with whom he shared a dormitory at prep. school.

The author links Anthony's shortcomings with his reluctance up to 1933 to recognize the present significance of incidents in the past. The reluctance is in turn due to the pursuit of a false (because unrealizable) form of freedom. Anthony wishes to be detached, not merely from other people but also from his own deeds, or omissions, whereas the condition to which he should be aspiring is that of 'non-attachment'.

Huxley's first formulation of the ideal of non-attachment is presented in *Ends and Means* which was published in 1937, the year after the appearance of *Eyeless in Gaza*. It is likely that at the time of the novel he was working towards a clear understanding of the distinction between detachment and non-attachment, two conditions which look alike but are antithetical. The detached man will simply not care, while the non-attached man will repeat Eliot's entreaty in 'Ash Wednesday', 'Teach us to care and not to care'. It is at the opening of the third part of 'Little Gidding' that Eliot offers his most enlightening analysis of the difference between attachment, detachment (meaning 'non-attachment', in Huxley's terminology) and indifference, and of how the memory should be used for the 'expanding of love beyond desire'. Compare the question Anthony Beavis puts to himself in an early entry in his diary : 'How to be simultaneously dispassionate and not indifferent, serene like an old man and active like a young one?' (p. 86).

The chief reason for beginning the novel on August 30th 1933 is that the happenings of that day bring about the start of Anthony's regeneration. To begin with, Anthony is still in pursuit of a spurious freedom, but at the end of the day, we must presume, a change has begun to be wrought in the recesses of his mind. Certainly, only a week later (in Chapter Thirty-one) he agrees, against all his previous convictions, to accompany Mark Staithes to Mexico, and, by April 1934, in order to increase self-knowledge, he has started to keep a diary.

The second chapter in fact consists of some early, rather tentative entries in the diary, further jottings in which are presented from now on, chronologically, at appropriate intervals throughout the novel. In this fashion the record of Anthony's progress in self-knowledge and consequent self-change threads its way in and out of the narrative from Chapter Two to Chapter Fifty.

Thus Huxley begins at the hinging-point and moves immediately afterwards into depiction of some hesitant steps into a spiritually better future. It remains, naturally, to look back and see what forces and decisions (or driftings) have produced the Anthony Beavis of August 1933. In other words, one train of events and the process of deliberate self-development go forward from this point in time, while, concurrently, several crucial trains of past events which impinge upon August 1933 are narrated.

The first of these trains of past events begins, as it should, in Chapter Four (that is, after a brief return in the third chapter to the villa near Cannes, which is necessary in order that the reader shall keep his bearings) with the funeral in 1902 of Mrs Beavis. The implicit point of the fourth chapter is that the 'horrible deep hole in Lollingdon churchyard' will haunt Anthony until he appreciates that the death of his mother has set up in him, or reinforced, promptings to seriousness and even purity. A second, more explicit consequence of the funeral is that Anthony is forced into a close relationship with Brian and Mrs Foxe. The track of the narrative which begins in Chapter Four continues in three more chapters which are spaced out through the first third of the book. Anthony, by refusing to come to terms with the full meaning for him of the funeral, has—in the terms used later by Dr Miller—forced the conjuror to force certain cards upon him.

One of these cards consists of his attitude towards, and consequent betrayal of, Brian Foxe. The track of this narrative begins in the tenth chapter in which Brian, Mark Staithes, Gerry Watchett, and Anthony are observed together at Oxford. Nine further chapters portray the engagement of Brian to Joan Thursley, the circumstances of Anthony's kissing Joan for a bet, and the events immediately leading up to the discovery, in Chapter Fifty-two, of Brian's body.

I have omitted for the sake of clarity to comment on the start in Chapter Five of the narrative of Helen whom, like Anthony himself, we have initially glimpsed just before a turning-point. The happenings of August 30th 1933 are a turning-point for her as well, but she afterwards plunges into a different form of unenlightenment. Helen's progress (which amounts to a sub-plot, and, like so many sub-plots, is responsible for a good deal of the richness and value of the whole) thematically parallels Anthony's, for it too is a sequence of cause and effect. Even such a pure accident as the arrival of the dog, produces a certain effect on Helen because her previous deeds and attitudes have ensured that it will. But Helen's progress also provides contrast to the progress of Anthony, because her nature is emotional and her form of eyelessness and slavery consists of too much attachment. In addition, her end is not an improvement.

In fact from the point we have now reached in our survey there are two contrasting pathways into the future (that is, the period of time after August 1933). While Helen reacts to the incident on the sun-roof by hurling herself into a love-affair with Ekki Giesebrecht and into active communism, Anthony reacts to it by accompanying Mark Staithes to Mexico and by systematic reflection upon his own nature. The progress of both characters we glean partly from straightforward narrative and partly form entries in Anthony's diary. Anthony stumbles through experiences of pain and humiliation towards the right attitude at the same time as Helen is responding to somewhat comparable experiences by consolidation of her wrong attitude.

There is little doubt that the unwisdom of Helen's activities from the time when she leaves the villa near Cannes is intended to stress by contrast the wisdom of Anthony's activities. It is true that only two chapters deal directly and entirely with Helen's doings after August 30th 1933, while seven chapters are likewise devoted to the affairs of Anthony, but of the fourteen chapters which are made up of extracts from the diary, five importantly include comments upon

Helen's current behaviour or states of mind. Helen's joyful self-abandonment in the autumn of 1933, should be balanced against Anthony's dispirited attempts to discard old mental habits by undertaking the journey in Mexico. The change in Helen is swift but unstable because it arises from attachment to persons and things; the change in Anthony, though miserably slow, preludes a lasting betterment. Helen's love for Ekki Giesebrecht, which blossoms so swiftly in the early autumn, is the counterpart of Anthony's meeting Dr Miller in the following February; but Ekki's way is wrong and his execution fills Helen with hatred for herself and all mankind at about the time that Anthony is discovering through Miller a superior kind of love. The contrast is between two varieties of love and two varieties of loss of self. Helen's variety entails exclusiveness and narrowing; joy is experienced through the loss of contradictory impulses. Anthony's variety—or Miller's—entails inclusiveness and broadening out; joy comes as in childhood through the relative absence of desire for a consistent pattern. This opposition is repeatedly brought out in the extracts from the diary through which the events of 1934 and 1935 are mainly depicted. Thus, on June 1st 1934 Anthony records what he said to Helen earlier in the evening.

'I said our ends were the same, the means adopted, different. For her, end justified means; for me, means the end. Perhaps, I said, one day she would see the importance of the means.' (p. 327)

About two months later (Chapter Thirty-two) Helen and Anthony listen to Miller speaking at Tower Hill. Her reaction to Miller's refusal to be upset by an attack upon him is one of resentment, while Anthony is moved to admiration and further desire to improve himself. In the entry for August 4th 1934, Anthony notes that Helen is pinning all her hopes on economic and social reform and regarding reform of the private individual as irrelevant, impossible, or downright bad (because 'reactionary'). On August 10th Helen confides to Anthony that Ekki 'made her kind, truthful, unselfish, as well as happy. "I was somebody else while I was with him. Or perhaps I was myself—for the first time"' (p. 478). The change in Helen, being involuntary, and a concomitant of love for one person, is unsatisfactory. A few weeks later, in precise contrast, Anthony writes out in his diary his meditation on William Penn's statement: 'Force may subdue, but love gains; and he who forgives first wins the laurel.' The meditation is partly upon a kind of love which is diametrically opposite to Helen's in being impartial and deliberate.

The antithetical pattern of Helen's attitudes and Anthony's continues to the last chapter of the novel, in which Helen, on the anniversary of Ekki's abduction, is as disgusted with herself as ever, while Anthony finds a new release from fear and sloth in a meditation leading to tranquillity. The last chapter contains subject-matter apt to the diary but is not in diary-form, as if to suggest that the diary is no longer necessary.

The design of *Eyeless in Gaza* has now been sufficiently described, but perhaps some justification is still called for. I have in mind the words of a recent critic, Mr Peter Bowering.

'In spite of this [the point of Huxley's experiment], most critics felt when the novel appeared that the method was unjustified. It must be admitted that the device of the time shift is too mechanical; that the events of the past are recorded from outside by an impersonal narrator, whereas the treatment of time in the first chapter suggests a psychological method more after the manner of Virginia Woolf's *Mrs Dalloway*, in which the "remembrance of things past" takes place in the mind of the protagonist.'[7]

The only way to defend the 'mechanical' nature of the time-shifts is by reminding ourselves that Huxley has not abandoned (nor will he ever abandon) the novel of ideas. *Eyeless in Gaza*, no less than any of the other novels, is organized to promote conscious reflection upon the arguments it embodies; and, just as a survey of the musical pattern of *Point Counter Point* (conducted after the novel has been enjoyed) enhances both the meaning and the pleasure, so the barefaced correspondence of form to content in *Eyeless in Gaza* is itself creative, though not in the usual fashion of novelists. In effect, Huxley evidently said to himself (even as he plainly says to the reader) that the memory works haphazardly, but sequences of moral cause and effect can be isolated from the muddle. To ponder these sequences at times when the desire for self-change is pressing is an obvious step. After that—so the injunction of the novel runs— observe and record your more significant activities in accordance with what you have learned about your past. The exhortation is traditional. It reflects, for example, *Piers Plowman*, in which Ymagynatyf appears (Passus XII) at the time when the search for Do-well, Do-better and Do-best is held up for lack of suitable introspection and retrospection. (It is Ymagynatyf also who, appropriately to Anthony Beavis and the argument of *Eyeless in Gaza*, points out with historical examples that 'wit' or intellectuality can be an encumbrance.) Similarly, in the puritan scheme of conversion, as illustrated by the *Pilgrim's Progress*, the first step is conviction of sin.

The form of the novel illustrates this process of fruitful recollection and self-examination, and does so 'mechanically', partly because the process itself is 'mechanical', in the sense of being willed and deliberate. The art that conceals art (say, the shift at the very beginning of *Mrs Dalloway* from Clarissa's present sensations to recollection of her past at Bourton) would here work against Huxley's didactic purpose. What we have in *Eyeless in Gaza* is a kind of meditation whose organization is central to the problem that is being meditated. And, one might ask, if this is an acceptable thing to do in poetry (compare the *Four Quartets*) may it not also be acceptable in fiction? In any event a good deal of the detail 'within' the structure is sufficiently dramatic, and it is to this, the less obtrusive aspect of Huxley's art, that I shall now turn attention.

It will be recalled that A. E. Dyson has referred to 'something curiously and usefully disturbing about the rapid transitions between (say) Mary Amberley's youthful brilliance and her squalid degradation in middle age'. While it does not seem to have been among Huxley's principal objects to produce disturbing effects of precisely this kind, there is sometimes a covert thematic point in the placing of the chapters, or the placing of references within chapters. Often the point is one of a chain conveying a certain kind of opposition which Huxley is trying through art and through the reflections of Anthony Beavis to reconcile : the opposition between physical beauty and vigour on the one hand and decay or death on the other. In some fashion this contrast is present in all Huxley's novels (even, though unostentatiously, in *Crome Yellow*), but the shades, tones, and composition vary greatly from novel to novel. In *Eyeless in Gaza* the imagery is more vividly sensuous than it is elsewhere. Let us see, by way of example, how the effects are produced in Chapters Three to Five.

The abiding impression of the third chapter is produced by words such as these.

' "You look like a Gauguin," he said after a moment. Brown like a Gauguin and, curiously, it struck him, flat like a Gauguin too; for the sunburn suppressed those nacreous gleams of carmine and blue and green that give the untanned white body its peculiar sumptuousness of relief.' (p. 21)

In this novel Huxley's remarkable visual capacities are more prominently in evidence than they have been in the fiction since *Crome Yellow*. It is sufficient for him to place a few sentences of detached comment upon a scene within a context of reflection and analysis for the context to be materially altered. The alteration is a product of careful observation and an accurate, unfamiliar choice of words. In the above passage, for example, 'nacreous gleams' and 'carmine' are words which could have occurred only to one who combines the painter's eye with the writer's verbal sureness. In the end, because of the use of few phrases here and there throughout Chapter Three the abiding impression of that chapter is not so much one of thoughts against a background of a sun-roof as of a curious compound of reflections, recollections, brilliant Mediterranean colours, and sensuality.

In strong contrast, Chapter Four is about the day of the funeral of Anthony's mother.

'Slowly, hoof after hoof, the old horse drew them; slowly along lanes, into the heart of the great autumnal jewel of gold and crystal; and stopped at last at the very core of it. In the sunshine, the church tower was like grey amber. The clock, James Beavis noticed with annoyance, was slow. They passed under the lych-gate. Startlingly and hideously black, four people were walking up the path in front of them. Two huge women (to Anthony they all seemed giantesses) rose in great inky cones of drapery from the flagstones. With them, still further magnified by their top-hats, went a pair of enormous men.' (p. 32)

It is November but there is a St Martin's summer. The scene, like that of the third chapter, is infused with clear light, but the light is English rather than Mediterranean, lambent and autumnal. What the reader retains, apart from the thoughts of the characters, is a picture composed of black figures set against such a light, the black hole of the grave, and the coffin, 'a small terra-cotta box, hardly bigger than a biscuit tin'. The words of the passage which I have just quoted invite a leisurely, contemplative reading, but even if they are read quickly, a picture remains of the autumn colours, the church, the great black figures, and the plodding horse, so that once again the thoughts (Anthony's nervousness and discomfort, for example) are part of a characteristically Huxleyan whole. To divorce the two elements is a deliberate act, not required of a reader. Nor is it required that the reader should consciously contrast the picture or 'snapshot' presented to him by the third chapter with the picture given by the fourth, but the two kinds of sensuous impression, together with the different phases or aspects of the body (in the first instance a medium of detached sensuality and in the second instance that which is immured within a 'small terra-cotta box') sink as neighbouring features into the mind. Compared with the contiguities of earlier novels these effects are scarcely explicit, as if to offset the greater obviousness of the main design. Rather more explicit, though still not so heavily stressed as some of the contrasts in the earlier fiction, are the contrasts within these chapters. I refer of course to the play of Anthony's musings in Chapter Three, musings upon time, free will, and the dead body of Brian Foxe as against the Gauguinesque presence of Helen; and to the unfitting thoughts of persons present at the funeral of Mrs Beavis in Chapter Four.

One of these persons is Mary Amberley, and she is filled throughout the proceedings with 'secret bliss' because of her marriage and pregnancy. In Chapter Five we are swept immediately onwards to December 8th 1926 to meet Mary's second child now grown up, now proud, tormented and squeamish, engaged in forcing herself to steal offal. Yet another phase or aspect of the body is presented here, because the predominant sensuous impression of this chapter is of the flesh in its rawest, grossest state. There is mention of the smell of stale blood, of a 'drawn and decapitated corpse'. Helen steals the kidney and,

'As she dropped it into the basket, the idea came to her that for some reason she might have to take the horrible thing in her mouth, raw as it was and oozy with some unspeakable slime, take it in her mouth, bite, taste, swallow.' (p. 52)

This rather effective passage is a fair sample of the way in which the set of contrasts in Chapters Three to Five is completed. The contrasts are similar to the variations on a theme in *Point Counter Point*, but the greater concreteness, the richer colours, of *Eyeless in Gaza* promote a different sort of meaning.

More examples could be offered of effects gained by swift transitions, but an examination of the order of chapters shows that, for once in Huxley's fiction, such effects are not a leading aim of the arrangement. Much more important in this novel is the total impression conveyed by images which are not immediately connected but do become linked in the mind of the reader. We have already considered in a different light the most conspicuous of these chains of images—the chain which is made up of references to bloody, raw, or otherwise revolting aspects of the flesh. A good many of these references surround Helen (the dog, the kidneys, the abortion, the kitten that dies, and the killing of Ekki which, however, is not described), but there are others unconnected with Helen which also contribute to the total effect. These are as follows: the sick child in Puerto San Felipe; Anthony's illness at Tapatlan, and his physically painful fear at the same place when he is faced with an aggressive Mexican; the injury to Mark Staithes's leg and the amputation, and (though here again there is little description) the body of Brian Foxe. The impact of these events is enhanced by private reflections, conversations, and metaphors. For instance, in Chapter Forty-two Anthony describes in the diary one of his meditations.

' "Force may subdue." I visualize men using force. First, hand to hand. With fists, knives, truncheons, whips. Weals, red or livid, across flesh. Lacerations, bruises, the broken bone sticking in jags through the skin, faces horribly swollen and bleeding. Then try to imagine, in my own body, the pain of a crushed finger, of blows with a stick or lash across the face, the searing touch of red-hot iron. All the short-range brutalities and tortures. Then, force from a distance. Machine-gun bullets; high explosive, gases, choking or blistering, fire.' (p. 500)

As we isolate the features which are exemplified by this passage, it grows even clearer that a strong impulse of the novel is towards providing an attitude that will enable one to face steadily the various phases of the body from thing of beauty to thing being maltreated or sunk into a grave. The point is best made by referring to Huxley's description through Helen's eyes, of a picture of the martyrdom of St Erasmus.

'An executioner in fifteenth-century costume, with a pale shell-pink cod-piece, was methodically turning the handle of a winch—like Mr Mantalini at the mangle—winding the saint's intestines, yard after yard, out of a gash in the emaciated belly, while the victim lay back, as if on a sofa, making himself thoroughly comfortable and looking up into the sky with an expression of unruffled equanimity. The joke here was less subtle than in *Toteninsel*, more frankly a knock-about; but excellent, none the less, in its own simple way.' (p. 600)

One might easily be misled by the tone of this passage. The context is of Helen, unsuspectingly gay, wiling away the time until Ekki has finished his conspiratorial conversation : within a few moments she will find him trussed and ready to be tortured. But Helen's amusement at the picture is more than a simple piece of dramatic irony. Huxley probably thinks that his character is right to be amused at the naïveté of the artist, but he is also convinced that no answer short of that indicated by the painting (however simple-mindedly conceived) will suffice. The real irony lies in the fact that the artist, more than any modern sophisticate, is right. At the end of the novel, as a short step in the right direction, Anthony gets himself into a tranquil frame of mind before attending a meeting at which he is likely to be assaulted.

A good part of the function of the language in *Eyeless in Gaza* is the evocation of the sensuous—the pleasantly, the excitingly, the nauseatingly, and the agonizingly sensuous—so that all varieties can be included in the reckoning. For this reason (and not because he has a Swiftian loathing for the body) Huxley introduces such effects as the shift on the sun-roof from the erotic to the purely disgusting. Having vividly depicted Helen's body before and after the arrival of the dog, he makes it his task to promote in the reader a frame of mind that will accept and care for both; to arrive, that is to say, at an approximation (however laughable this might superficially seem) to the frame of mind of St Erasmus in the painting.

The sensuous element, which is so richly present in this novel, is joined by two other elements. The first bulks large and may be labelled 'reflective', while the second occupies only a few, climactically effective pages and should perhaps be called 'meditative'. Let us now turn our attention to a representative passage of reflection.

'And here, I suspect, lies the reason for that insistence, during recent years, on the rights of the body. From the Boy Scouts to the fashionable sodomites, and from Elizabeth Arden to D. H. Lawrence (one of the most powerful personality-smashers, incidentally : there are no "characters" in his books). Always and everywhere the body. Now the body possesses one enormous merit; it is indubitably *there*. Whereas the personality, as a mental structure, may be all in bits—gnawed down to Hamlet's heap of sawdust. Only the rather stupid and insentient, nowadays, have strong and sharply defined personalities. Only the barbarians among us "know what they are". The civilized are conscious of "what they may be", and so are incapable of knowing what, for practical, social purposes, they actually are—have forgotten how to select a personality out of their total atomic experience. In the swamp and welter of this uncertainty the body stands firm like a Rock of Ages.' (p. 148f)[8]

Although these remarks are supposed to be little more than notes for a chapter of Anthony Beavis's book, 'Elements of Sociology', they could, with scarcely any alteration, appear as part of an essay under the author's own name. This amounts to saying that we are dealing with a piece of perfectly lucid exposition of a sort that has often been thought unsuitable for prose fiction. But the presence of such passages in this novel is fitting (and, indeed, necessary) because they exemplify something of Anthony's mind and stages in his development. In other words, the 'essay' manner is a feature of the dramatization, and the reflective parts of *Eyeless in Gaza* are of a piece with the (more numerous) non-reflective parts. The comment upon the action is itself a fragment of the larger action; and so brings about a proper fulfilment of the novel of ideas.

The idea developed in this passage, and throughout Chapter Eleven, is a key one not only in Anthony's process of enlightenment but also in the author's own progress. We have seen Huxley from the time of *Crome Yellow* wrestling with the problem of his lack of a sense of rigid selfhood. Other people than Denis Stone, Gumbril, and Philip Quarles seemed to have readily definable personalities, to know how to 'select a personality out of their total atomic experience', or, more probably, failed to have sufficiently atomized experience. Hence, partly, Gumbril's farcical assumption of the role of Complete Man. At the time of *Point Counter Point* an inadequate answer (known, even then, to be inadequate) was represented by Mark Rampion's particular way of accepting variegatedness and dismissing Manichaeism. To Lawrence himself, though this is scarcely touched on in the portrait of Rampion and is analysed only now in Chapter Twenty-six of *Eyeless in Gaza*, unity was not to be sought on the conscious level but through an assertion of barely definable impulses.[9] Now, in *Eyeless in Gaza*, there emerges the answer that Huxley will elaborate and modify, but never abandon, for the rest of his life. Briefly, this solution consists of what might be called 'upward self-escape', meaning not the adoption through will-power of an alien personality, but rather a greatly heightened degree of awareness, in which condition the bundle of habits and self-images which makes up the unenlightened ego is discarded.

A not inconsiderable proportion of the novel is couched in a style roughly like that of the passage we have just examined. In addition to Chapter Eleven, which mainly consists of the notes on the 'Elements of Sociology', all fourteen diary chapters contain the same analytical and expository use of language (though taking the form of rough notes), and elsewhere the manner is often present in renderings of Anthony's thoughts and conversations. Therefore there is enough serious reflective language in the novel for such language to make a weighty aesthetic contribution. The chief final effect of *Eyeless in Gaza* arises from a curious blend of sensuousness (sometimes rather detached, as in the passages about Brian and Joan, sometimes quite immediate as in the depiction of Helen's reactions to the kidney which she has stolen) and expansive, analytical thought.

The same kind of blend occurs in the *Four Quartets*, and like Eliot's poem, or series of poems, Huxley's novel ends with language of absolute assurance. All the tensions of daily life have departed. There is no need to think, in the ordinary sense, and the senses have ceased for a time to invite distractions.

'Peace at the tip, as it were, of a narrowing cone of concentration and elimination, a cone with its base in the distractions of the heaving surface of life and its point in the underlying darkness. And in the darkness the tip of one cone meets the tip of another; and, from a single, focal point, peace expands and expands towards a base immeasurably distant and so wide that its circle is the ground and source of all life, all being. Cone reversed from the broken and shifting light of the surface; cone reversed and descending to a point of concentrated darkness; thence, in another cone, expanding and expanding through the darkness towards, yes! some other light, steady, untroubled, as utterly calm as the darkness out of which it emerges. Cone reversed into cone upright. Passage from wide stormy light to the still focus of darkness; and thence, beyond the focus, through widening darkness into another light. From storm to calm and on through yet profounder and intenser peace to the final consummation, the ultimate light that is the source and substance of all things; source of the darkness, the void, the submarine night of living calm; source finally of the waves and the frenzy of the spray forgotten now. For now there is only the darkness expanding and deepening, deepening into light; there is only this final peace, this consciousness of being no more separate, this illumination . . .' (p. 619f)

This rather long quotation is, nevertheless, only a small part of Anthony's concluding experience, expression of which occupies about nine pages. To begin with, he thinks in a normal manner about the possibility of being assaulted at the pacifist meeting; that is, he imagines himself being hurt and afraid and he starts to invent excuses for not attending. From this frame of mind he proceeds to equally normal (and therefore unconvincing) musings about the unity of all life, in an attempt to remove his fears, for are not he and his enemies ultimately one? There follows a detailed consideration in terms of his own experience and in the terms of biology and psychology of the fact of unity. So far, Anthony is still thinking, in the ordinary sense of the word. The process leads to a brilliantly lucid account of the paradox that while unity is a fact, diversity, which is evil, is the very condition of life.

At about this stage Anthony ceases to reason and explain, and moves to seeing with his mind's eye the illustration of the paradox in the shape of a cone. Concentration upon the cones, which constitutes not an evasive fantasy but a valid way of apprehending the nature of reality, produces conviction. Meditation, in other words, has succeeded reflection, and is succeeded in turn by the condition to which Huxley has always striven—the condition in which apparently limitless variety and conflict are simply accepted, and one is no longer the tormented centre of the universe.

For the first time in Huxley's novels a conclusion is unqualifiedly optimistic. In Anthony's end is his beginning, and for the author, too, a watershed has been reached. The half-way mark in Huxley's writing career, from *The Burning Wheel* (1916) to *Island* (1962), comes in 1939 when *After Many a Summer* was published; and in a valuable as well as a merely chronological sense *Eyeless in Gaza* represents the close of the first period. We have so far examined the variety of techniques which Huxley used to make sense of his experience, but from now on, excluding *Ape and Essence*, we shall be observing degrees of success in the techniques used to disseminate certainties. At the time of *Eyeless in Gaza* Huxley is already sure of himself, but it is a recent sureness arrived at, presumably, by routes sufficiently similar to Anthony Beavis's (I do not suggest a great deal of biographical correspondence), and therefore needs the clarification which writing a novel brings.

It is a triumphant close to a period, at least in the sense that a search of the utmost rigour has been concluded. It seems possible that between *Crome Yellow* and *Eyeless in Gaza* Huxley overlooked no alternative to the perennial philosophy and no loophole in the arguments for it. But the book is also a considerable literary feat because it pushes the novel of ideas as far as possible in the direction of the novel proper without losing the distinctive characteristics of the former or dealing less than ably with the requirements of the latter.

Part *Two*

NOVELS OF CERTAINTY

After Many a Summer (1939)
Time Must Have a Stop (1944)
Ape and Essence (1948)
The Genius and the Goddess (1955)
Island (1962)

7

After Many a Summer (1939)

It has commonly been contended that Huxley's later fiction, beginning with *After Many a Summer*, is less well-organized, and indeed
less passable as imaginative literature, than the earlier novels and
stories. Peter Bowering, for example, who has many enlightening
and appreciative things to say about the later novels, nevertheless
makes the following assertion :

'This lack of interest in form, which characterises all Huxley's later
work, was accompanied by an increasing preoccupation with the
didactic content of the novel, and at this point, as most critics have
observed, the moralist began to take precedence over the novelist.'[1]

Very seldom in fact does one find agreement with Christopher
Isherwood, who writes : 'I am one of those who maintain that nearly
all of Huxley's best work was done in the latter, American half of
his life.'[2]

Mr Isherwood may have been swayed by a liking for the teachings
in the 'American' novels, while the views of some critics in the
opposing, majority party may have been strengthened, if not entirely
formed, by a detestation of the same didactic content. My own view
is that the positive ideas one meets are of great interest, but that
in trying to embed the communication of these ideas in various
fictional worlds, Huxley made some structural mistakes. It seems to
me also that the later novels as compared with the earlier exhibit
a reduction (though certainly not a disappearance) of delight in the
surface of life. It is significant that four of the last five novels have
fantastic features while the fifth—*The Genius and the Goddess*—
eschews a dramatic in favour of a descriptive mode of presentation.

All this, however, does not mean that in becoming a preacher

Huxley ceased to be an artist: on the contrary, he continually attempted to teach amusingly, partly through style and partly by incorporating openly didactic material into parts of the books where most of the material is disguised and metaphorical. In effect, the stories from now on are parables, aspects of whose meanings are here and there plainly stated. Far from losing interest in form, as Mr Bowering maintains, he carried on seeking the right form for saying as effectively and entertainingly as possible what he wished to say.

Moreover, though Huxley from now on is generally sure of his own beliefs, and expounds them with great clarity, it does not follow that the expositions of belief can be lifted clear from each novel, leaving behind only adornment or illustration. For all his facility with abstractions, Huxley's cast of mind continues to require the concrete, the metaphorical, even the poetic, for total expression. Therefore, while it will be necessary in this second part of the study to notice such shortcomings as I have mentioned, my aim is still to define (by the usual methods) the whole meaning of each novel.

With these generalities in mind let us begin to examine *After Many a Summer*, Huxley's first attempt at constructing a parable.

The book is not an enquiry as are so many of the earlier writings; nor is it an account of a journey to truth, as is *Eyeless in Gaza*. In this seventh novel the truth is precisely, unambiguously expressed almost from beginning to end, while various forms of error are concurrently illustrated. For this reason it is incorrect to say, as one critic has said, that 'the philosophic divagations are inserted . . . somewhat arbitrarily, and tend to destroy the balance of the book'.[3] Mr Propter's remarks are not divagations, the placing of them is planned, not arbitrary, and the balance of the book is, in one sense, exactly what they provide. This is the feature of the design of the novel to which I shall first pay attention, but, as a preliminary, it is necessary to give more consideration to the usual criticism of Propter as a character and to Propter's ideas. The criticism is adequately represented by the words of a contemporary reviewer, Derek Verschoyle.

'With Mr Propter, as a character, he displays little skill of any kind. His failure with him is a matter of proportion, for while there can be no two opinions of the interest of what he says, the effect of his monologues, which occur too frequently and at infinitely too great length, is to make the book profoundly static, and to destroy the effect of what has preceded them. It does not matter that his philosophical lectures would not be credible in a person in real life; it does matter that they have the effect, not of elements in a work of fiction, but a series of casual tracts.'[4]

Huxley may have been influenced by remarks of this kind, in spite of the fact that he once stated that he had never read his critics,[5] because it was in the writing of his next novel, *Time Must Have a Stop*, that he took pains to space out, to reduce, and to integrate the straightforwardly didactic material, and in consequence was pleased with what he regarded as a superior technical achievement.[6] Nevertheless, the examples of *Time Must Have a Stop* and *The Genius and the Goddess* incline one to acknowledge the justice of Mr Verschoyle's remarks. The truth of the matter is that Mr Propter talks too much in relation to the rest of the novel and is barely involved in the action. The lengthy expression of serious ideas can artistically be included in a novel when the novel as a whole is big enough to contain them comfortably and when the utterer of the ideas lives and suffers (as, for example, when Dostoevsky causes the complex Ivan Karamazov to hold forth against Christianity for two profoundly interesting chapters).

In fact, Propter talks for about seventy out of the three hundred and fourteen pages of the book, and there are other places where a character (Pete Boone or Jeremy Pordage) thinks about Propter's words. Nearly a quarter of the novel provides both an analysis of the various stupidities and wickednesses which are manifested in the other three quarters, and positive recommendations as to how to improve the quality of life. Propter repeats himself a good deal (usually with interesting variations) so that it is not difficult (and is useful) roughly to summarize his main points.[7]

Propter's views rest upon a basic assumption that the nature of things is universal and everlasting. In one way or another his remarks continuously support the first of the two fragments of Heracleitus that T. S. Eliot used as epigraphs to 'Burnt Norton': 'Though the law of things is universal in scope most men act as if they had insight of their own.' Thus, Propter is again and again pointing out that all deeds carry their own characteristic, inescapable consequences; that one can never get something for nothing; that political revolutions produce at best a balance of good and bad; that God is not mocked; that life is 'not fair'; that 'from him that hath not shall be taken away even that which he hath'.

Perhaps the most fundamental of the timeless laws that Propter expounds is concerned with the nature of time itself. Actual good, says Propter, is outside time. In so far as a man looks before and after and pines for what is not, he cannot think good thoughts or perform good acts. The human personality, which ideally should be transcended, is realized only by reference to past and future. To the extent that a sense of past and future is lost, a sense of personality is also lost, and the individual becomes capable of good. Although this ancient wisdom is more memorably expressed in the *Four Quartets*, no other modern author can have expressed it more comprehensively than Huxley.

Mr Propter also discusses man's amphibian nature. He is no Manichee for he regards both flesh and spirit as good. It is not clear whether or not he can be classed as a humanist, since humanism contains so many variations of belief and emphasis,[8] but he does assert that it is a mistake to believe that the human will can somehow prevail over the pre-ordained nature of things, and also that the strictly human sphere is the sphere in which spirit and flesh are both frustrated and perverted. When one's bodily functions are in order, when one's senses are responding naturally to whatever stimuli they are receiving, all is well. Bodily appetencies and aversions, unprovoked and untouched by thought, are right and proper. The spirit, on the other hand, is the mode of consciousness by which it is possible to apprehend the nature of the world without personal desires and aversions. 'All shall be well, and all manner of things shall be well.'[9] In other words, the nearer one approaches the purely animal or the purely spiritual, the better (and the more healthy) one becomes. Error resides in the wretched ego. In an essay Huxley remarks that Swift 'could not forgive men and women for being vertebrate mammals as well as immortal souls.'[10] Mr Propter is perfectly happy that man should be both, and is only concerned about the difficulty of being either satisfactorily.

Propter accepts Cardinal Bérulle's definition of man as 'a nothingness surrounded by God, indigent and capable of God, filled with God if he so desires', and accepts John Tauler's definition of God as 'a being withdrawn from creatures, a free power, a pure working' (p. 90). Familiar difficulties (in what way is God both a 'being' and a 'pure working'? in what sense is He 'withdrawn from creatures' yet immanent?) are not enlarged upon, but Propter's chief wish is clearly to the effect that man should recognize his own nothingness and should desire to be filled with God.

That is the substance of Mr Propter's teaching, though it should be added that he also proposes a form of social organization—a kind of Jeffersonian democracy—in which his traditional message has the greatest chance of being acted upon.

If we now place Propter's words on one side of the scales, as it were, we shall readily see that the rest of the novel must be placed on the other side. It could be said of almost every novel that its subject matter, including the virtues it celebrates, is in flat contradiction to Propter's notions, but here the contradiction is deliberate and heightened, and made to be the main feature of the structure. Every character except Propter thinks and acts falsely; the locale, especially Jo Stoyte's house, lends itself to the boosting rather than the diminution of ego; the news (from Spain) is of what Propter thinks of as wasted or evil efforts; there are marked obsessions with time and 'progress'; there is a common assumption that the nature of things is constantly changing or can be caused to change to suit a particular case. Partly for the purpose of illustrating the constancy of wrong-headedness, many present attitudes are implicitly matched with attitudes revealed in the Earl of Gonister's notebooks, which cover the period from about 1770 to 1834.

There is some subtlety and complexity in the details of this contradiction or balance, mechanical though it undoubtedly is. For instance, a character's views are sometimes a parody of, rather than a simple opposition to, the correct views and in this respect the novel reveals Huxley's apprenticeship in techniques which he uses much more skilfully in *Time Must Have a Stop*. There are, moreover, many correspondences between forms of error. The systematic nature of the balance that Huxley has arranged helps the novel to be a sort of artificial comedy, incorporating fantastic features. The characters clearly are exceptional and some of them are even somewhat grotesque. John Wain has complained, 'What on earth has this [much of the sexual activity] to do with the life of a normally poised human being?'[11] But Huxley evidently wanted to present common human tendencies writ large. The book illustrates some attitudes to love, to money, to politics, to the intellectual life, to death, by the comic technique of isolating them.[12]

The environment of the novel expresses and fosters ways of life diametrically opposed to the ways advocated by Propter. The sky-signs, billboards, and buildings of Hollywood, seen in the first chapter by a consummately un-American Jeremy Pordage, offer and crudely mix a variety of substitutes for the animal and spiritual spheres. Church, cemetery, restaurant and lingerie shop are equated as things to be sampled or consumed. Moreover, the supposedly carnal offerings of the billboards ('Thrillphorm Brassieres', for instance) are as far removed from the simply carnal as the 'spiritual' offerings ('Go To Church And Feel Better All The Week') are from the truly spiritual. The human ego has reached out and drawn the upper and lower forms of purity into its defiling clutch.

Another aspect of this debasement is revealed through the rich houses in the residential quarters of Hollywood. Here the modern human ego shows itself unable to express even some kind of unity, because the houses are in styles borrowed from past or distant cultures. Of this aspect Jo Stoyte's house, out in the San Fernando Valley, is the most monstrous example.

The Gothicity of the house indicates not only that Stoyte is a modern baron wielding power like his medieval forerunners, but also a baron who has nothing uniquely his own to assert. The interior of his house is a mish mash of plundered or copied things, having little or nothing in common but their owner. Thus, by a paradox, nonentity becomes conspicuous and forceful. What this means is that Jo Stoyte has first to find a personality before he can, in accordance with Propter's teaching, set about losing it. (And of course Stoyte is a representative figure.)

The most striking incongruity in Stoyte's house is found in the great hall, from opposite ends of which El Greco's *Crucifixion of St Peter* and a magnificent nude by Rubens face each other. Death and sexuality (both given order and beauty by the paintings) are the extreme elements, which not only Stoyte but this part of California as a whole have attempted to amalgamate by taking the stings out of both of them. Propter, on the other hand, will argue that these elements can properly be combined, stings and all, by abnegation of the ego. The 'no-track' mind which Stoyte's house expresses is a parody of the proper acceptance of multifariousness by the humbled ego. According to Mr Propter, any one of the usual forms of unification (religious, political, intellectual) is even worse than 'no-track idiocy'. In this way the continuity of Huxley's thinking down the years is again illustrated. So much in novel after novel stems from that conversation between Denis Stone and Anne Wimbush in Chapter Four of *Crome Yellow*. Reading the novels chronologically, we see ever more clearly that the uncertainty of the young author's attitude towards Anne was due to a feeling that some sort of 'paganism', some sort of acceptance (though not necessarily Anne's) was superior to the imposition of order by the ego.

At this moment, however, it is necessary chiefly to stress that Jo Stoyte's house, while being a distinct and credible place, is also a formal feature in a way that is not true of Crome or the Palace of the Cybo Malaspina (though it is true to some extent of the London of *Antic Hay*). The house does not merely express a particular mind (Stoyte's), or the general state of Southern California, or, even more generally, the entire mental condition in which mutually irrelevant things rub shoulders. The house is both bizarre and the expression of a normal, widespread condition. In this way Huxley has composed the equivalent of an allegorical painting. In the centre foreground, so to speak, is a fantastic building. A little to one side of this building is a small and decent house (Propter's) which somehow demonstrates the absurdity of its neighbour. This is but one aspect of Huxley's allegory.

Moving around and within the house are human figures, at once distorted and commonplace. The personages of *After Many a Summer* may have been deliberately chosen to represent (even, in some instances, by their very grotesqueness), first, conditions of the late 1930s, and, secondly, lasting features of the human condition. Such people as Stoyte himself and Dr Obispo are representative in the sense that such unusual people as Palmerston, C. L. Dodgson, W. G. Grace, are said to be representative Victorians. One cannot know whether or not Huxley at any stage in the writing of his novel had in mind the systematic arrangement of characters that I am about to discuss. However, the outcome is plain : the characters offer—less tangibly and more schematically than one would have hoped—a variety of attempts to controvert or ignore the nature of things.

Virginia Maunciple—to consider her first—accepts the social order, but not the psychological. To her there is nothing in the least questionable about 'Uncle Jo's' riches as contrasted with the poverty of the transients, or about his manner of obtaining riches. Hers is a child's acquiescence in the social scheme and a child's ignorance of the psychological scheme. She wishes to hold on to all things which give pleasure or a sense of security without seeing that the incompatibility of some of these things will automatically undermine pleasure and security. That you cannot get something for nothing is one of Propter's beliefs and, in the later part of his life, one of Huxley's reiterations : Virginia persists in supposing that you can.

Many of Virginia's characteristics are like distorted reflections of characteristics that Propter recommends. Her vices are the sort that the Devil would encourage when misleading some innocent person about the real meaning of Propter's words. Up to a point she accepts the world as it is. She likes, so far as possible, to be amiable and accommodating, rejecting nobody on narrow moralistic grounds. She lives in the present, occupying what Huxley calls a 'mindless eternity', so that when Jo Stoyte asks her what kind of gift she would like if he makes the money he expects to make she is nonplussed. Similarly, she seldom, if ever, recalls the past. In short, her behaviour is what some uncomprehending person, on being told that Propter in effect enjoins us to take no thought for the morrow, would conclude to be the right behaviour. Virginia's response to distant political events is free from the partisanship and idealism that Propter condemns. Her indifference is childlike, but to be agitated in the manner of Pete Boone is represented as being even worse. If Virginia's accommodation to the conditions of life, partial though it is, is used as a burlesque of 'upward self-transcendence', her mode of 'downward' self-escape is likewise a caricature of the true purity of the animal sphere. The forms of love-making to which Dr Obispo introduces her (after some preliminary translating of *Le Portier des Carmes* and *Cent-Vingt Jours de Sodome*) induce perfectly coordinated workings of the body and exceptional absence of self-consciousness. But afterwards comes a sense of self more painful than any Virginia has known before, and her awakening to a new and miserable sense of her own condition is a major step away from her previous innocence. For innocent in a way she has been up to now. The white *décor* of her bedroom, the white yachting-cap she wears, her short upper lip, her assumption that the Virgin is merciful and will watch over her, even the elements of charity in her feeling towards Jo Stoyte, have all expressed or constituted a kind of childlike purity which is used to offset and stress by contrast the adult, knowing purity which it is the main purpose of the book to commend.[13]

What happens to Virginia is a direct product of her character. Pursuing pleasure and self-annihilation she becomes enslaved to Obispo and acquires increased self-knowledge. Fearing pain and crudity (childbirth, for instance, and the water-spouting breasts of

Giambologna's nymph) she brings about, or helps to bring about, the shooting of Pete Boone and is at last faced with the disgustingness of the Earl of Gonister's housekeeper. As she and Stoyte look through the bars in the cellar of Gonister's old house they see a logical extension of their own desires and roles.

The portrait of Virginia Maunciple is an attribute of the form of this novel, in which we are presented with an assemblage of embodied ruling passions whose thoughts and utterances (together with a few physical actions) are offset against wisdom and goodness as the basic feature of the design. There is one central melody (the words of Propter) to which the other melodies, being variations or distorted echoes, owe their existence. The attitudes of Pete Boone, for instance, are included for the sole purpose of being discredited, explicitly by Propter and implicitly by the author's own style. We are given to understand that Pete's enthusiasm for soldiering is likely to sustain rather than undermine the very evils against which he thinks he has been fighting, since the enthusiasm and the evils are bound up together.

Through the cardboard figure of Pete Boone Huxley attacks all idealistic thinking. Pete's particular ideals are normal for their time and place, since they are to do with patriotism, social justice, scientific progress, and romantic love; but other ideals commoner in other periods of history are equally susceptible to the same criticism. The story of Pete, like the story of Virginia, is designed from beginning to end to reveal the consequences of a particular error. His death seems accidental but is a product of his nature and beliefs. It is also ironic because, in addition to being a futile—if unwilled—sacrifice, it takes place as he is on his way to the top of the keep to meditate upon Propter's words, which are now beginning to influence him.

If Miss Maunciple and Pete Boone are allotted ends which accord with their natures, Jeremy Pordage suffers no fate except to remain himself. He has the distinct functions of enabling the reader to see California through alien but swiftly comprehending eyes and providing the necessary link between present activities and the activities of the Earl of Gonister. It is likely that there are also elements of self-parody in Huxley's presentation of Jeremy Pordage. Denis Stone, one might say, has matured along the wrong lines, and lost little of his ineffectualness; Gumbril's hedonistic dreams have (regrettably) come true. Here, once again, is something of the spectatorial detachment of Chelifer, of Philip Quarles in the days before he met Mark Rampion, and of Anthony Beavis before his conversion. But Pordage, in his character rather than in his words, is a more purely comic and less impressive figure than any of these others because he has no struggles in which we are caused to take an interest. He has retreated into various bolt-holes and now suffers no more than minor embarrassments and humiliations.

Jeremy's principal thematic function, however, is not unlike aspects of the functions of Chelifer, Quarles, and Beavis, that is, to bring out through conversation and private reflections the wisdom of the positive character. As so often, Huxley needs the presence of an intelligent and well-informed sceptic, but now he needs him not to test the theories of the wise man, but solely to allow the wise man to produce for the benefit of readers his subtlest and most convincing arguments. This happens principally in Chapters Eight, Nine, Eleven, and Twelve, which consist of a long, interrupted conversation between Propter, Pete Boone, and Jeremy. Pete Boone can put certain elementary but sensible questions to Propter (about the value of self-sacrifice, for instance), but a Jeremy is needed to provoke Propter into comment upon some words of Molinos, the seventeenth-century Quietist.

The very same words have earlier in the day been discussed by Dr Obispo, a fact which exemplifies a major feature of the structure of this novel. Dr Obispo is of course the Mephistopheles of *After Many a Summer*. Peter Bowering excellently puts the matter as follows:

'Dr Obispo and Mr Propter, representing the conflicting ideologies in the novel, are symbolic manifestations of the material, spiritual motifs referred to earlier. Delineated with an almost allegorical simplicity, they hover around Stoyte like the good and evil angels round a tottering Faustus, Obispo tempting with his promise of rejuvenation, while Propter offers the more permanent, if less immediate, attractions of enlightenment.'[14]

Certainly there is a strong Faustian theme running through this novel. On the one hand we are told repeatedly of the Nature of Things, pre-ordained, unamenable to human subversion; on the other hand are the various, more-or-less naïve attempts to subvert the perennial scheme. Jo Stoyte, though he seems an unlikely Faust-figure at first glance, does give up everything else in pursuit of the sort of knowledge that brings power and riches. In particular of course he wants prolongation of life, and continues to want this even when, at the very end, it becomes apparent that as he grows older he will grow downwards into a foetal ape. And Obispo is the Mephistopheles of the novel, not only because he tempts Stoyte with the prospect of long life, but also because he—much more than Jeremy Pordage—is the character who understands so much of what Propter understands, but reacts to his understanding evilly. These two, Obispo and Propter, stand above the other characters in shared knowledge and unillusionedness, but Obispo collaborates with evil while Propter resists it.

Like Marlowe's Dr Faustus in his early dealings with Mephistopholis, Jo Stoyte, in paying his physician, supposes that he is master when he is really becoming a slave. Obispo's universal cynicism recalls Marlowe's Mephistopholis who knows that,

> '. . . where we are is hell,
> And where hell is, there must we ever be.'

But the irony is that Mr Propter would agree with these words, adding only that in so far as we can contrive to be nowhere by losing an improper sense of self and time, then hell will disappear. Huxley emphasizes the similarity in polar opposition of these two characters by having Pete Boone comment upon their common cynicism. He emphasizes it also by having them both discuss Molinos's words to the effect that one should love God as He is in Himself and not as He is in one's imagination. Obispo concludes that God is nothing and that one cannot love nothing; Propter believes that God is no-thing and that no-thing is precisely what one should love because one cannot then be loving an extension of one's own ego.

If God is no-thing but a 'pure working', man also is a nothingness in the sense of having no self-supporting significance. At the beginning of the eighth chapter Propter draws together some words of Cardinal Bérulle and some of John Tauler to produce the following thought:

'Man, then, is as nothingness surrounded by, and indigent of, a being withdrawn from creatures, a nothingness capable of free power, filled with a pure working if he so desires.' (p. 90)

Obispo's beliefs and behaviour constitute a perversion of these words. He, too, seems to believe that man is 'as nothingness', that God is absent and therefore in a sense 'withdrawn from creatures', and that man is capable of 'free power'. But to Obispo the nothingness of man means that men can use one another as they wish, the absence of God means that it is foolish to bring Him into account at all, and man's free power is simply man's own non-moral, non-significant will. Obispo, like any Mephistopheles (and like Propter), knows that not being with God is the condition of hell, and he is resolved to make the best of this condition by whatever activities (the love-making with Virginia, the experimentation with Stoyte) help to bring others to a realization of the condition. Thus he and Propter are each engaged in stripping people of their illusions. Both inform Pete Boone that his political ideals are false, both contrive to remind Stoyte of his fundamental helplessness, both humiliate Jeremy Pordage. The result of Obispo's scientific experiments will be—as he thoroughly understands—not to benefit people but to detain them even longer and even more ineluctably in the condition of hell. The handsome Levantine facet of Obispo, his wolfish smile, his production of pills and other 'magical' cures, his words which are often absolutely true but which he (like the witches in *Macbeth*) knows will be misunderstood or disbelieved, his mischievous activities which principally cause the killing of Pete Boone, all combine to place him nicely in the Satanic tradition.

So far I have been trying to illustrate by detailed comment upon the characters one contrived way in which the book is unified. The other principal way is more satisfactory, I believe, because it consists of a network of allusions, probably produced, without conscious contrivance, by the intensity of the author's feelings. One of the plainest motifs in this network has to do with death and burial. Huxley himself and his least deceived characters, Propter and Obispo, regard fear of death rather than death itself as the real enemy. Obispo says to Jo Stoyte, 'If you're always scared of dying, you'll surely die. Fear's a poison; and not such a slow poison either' (p. 37). But Stoyte remains terrified of dying, so that his enormously profitable cemetery, the Beverley Pantheon, which is designed to minimize, sentimentalize, or otherwise distort the meaning of death, fails to give him any of the reassurance it must give to many of his customers. The cemetery, with its nubile statues, perpetual soothing music and cosy chapels, epitomizes the confusions and confused attempts to evade the Nature of Things which the book as a whole is largely about. Tennyson's line, 'And after many a summer dies the swan', means of course that everything including the swan (and including the Earl of Gonister's carp and the Earl himself) must eventually 'lie beneath'. When, very early in the novel, Jeremy

152

Pordage says to a girl in the Western Union office, '*You* know, the bourne to which no traveller goes, if he can possibly help it' (p. 8), he is being caused to announce (though the remark does not seem relevant to anything at this stage) the theme of attempted evasion of death. The Beverley Pantheon, to which Jeremy will shortly be introduced, has a Tower of Resurrection, which, no doubt, subtly implants into many visitors a vague irrational optimism. Every gallery of the Pantheon has over its entrance a scroll which asks, 'Oh, Death, where is thy sting?' and the surrounding erotic statuary, which ought to remind visitors of what in death is lost, actually makes people feel more cheerful.

Death and attitudes to death probably constitute the most frequently recurring note in the novel. Pete Boone is killed and so are many anonymous slaves in the Earl of Gonister's ships, many anonymous persons in the Spanish Civil War, at least one woman seduced by Gonister, people ill-treated by the Marquis de Sade, and several animals experimented upon by Obispo. The baboon mother who refuses to release her dead baby is an animal counterpart to some of the human beings.

A concomitant of this theme is the theme of burial. Many people in this novel who deny themselves, or are denied, the full spiritual life go down into the earth, into cellars, into subterranean or submarine places. Sometimes they are fighting against death and do so, ironically, by prematurely burying themselves. In order to escape transportation or confinement in a madhouse, Gonister has to hide in what amounts to a grave. It is less necessary that Pordage's studies (an '*Ersatz* for the experience of eternity'—p. 104) and Obispo's experiments should be conducted below ground level, but Huxley so places these men's workrooms to emphasize that their work is spiritually deathly. To the same cellars are brought embalmed nuns from a convent wrecked in Spain, there to join many historical relics and the animals upon which Obispo is—often fatally—experimenting. The slaves in the holds of Gonister's ships undergo a living death as do some of the prisoners whom Gonister observes in their cages at Newgate.

These cages are sometimes on the surface rather than in dungeons so that they also become part of another motif which is concerned with bondage and liberation. Alongside the psychological states of enslavement and freedom which Propter discusses and which are regularly dramatized, there are many references to more obvious forms of captivity. The prisoners at Newgate clearly resemble the slaves herded below decks in Gonister's ships; the men in cells at San Quentin, to which prison Jo Stoyte is liable to be sent; the girl, Kate, whom Gonister confines in his cellars; the girls whom Sade likewise detained, the inmates of the Bastille; comrades of Pete Boone put in concentration camps; the baboons encaged in the grounds of Stoyte's house, and the monkeys in his cellars. The question here is not mainly one of just as opposed to unjust forms of imprisonment, but Propter does inveigh against opportunities in present and past social systems for man to exercise power over man. His emphasis, however, is only partly on the removal of abuses, since he also stresses the right way to face injustice. The way Propter advocates is to regard yourself as at least partly responsible for your own misfortunes. No accident is purely an accident but is 'the collision of a train of events on the level of determinism with another train of events on the level of freedom' (p. 289). There are murderees as well as murderers; there are people who invite suffering as well as people who wish to inflict it, and this is true not only in the commonplace sexual sense.[15] It is the extent of Huxley's application of this concept which many people would find difficult to accept. Huxley causes Propter to assert that the stupidest text in the Bible is 'They hated me without a cause' (p. 94), and to argue that even the victims of the most flagrant injustices are in part the authors of their own misfortunes. The effect of this assertion is to combine all the categories of human prisoners that I have mentioned into one exemplary theme. While it is obvious that no agency other than Gonister's own will is responsible for Gonister's incarceration, it is less obvious that a typical slave in one of Gonister's ships brought himself to that condition. But Propter recalls the action of St Peter Claver who went down into the holds of slave-ships at Cartagena not only to comfort the inmates but also to remind them of their sins. In a faintly similar way Propter explains to the wretched transient from Kansas about the chain of cause and effect which has led to the latter's distress. The transient could have taken evasive action (or, presumably, invited his fate like a martyr) but instead he declined in slow stages through what Propter regards as a reprehensible lack of awareness. The harsh realism of this attitude, in running counter to much modern, liberal thinking, is no doubt one reason why Propter has been heartily disliked by some readers.

It seems that unawareness is the sin which afflicts all the characters in the book except Propter and Obispo, for even Jeremy Pordage and the Earl of Gonister are sometimes surprised by the results of their own actions. And this kind of 'stupidity' embraces in one pervading theme all the named and nameless victims of actual physical bondage as well as those leading characters whose form of bondage is attachment to the ego. When the Earl of Gonister writes in his notebook, 'The Bastille is fallen. Long live the Bastille!' (and when he speaks to the House of Lords in favour of the Great Reform Bill) he is simply expressing his conviction that mankind will always be divided into top-dogs and underdogs, but to the reader the comment is also an item in a network of parallels and allusions.

The motifs that I have discussed separately are of course inter-woven with one another. Whenever there is a reference to imprison-ment, for example, there is a clear connection not only with other references to imprisonment but to death and burial allusions as well. The simian motif is likewise connected to all the others. There are monkeys and monkey-like human beings, and all have to do with degrees of freedom, the quality of life, the fact of death, and the Nature of Things. The point of the monkey-references, I believe (because it is not made explicit), is that man differs radically from other animals not in the greater scope of his consciousness as such, but in the fact that this greater scope includes the ability to be conscious of consciousness. The man who most exercises this ability, which points the way to 'essence' as opposed to 'ape', is the man who least leans towards monkeyhood.[16]

This, rather than simple comparisons in respect of such activities as copulation, is the real point of the monkey-references in the novel. When Virginia, on seeing two baboons copulating, exclaims, 'Aren't they cute! Aren't they *human*!' (p. 82) we are having brought home to us the kind of simple comparison upon which subtler parallels are based. (The incident with the two baboons also foreshadows the closing scene of the Earl of Gonister and his ex-housekeeper.) It is through the thoughts of Jeremy Pordage in Chapter One of Part Two that the range of the comparison is conveyed.

'One scratched like a baboon, he concluded; one lived, at fifty-four, in the security of one's mother's shadow; one's sexual life was simultaneously infantile and corrupt; by no stretch of the imagination could one's work be described as useful or important.' (p. 196)

These words help to form the conclusion of a train of thought whose theme is the acceptance by Jeremy of what may as well be called his 'baboon-nature'. The point is that Jeremy's self-understanding (which is acute) and the self-understanding of his mother (who has read all the literature about possessive mothers but avowedly continues to be possessive) amounts to nothing of spiritual consequence because the one un-apeish step, the step towards non-attachment, has not been taken. If this is true of Jeremy whom Propter describes as a scholar and a gentleman, how much more plainly is it true of Jo Stoyte who is almost entirely possessed by his fears and rages, whose chest—we are more than once told—is a 'thick barrel of hairy flesh', who lets out inarticulate bellows as he rushes to find his gun, and who finally envies the Earl of Gonister. Stoyte is one of the rich whom Dr Mulge, the president of Tarzana College (the name, 'Tarzana', has been chosen for obvious reasons) knows to be 'like gorillas, creatures not easily domesticated, deeply suspicious, alternately bored and bad-tempered' (p. 75). But Dr Mulge himself is some variety of monkey, and so is everyone else except Propter. This is the reason why actual monkeys are presented so often and partly why so many references are made to people in cages of one sort or another. Even Obispo is merely a clear-sighted animal ('wolfish' is the usual adjective) and the same is true, in a rather different way, of the Earl of Gonister.

Gonister recalls the vision of evil in *King Lear*, for he, like the villainous persons of that play, uses his human wits for obtaining prey. He is a 'fox in stealth', a 'wolf in greediness', a 'lion in prey'.[17] He is intended to be an historical counterpart to Jo Stoyte in his riches and his ways of obtaining riches, but of course he is a markedly more impressive and more intelligent character. After reading the Marquis de Sade he concludes (and the conclusion is meant to be a distorted reminiscence of Propter's words) :

' "In relation to Pain, that empty word, Infinity, comes near to having a meaning . . . For this reason, the infliction of Pleasure can never be so delightful to the aspiring Mind as the infliction of Pain. To give a finite quantity of Pleasure is a merely human act; the infliction of the Infinity we call Pain is truly god-like and divine." ' (p. 257)

As these words show, one of the purposes of including Gonister in the novel is to dramatize the most hubristic of false responses to the Nature of Things. If Obispo recalls Mephistophelis, Gonister is Luciferian. Obispo nowhere claims to have an 'aspiring mind'; nowhere attempts to justify or embellish his actions. Even his researches into the prospect of longevity are a form of amusement undertaken by one who knows he cannot defeat nature but is glee-ful in encouraging others to suppose that they can. Gonister, on the other hand, would rival God. This means that instead of seeking to lose a sense of time, he tries to master time, and so becomes time's principal victim. He so successfully extends his ape-like ego as to cause it to devour his human nature. The themes of death, burial, imprisonment and monkeyhood all move towards the single focal image of Gonister in his underground cage. The concluding scene represents in little the entire novel, which Huxley saw as 'a kind of fantasy, at once comic and cautionary, farcical, blood-curdling and reflective.'[18]

This list of accurate epithets does not include 'realistic', from which we might conclude that even the non-fantastic parts of the book were intended to possess little more than the kind of verisimili-tude one finds in the most artificial comedy or in allegory. Unfortun-ately, the reader, through no fault of his own, expects something less schematic and less blatantly didactic than he gets: this is the central weakness of Huxley's first attempt to teach delightfully.

8

Time Must Have a Stop (1944)

'But Hotspur's summary has a final clause : time must have a stop. And not only *must*, as an ethical imperative and an eschatological hope, but also *does* have a stop, in the indicative tense, as a matter of brute experience. It is only by taking the fact of eternity into account that we can deliver thought from its slavery to life.' (p. 292)

The main structure of the novel is designed to persuade us of the truth of these words. Huxley's target is plainer and his aim is surer than ever before or afterwards in the fiction. To say this is not to assert that *Time Must Have a Stop* is the best of the novels (though Huxley himself thought so[1]) but merely to mention that the ambiguities of the earlier fiction are still absent while the message of the later fiction is narrowed to one clear point.

For all its richness and variety of dramatic detail the narrative drives forward concentratedly towards the clear point. Many seemingly incidental things further the momentum. In effect we are shown what Yeats called 'the foul rag-and-bone shop of the heart'[2] and various 'ladders' by which people seek to climb upwards. All ladders but one are sooner or later knocked away and the rightness of the remaining ladder is both argued and demonstrated with the full force of the author's conviction. The procedure is familiar, having been used again and again since the time of *Those Barren Leaves*, but here are noteworthy refinements which produce a subtler fusion of the elements of the novel. Much less than usual does Huxley tell us what to make of an occurrence, and many of the arguments or attitudes (though not of course Bruno Rontini's) seem less important than they really are. To illustrate these remarks I shall first consider the nature of the particular ladder which Sebastian Barnack, until the time of his conversion, thinks he will climb.

At the outset Sebastian, among his other activities (for Huxley seems to have been unusually determined not to halt the flow of action), reflects upon 'Endymion' and polishes the phrases of his own projected poem whose theme will be the 'historical squalor that was Greece and the imaginary glory' (p. 5). The squalor consists of pain, dirt, slavery, sensuality, and sophistical argumentation, while the glory is summed up in the phrase, 'the incandescent copulation of Gods'.

> 'And all the while, dazzling upon a thousand
> Islands in the hyacinthine sea,
> What bulls, what boys, what frenzy of swans and nipples,
> What radiant lusts, like a red forge panting up
> From fire to purer fire, to Light Itself—
> The incandescent copulation of Gods.' (p. 7)

To the youthful Stephen 'Light Itself' means a barely imaginable state of ecstasy, an intensification of some compound of the pleasurable ecstasies which people now and again experience in life. He despises the humdrum, the ugly, and the incoherent. We are shown in the early chapters the extent to which Sebastian's life is made up of these despised elements and his ways of counteracting them by composing poetry or fantasies. The poetry faces the squalor but takes it up into a verbal universe of order and beauty, while the fantasies simply exclude squalor. Of course these early chapters offer principally a characterization of Sebastian and of other figures who surround him, but Huxley builds into the characterization, here and later on, a number of images and references which expand beyond their immediate function.

On the road where Sebastian's father lives there is a Primitive Methodist chapel whose appearance is magically transformed when the gas-lights come on in the evening.

> 'Little squalor! transfigured into Ely,
> Into Bourges, into the beauty of holiness;
> Burgeoning out of gas-light into Elephanta;
> Out of school-treats, out of the Reverend Wilkins,
> Flowering into Poetry . . .' (p. 30)

Sebastian ponders the question of which is real—the dreary pieties and the plainness of the chapel in the daytime, or its loveliness at night, which is a product of 'bright little details and distinctions fading upwards into undifferentiated mystery' (p. 30). The reader is going to be led to the implicit conception that both are real, that the night-time beauty of the chapel, like Sebastian's notion of 'Light Itself', is a dim earthly sign of the 'Brightness beyond the limits of the possible' (p. 139) which Eustace Barnack will experience after death. The chapel and the projected poem are crude paradigms of the true relationship between man's existence and (in Huxleyan terms) his Final End. The particular form of squalor which is dreariness changes into the 'beauty of holiness'; the varied squalors that were Greece move upwards in Sebastian's naïve imagination into 'the incandescent copulation of Gods'. Sebastian is an aesthete who entertains adolescent sexual fantasies, so the ladder which he fancies himself climbing is the wrong one, but to the reader it grows into a distorted reflection of the right one. For example, the phrase, 'the beauty of holiness', is apt and might be used by Bruno Rontini, but Sebastian doesn't know what it really means.

The chapel, or Sebastian's apprehension of the chapel, obscurely burgeons throughout the novel. It is alluded to again only once, when Sebastian is shown the dome of the Cathedral of Florence (which also is darker above than below) but it serves to summarize features of the earnest, righteous political activities of John Barnack, the well-meaning charity of Daisy Ockham, the funereal Poulshot household, the philistinism of a chartered accountant called Tendring, Susan's married life, and the world of chilblains and church boys' clubs from which Veronica Thwaile felt impelled to escape. Huxley's imagination seems here to be working more Dickensianly than it has often done. Images, characters and incidents are fused either without a great deal of conscious contrivance or with an unusual preference for clandestine effects.

Throughout the period of Sebastian's unregenerateness, similar clues and images are scattered. 'Perhaps dirt is the necessary condition of beauty,' conjectures Professor Cacciaguida (p. 35)—recalling Mustapha Mond and one of the arguments of *Brave New World*— and Sebastian is delighted by the style of the Professor's ensuing remarks. But the Professor, though an anti-fascist, is not a pleasant or enlightened man, and while he merely displays to Sebastian his conversational prowess, he conveys to the reader perfect Huxleyan axioms. This is not an instance of the simple use of a character to communicate the author's own ideas, but rather it is part of a pattern in which many characters are caused to utter partial or misinterpreted truths. We learn, for example, that Eustace twenty years earlier wrote to his mistress, Laurina, 'God alone is commensurate with the cravings you inspire' (p. 97). The words were once a lover's sincere hyperbole; now they are to Eustace a source of amusement, but to the reader they suggest a Dantesque or Platonic ladder which Eustace might profitably have ascended.

Shortly after his arrival in Florence, Sebastian begins to conceive another poem, and this new conception neighbours the truth even more closely than the partly-composed poem on ancient Greece.

'It would be something like "Tintern Abbey", like Shelley's thing on Mont Blanc—but of course quite different and contemporary. For he would use all the resources of non-poetic as well as of poetic diction; would intensify lyricism with irony, the beautiful with the grotesque. "A sense of something far more deeply interfused"—that might have been all right in 1800, but not now. It was too easy now, too complacent. Today the something interfused would have to be presented in conjunction with the horrors it was interfused with.' (p. 135)

The description could be applied, with only a little brashness, to the novel itself. *Time Must Have a Stop* contains not only the mention of the something interfused but also an attempt to reproduce it. And the something interfused occurs in conjunction with grotesqueness and horrors—with, for example, the manner of Eustace's death and the bayonetting of Jim Poulshot. Behind the simple irony that the spiritually unfledged Sebastian should produce an idea which, on the verbal level, resembles the whole idea of which he is a part, lies an author's message (nowhere stated) to the effect that truth often becomes apparent if one pays serious attention to what one is thinking or saying. To Sebastian the something interfused is just an exhilarating idea; for a first step towards enlightenment all he has to do is to take it seriously.

Sebastian has other intellectual apprehensions of truth most of which he sees as contributions to his poem. It occurs to him as he recollects a physics lesson he received at school that the cosmos has a primal pattern of atoms and molecules out of which comes, first, the chaos of inanimate things and then the more elaborate patterns of living things. From this observation he moves to the conclusion that people should strive for a way of living that embraces, rather than trying to reduce (as at present), the complex patterns of their separate individualities. Sebastian sees a beetle crawling across the knee of the statue of a goddess and realizes that the beetle and he, the observer, have different views of what the beetle is doing. Clearly no partial view is acceptable. This is particularly reminiscent of *Point Counter Point*, not least in that Lord Edward Tantamount, on reading some words of Claude Bernard, becomes excited by the idea of universal interconnectedness, the full implications of which he does not understand or is not capable of acting upon.[3] And, of course, Huxley has regularly given to unsatisfactory personages ideas which he himself was currently entertaining. One development apparent in this novel is that the scattered ideas are more closely woven into the texture of the narrative. Another development is that there is an increase in the number and subtlety of the occasions on which ideas operate on different levels. On the first level they could be seen simply as pieces of characterization, and therefore be dismissed by the unwary as things thought at particular moments by obviously unenlightened people. On the second level they might be lifted from their context and even anthologized as Huxley's own reflections. On the third level they could be put back into the novel, so to speak, and then seen as elements in a pattern of which we, the readers, have a complete view. Everything makes sense in relation to the 'Brightness beyond the limits of the possible', but each thing makes a different and lesser kind of sense in its immediate context. Huxley treats the words from Hotspur's dying speech rather in this way. On Huxley's reading, what Hotspur says is profound, though he has not been up to now, and perhaps is not even now, a profound man. Therefore, unless Shakespeare simply took the opportunity to deliver himself of some sentiments, Hotspur has suffered a change in his dying moments, or like Huxley's characters, doesn't fully understand his own words. But the sayings of the people in *Time Must Have a Stop* are all plainly in character.[4]

By the end of Chapter Twenty-six Sebastian has talked at length with Bruno Rontini and been presented with some leading features of Bruno's philosophy. He finds these features interesting, novel, oddly impressive, but above all apt for inclusion in his stock of general ideas. The right way has been pointed out to Sebastian and it remains for him to cross the enormous gulf from theoretical approval to ardent practice.

It is not only Sebastian through whom the author composes his pattern of notions which mean one thing in their immediate context and quite another in the light of the whole novel. We judge other characters, or some remarks of other characters, in one way when they are first presented to us and in a different way when we close the book. Daisy Ockham, for example, appears on the first page and is seen partly through Sebastian's eyes as an irritating and foolish woman. She quickly leaves the stage, so that we take her to have been a mere convenience for introducing Sebastian. After her unexpected reappearance she grows more acceptable. The maternal kindness and the lack of a sense of her own importance are not treated with even the mild irony with which similar characters (such as Mrs Chelifer) have been treated in the past. But some of her remarks still sound faintly absurd. Eustace's money, she maintains, must be used as God wishes. She reaffirms that God is Love. She asks Sebastian why he bothers so much with art.

'She hadn't bothered—except, of course, negatively, inasmuch as she'd always felt that the whole business was profoundly unpleasant. And, in spite of her mother's vague but fearful warnings about the male sex, her darling Francis had really bothered very little. So why did other people find it necessary to think and talk so much about it, to write all those books and poems, to paint such pictures as this thing they were now looking at? Pictures which, if they weren't Great Art, one would never dream of tolerating in a decent house, where innocent boys like Frankie, like Sebastian here . . .' (p. 204)

The point is that Daisy's thoughts distortedly foreshadow sentiments of Bruno Rontini, and therefore of the author. We later learn that art is a distraction from God, a means of expressing or contemplating that which you do not wish to act upon, a species of ego-projection, even a sexually corrupting influence in Daisy's narrow sense. Thus in these words Huxley is characterizing Daisy and, almost subliminally, supporting his own message. He later comes to terms with the problem of simple goodness (a problem which occupied him even at the time of writing *Antic Hay*) by causing Sebastian to consider the Buddhist distinction between compassion and Great Compassion, between pity as an emotion, and pity informed by principle and insight into the nature of things.

However, the character who most distinctly plays a dual role is Paul De Vries. His function as lover of Veronica Thwaile is really subordinate to his function as deliverer of a pseudo-Huxleyan message. A recent critic, Mr Jerome Meckier, makes a similar point.

'Paul hopes to be a "humble bridge-builder", to set up "an international clearing house of ideas" in the hope of formulating some "scientific-religious-philosophic-synthesis for the entire planet". As de

Vries continues to talk, he sounds more and more like a satiric portrait of the Huxley who wrote *Point Counter Point* in the hope of finding a musical composition in prose into which all the variations of characters, opinions, and events could fit harmoniously.'[5]

But Paul sounds like a satiric portrait not only of the earlier Huxley who wrote *Point Counter Point* but also of the later Huxley who wrote *Island*. A 'scientific-religious-philosophic-synthesis for the entire planet' is exactly what Huxley was after all his life and offered to us in his last novel. The picture of her husband that Laura Archera Huxley gives us in *This Timeless Moment* bears at times a superficial resemblance to the picture of Paul De Vries, in that both move about to European and American academic conferences always in search of modes of synthesis. And of course Huxley, more than any other modern writer, was never content with a merely scientific, or religious, or philosophic viewpoint.

There can be little doubt that De Vries constitutes self-parody. He is Huxley without the ingredient of ironic humour. The circle of Paul's awareness lies inside, but not very far inside, the circle of Huxley's own. For Paul is meant to be highly intelligent and knowledgeable. But we are led to fancy that anything Paul says, however reasonable (and however much it resembles Huxley's remarks in essays), cannot possibly be true because of his rather absurd nature. In fact a good deal of what he says is entirely true when seen from the one clear vantage-point which finally governs the book. The synthesis which Huxley himself, as an artist, gains by this method is more subtle than any he has gained before. The elements flow together now. Broadly speaking, as we have seen, the earlier fiction displays patterns of attitudes tensed against one another and reconciled in the form of the whole. Something similar is still manifest in *Eyeless in Gaza* where one right attitude (Miller's and the converted Anthony's) qualifies the others. In *After Many a Summer* there is yet a deliberate 'artificiality' in the arrangement of Propter versus the rest, but some wrong attitudes are parodies rather than plain reversals of Propter's. The technique of *Time Must Have a Stop* can in part be seen as a considerable refinement of the technique of parody. Through Eustace Barnack's experiences after death we are told of what Shelley called the 'white radiance of eternity', and two characters, Bruno and the Sebastian of the Epilogue, have a conviction about the way to prepare oneself for absorption into the radiance. The attitudes of other characters, including of course the earlier Sebastian, are 'stained' by the 'dome of many-coloured glass'. Truth reaches them after a process of refraction. But we, the readers, can see the relationship between pure and refracted truth.

This is how we should understand a good many of Eustace Barnack's remarks in his excellent talk with Sebastian immediately before his death. Eustace, the last in the line that began with Scogan, makes trustworthy judgements about the nature of the world. Though he talks for effect he does not talk only for effect. In ranging himself in the ranks of the Old Man of Moldavia (Confucius) rather than the ranks of the Old Man of Port Royal (Pascal) or the Old Man of Corsica (Napoleon) he is expressing Huxley's distaste both for power and for introverted self-torment.[6] His admiration for Chaucer is the author's own.[7] His cynicism about 'Inevitable Progress', which is reminiscent of Propter, also recalls *Proper Studies*. It is not too much of an exaggeration to say that Eustace Barnack's views on the nature of the world are Huxley's minus the all-important element of respect for the spiritual life. Later, Bruno Rontini gives us the answer to Eustace (as to everyone else of importance) in specific terms. Chaucer is very fine, but one mustn't disregard the close of the *Paradiso*. Being a poet is all right if exercising negative capability doesn't cause one to overlook cultivation of the 'inner not-self'.

Veronica Thwaile, too, despite her depravity (or rather because of it) hits on a truth in her belief that the essence of life is shamelessness, and that 'dying is even more shameless than living' (p. 149). Veronica is simply delighted to observe that shame is a conditioned reaction which can swiftly be overcome by events in life and is obviously annihilated by death. Huxley shows us experiences after death that are shameless, thus expanding the significance of Veronica's remark, and causes Bruno to argue that Sebastian's response to the 'shamelessness' of the seance ought to be one of preparing himself for dying. It might be added that even the autocratic Mrs Gamble is supposed to be both ridiculous and not ridiculous in her anxiety to hold seances.

The unifying pattern that I have been examining is built upon a straightforward narrative whose main track concerns the details of an offence and retribution for the offence. As Sebastian sows so he reaps, though the main sufferer is Bruno Rontini. Bruno speaks of the 'genealogy of offences' and we are presented with one such line of descent. This feature of the novel is reminiscent of Anthony

Beavis's betrayal of Brian Foxe. Initially Sebastian is invited to Tom Boveney's party for which he will need evening dress, but his father, on socialist principles, will not buy him such frippery. Immediately afterwards Sebastiain goes for a holiday at his Uncle Eustace's house in Florence, and, as it happens, Eustace on the day of Sebastian's arrival buys a Degas drawing from M. Weyl, an art-dealer. Just before his death that evening Eustace presents Sebastian with the drawing, and Sebastian, having little use for the Degas and much use for evening dress, the next day sells the drawing to Weyl without knowing that Weyl was the previous owner. When Daisy Ockham arrives to review her inheritance she offers to buy Sebastian a suit of evening clothes. At the same time it begins to be assumed that the drawing has been stolen : perhaps the gardener's little girl filched it. In a panic Sebastian tells his entire story to Bruno Rontini, who goes to Weyl's shop and, by threatening the art-dealer in some fashion, regains the drawing. In revenge Weyl denounces Bruno to the fascists. One result of Bruno's arrest and imprisonment (and indeed of the whole sequence of events) is Sebastian's conversion.

There is little need to comment on the manner in which this basic narrative thread is made up of the 'parents, ancestors, collaterals' and 'descendants' of a particular offence. Sebastian's overweening anxiety not to look a fool over the matter of the evening clothes is the principal agency of the evils, but John Barnack's intransigence and Mrs Gamble's readiness to assume that servants steal contribute to Bruno's suffering. There are many tiny moments, gestures, trifling pieces of egotism that also aid the process. Huxley ably makes his point about the interrelatedness of evil and the need for unsleeping vigilance. What requires much more comment is the design of anticipations, parallels, repetitions, woven around the basic thread.

One of the motifs in this design appears on the first page of the novel when Daisy Ockham gazes maternally upon Sebastian in the vestibule of Hampstead Public Library and offers him chocolates. What seems a mere device for beginning a story can later be seen as part of a sequence concerning Sebastian's charm. His name implies that he will invite arrows, but the suffering later turns out to be more of a spiritual than a physical kind. Despite the arm lost in a battle in the Western Desert, Sebastian's fate will lie in his difficulty in resisting help and attention (especially from women) and thus learning morally to stand on his own feet. From the standpoint of the book, though not by worldly criteria, he is therefore a sufferer.

Sebastian's nature is clearly presented from the outset when Daisy

Ockham is moved to give him chocolates, and later, in the same way, she offers to buy him evening clothes. A little later in Chapter One we observe Susan Poulshot's similar impulses towards Sebastian. At the end of Chapter Five Susan comes to Sebastian to comfort him as he lies weeping in his bed. The motif is taken up again at the close of the twenty-third chapter when Daisy Ockham likewise visits Sebastian in his bedroom in Florence, and there consoles him, feeling almost exactly the same as Susan earlier felt. Shortly after Daisy's departure, Veronica Thwaile also comes to Sebastian's bedroom to provide her own, radically different ministrations. The sequence is strictly superfluous to the main narrative around which it is entwined, and its purpose is chiefly thematic. The repetitiveness is of course not the result of a failure in Huxley's powers of invention, nor is it simply that he wishes, above all, to stress Sebastian's character. He gains a kind of rhythmic effect, as in the earlier novels, but does so unemphatically. E. M. Forster has famously drawn attention to literary techniques of this sort, using as an example the repetition of the 'little phrase' from Vinteuil's music in *À La Recherche du Temps Perdu*.[3]

A somewhat similar sequence begins in the second chapter when we learn about Sebastian's imaginary love-affair with an imaginary Mrs Esdaile. This lady of fantasy, whose name Sebastian found in a telephone directory and whose pale, oval face he found in a book of Victorian engravings, is used by him partly for his inward pleasure and partly as a means of teasing Susan Poulshot. Shortly afterwards, Sebastian's real sexual experience, consisting of one humiliating escapade with a prostitute, is described. This brief pattern of beauty and refinement followed by descent into the comically sordid foreshadows Sebastian's experiences with Mrs Thwaile. She, who resembles the Mrs Esdaile of fantasy, introduces him to a frenzied form of love-making shockingly different from the elegant lasciviousnesses he has imagined. The descent with Veronica is thus anticipated by the descent (sufficiently different yet sufficiently similar) earlier described. Mrs Esdaile and the prostitute in blue are used both to explain Sebastian and—since other means of explanation could have been invented—to aid a design.

It is worth noting as part of the same, or similar, technical devices the many references in Chapter Four (the scene of which is the Poulshot household) to death, imminence of death, the nature of the next world, the Gaseous Vertebrate, and other religious subjects. In one sense there is here yet another body of uncomprehending allusions to matters which, in similar phraseology, we are later going to be persuaded to take seriously, but at the same time the allusions are ironic anticipations. Eustace's last day in Florence likewise contains many omens of his death and of his experiences after death; and yet, most effectively, his dying comes as a surprise.[9] We, no more than Eustace, attach the right significance to the events of his last day, and we are as heedless as he even when, shortly before the death-throes, he takes on a resemblance to Faustus by reciting, '*O, lente, lente, currite, noctis equi*'. The point of this particular piece of ironic anticipation (and by extension the entire portrait of Eustace's unpreparedness) becomes clear when Eustace, struggling for life, finds he cannot scream out 'Ah, Christ! Christ!'—almost the very words of Marlowe's Faustus.

There is one important formal feature which I have so far scarcely mentioned. Eustace Barnack's death occurs less than half way through the novel, but we remain in touch with him until nearly the end. Eustace's experiences after death are woven in and out of the earthly doings of the other characters, and in fact six chapters are wholly or partly taken up with the spirit of Eustace. The puzzling elements in these chapters have recently been explained by Peter Bowering who has related the chapters to the *Bardo Thödol* or *Tibetan Book of the Dead*, a 'Mahayana Buddhist text describing the intermediate state between death and rebirth.'[10]

'The *Bardo Thödol* is divided into three parts, all of which are easily recognizable in Huxley's novel: first, the Chikhai Bardo which describes the happenings immediately after death; then the Chönyid Bardo which deals with karmic visions and hallucinations; and finally, the Sidpa Bardo which is concerned with the events leading up to reincarnation.'[11]

For full understanding of what Huxley is driving at it is necessary to know these facts, and the many others which Mr Bowering offers in this connection. In the past, however, one of the most pressing questions about Huxley's presentation of life after death has not been concerned with his meaning (which is clear enough on a careful reading) but with his degree of seriousness. Eustace is comic and grotesque, though not unlikeable, both before and after death. Aspects of the post-mortem situation are farcical. One wanted to know, therefore, how seriously Huxley took these matters. It is now plain that he took them seriously as a feasible explanation of psychic phenomena while at the same time allowing his sense of irony to reach beyond the grave. Even purgatory is a kind of prodigious joke played upon those who have refused to anticipate it. Eustace's purgatory is ludicrous in something of the proportions that his life was ludicrous. Huxley has thought up an explanation for the bathos of so many supposed spirit messages while at the same time attempting to turn the joke around on those whose interest is eclipsed by the bathos.[12]

There are two factors involved in the formal arrangement of Eustace's experiences after death: first, Huxley's simple need, as a craftsman, to space out his material, and secondly his desire to relate what is happening to the spirit of Eustace to what is happening among the living in Florence. Apparently it proved necessary or convenient to depict a version of the three *Bardo* stages through the course of six chapters. The first of these, Chapter Thirteen, principally portrays an awareness of the Clear Light of the Void, but at the end of that chapter Eustace becomes aware also of himself, as something distinct from the Clear Light. He is now moving into the second stage, the 'Chönyid Bardo which deals with karmic visions and hallucinations'. Throughout Chapters Fifteen, Seventeen, Twenty, and Twenty-five, the spirit of Eustace remains in the Chönyid Bardo, recollecting significant events of his life on earth, having visions of the future, and answering questions asked by persons at Mrs Gamble's first seance. The Clear Light is still manifest, but Eustace is progressively succeeding in ignoring it. This phase continues into Chapter Twenty-eight, but because Eustace now begins to realize that the Weyls (who are present at the second seance) can be caused to be his parents in his next cycle of earthly life, he may be presumed to be moving into the third phase, the Sidpa Bardo.

The phases thus flow into one another and do not correspond to the beginnings and endings of chapters. (Of course it would be confusing for us if they did.) The interwovenness of the *Bardo* sequence with the sequence of earthly occurrences supplies an implicit commentary to support the explicit remarks of Bruno to Sebastian and Sebastian's notes in the Epilogue. The general frame of reference embraces at one end of the scale the Clear Light (depicted almost continuously in Chapter Thirteen and less and less frequently in the other *Bardo* chapters), and at the other end of the scale the preoccupations of the living characters. This, we might say, constitutes the first irony. The second irony consists in the fact that Eustace's 'ego' (if we may call it that for convenience) struggles against the Clear

169

Light on the 'other side', while in Florence various other persons' egos are asserting themselves in what Huxley regards as the usual imbecilic fashion. There are numerous subsidiary ironies.[13]

Initially Eustace's painful death is followed by the brief scene in which Sebastian retires to bed cheerfully considering, among other things, how he will work into his poem the something far more deeply interfused. While Sebastian is thus engaged, the dead Eustace has been made aware of—or has been merged into—the Clear Light, which is, or is the essence of, the something interfused. Next day as Eustace's 'ego' starts to recall the phrase, 'backwards and downwards' (a piece of his own earlier cynicism and a sign of the route he will eventually take back into life), Sebastian awakens to the delights of the senses, for it is a beautiful morning in Florence. The beauty of the morning contrasts both with the thoughts of the disembodied Eustace and with the sight of servants carrying his dead body out of the house. Chapters Fifteen and Seventeen contain Eustace's recollections of significant moments in his life, some of which are spiritual and some sordid. These recollections are interrupted by the presentation, in Chapter Sixteen, of Veronica's sexual stratagems.

The second part of the seventeenth chapter takes us back and forth between the people at the seance, longing for reassurance or amusing themselves, and Eustace also amusing himself in something of his old way. They ask typically unenlightened questions and he gives typically mischievous answers, which, however, are vulgarized by the intermediary, a child killed in the San Francisco earthquake. In Chapters Eighteen and Nineteen Sebastian is occupied with taking the Degas drawing and selling it to the rapacious Weyl. Eustace's thoughts in Chapter Twenty about various 'triumphs' of human progress are borne out by the events which either take place or are commented upon elsewhere in the book. The thoughts are meant to be valid, since in relation to the Clear Light most human aspirations are vain, but during these very moments in which Eustace's irony is hitting targets he becomes the target of a greater irony. The cynic is right but the ultimate absurdity is that he should prefer his cynicism.

The earth-bound comedy continues in Chapters Twenty-one to Twenty-four, as Daisy Ockham arrives, as Sebastian panics over the drawing, and as Veronica comes in the night to Sebastian's bedroom. In Chapter Twenty-five, however, Eustace's visions of future earthly happenings sharpen the comedy. For example, we have been amused by the young philistine, Jim Poulshot, and now we are presented with a vision of his ghastly death at the hands of Japanese soldiers. The point of Huxley's satire here is that the manner of Jim's death is a result of what Jim and nearly all the rest of mankind are like, so that our earlier amusement needs to be qualified (though not obliterated) by the later incident.

Chapters Twenty-six and Twenty-seven resume the comedy in Florence, interrupted by Bruno's sane remarks, and then, finally, in Chapter Twenty-eight, Eustace is happy to discover an opportunity to climb back on to the wheel of life. His spirit struggles through frantic agonies in order to be re-embodied, and after that of course it will experience all the usual forms of suffering and impurity. This is the final irony.

Much of the persuasiveness of the teaching of this novel depends on the acceptability of the *Bardo* sections. In the past Huxley has relied on more orthodox forms of argument and demonstration, but now the orthodox methods are reinforced by depiction of the afterlife. The risk involved in this mode of attack lies in the fact that any weaknesses in the *Bardo* sections might actually undermine, instead of supporting, otherwise convincing arguments in the rest of the book.

Huxley is fundamentally serious in the parts devoted to the spirit of Eustace, though he is obviously not solemn. Any ordinary ridicule that someone might think of heaping on these parts has already been incorporated into them. This is why D. S. Savage, for instance, has mistaken his aim.

'And the anti-climax of the disembodied Uncle Eustace's eventual choice of reincarnation out of the "living uterine darkness", the "vegetative heaven" of Mme Weyl, should serve, at least in the mind of no uncommonly penetrating reader, to put Huxley's "mysticism" in its proper, very humble place.'[14]

But the anti-climax (which is of course intentional) does not in itself invalidate Huxley's 'mysticism', and the absurdity of Eustace's choice is precisely Huxley's own, comic point. The dubious feature of the *Bardo* sections is in truth that they enable Huxley to have his cake and eat it. What these sections postulate is of great importance to the argument of the book, but healthy scepticism (on our part and perhaps on Huxley's too) is partly forestalled by the built-in satire.

What also might help to invalidate the mysticism is the quality of the language, for Huxley has composed an unwhimsical fantasy about ineffable spiritual states which neither he nor anyone else has ever experienced, and which we have no strong reasons for supposing occur after death.

Chapter Thirteen, the chapter portraying Eustace's experiences immediately after death, proceeds for the most part in a succession of short paragraphs. Until nearly the end there is no mention of Eustace, for he is not aware of himself. The syntax is organized to convey sensations with only the minimum indication of an experiencing subject. For a time indeed there is a state of awareness which is both subject and object, or neither, except that it feels itself to be defined in relation to an absence of something else. Perhaps Huxley's technique here is only an extension of techniques used by authors when they wish to convey some comparatively normal condition of pain, pleasure, or serenity, whose intensity almost drives away the sense of a separate self. We may recall that Huxley has attempted something of this kind before when Gumbril, listening to Mozart's G minor Quintet, imagined the sensations of a fever so acute that 'Body and mind are indivisible', and when Anthony Beavis deeply meditated.

The opening paragraph, probably for the purpose of giving the reader his bearings, is a straightforward continuation of the previous scene of Eustace's dying moments.

'There was no pain any longer, no more need to gasp for breath, and the tiled floor of the lavatory had ceased to be cold and hard.' (p. 136)

But shortly afterwards the language directly expresses the post-mortem experiences, with no references to earthly phenomena such as tiled floors or coldness.

'The awareness knew only itself, and itself only as the absence of something else.

'Knowledge reached out into the absence that was its object. Reached out into the darkness, further and further. Reached out into the silence. Illimitably. There were no bounds.

'The knowledge knew itself as a boundless absence within another boundless absence, which was not even aware.' (p. 136)

These words attain as much impersonality as is compatible with consciousness. The subjects in these paragraphs are simply 'the awareness' and 'knowledge'. There is no one who is aware or who possesses the knowledge. To further the impersonality Huxley includes, here and later on, a number of sentences which have no grammatical subject, as, for example, 'Reached out into the silence'. Even the one-word sentence, 'Illimitably', is used not solely to stress the ideas of limitlessness but also to enhance the impression of some unbounded, and therefore certainly impersonal, thing reaching out for ever. The phrases minimize the notion of finitude.

The short, broken paragraphs largely made up of equally short and broken sentences compose a series of brief descriptions of phases in a metamorphosis. The point of the jerky syntax is that one thing does not flow into another, but simply changes into the next thing unexpectedly. Each phase seems set to last, or, alternatively, fails to contain an indication of what is going to succeed it, and then, without warning, another phase has begun. It is analogous to watching some chemical process which one has never watched before and scribbling down notes. Long or complex sentences, on the other hand, would suggest that the phases of the process were known in advance.

By his technique Huxley produces a drama whose participating forces are supposed to be impersonal but which are personal enough to arouse self-identification. Eustace's spirit has a story and a development, not merely later on when Eustace has regained some sort of self-awareness, but even here. There is conflict, pain, and growth. From the point of view of the reader there is the usual desire to know what is going to happen next, not as when watching a chemical process, but in the normal way of fiction. The reader identifies himself with the awareness as though the awareness were a character, which in some sense it probably is.

Gradually the awareness with which the reader is identifying himself becomes aware that it is known by some other awareness. It shifts to conceiving of itself as object. From this point the drama truly develops, for the light starts to devour the first awareness. The paragraphs continue to be short, broken from one another, sometimes beginning with such words as 'suddenly' or 'abruptly'. The first awareness is still undergoing a metamorphosis.

Huxley causes the light to seem supremely attractive.

'Brighter, brighter, through succeeding durations, that expanded at last into an eternity of joy.

'An eternity of radiant knowledge, of bliss unchanging in its ultimate intensity. For ever, for ever.' (p. 138)

And yet, since the light is so impersonal and seeks to annihilate personal consciousness, most readers must surely range themselves against it, even as the spirit of Eustace, knowing itself to be contemptible, nevertheless refuses to yield. This is probably not contrary to Huxley's intention, for while he is not, so to speak, of the devil's party, neither is he straightforwardly seeking to justify the ways of God to man. It is clear from Huxley's manner that he is saying in effect: 'Here is what may very well be the supreme choice lying behind all others; what is your reaction to it?'

The result is that even in the seriousness of the thirteenth chapter there is an element of comedy, and as we proceed into the rest of the *Bardo* chapters the comedy increases and grows more orthodox. Eustace's spirit gradually becomes more akin to Eustace in the flesh; the observations of past, present, and future flow back into the main current. Thus the *Bardo* chapters are compatible with the rest of the novel in tone, even as they are a smooth feature of the structure.

In these ways Huxley conveys the zenith of the positive values of the book. Lower down the scale come the comments of Bruno Rontini and the reformed Sebastian, and these mainly take the form of polemical exposition. Bruno's spoken words and Sebastian's notes are often similar in style but not identical, because Sebastian is an appreciative student rather than a saint. Both are assertive, allusive, aphoristic, logical; but Sebastian, as befits his nature, his occupation as a playwright, and the medium of a private note-book, pursues his ideas in more detail. He thinks out the implications of certain concepts which Bruno has so fully absorbed that he has little further need to think about them. Huxley has thus split the communication of his own notions, giving the serene acceptance of them to one character and a marginally more questioning attitude to another. This is a sound procedure, since variety, which was lacking in *After Many a Summer*, is here achieved, and because the reader is enticed both by the conviction of one character and the intelligent exploration of another. The technique is similar to that of *Eyeless in Gaza*, in which certainty was voiced by Miller, while comparatively cautious—and therefore disarming—examination was conducted in Anthony's diary.

Everywhere in the book, in the positive passages no less than in the much more numerous areas of criticism, satire and story-telling, there is distinct forward movement and reasonable economy of effect. The narrative is not held up and matters are not contemplated at considerable length. In terms of pace this novel lies midway between the swiftness of *Brave New World* and the leisureliness of *Crome Yellow*. Here and there occur passages of description reminiscent of *Crome Yellow* and *Those Barren Leaves*, but they are few and comparatively brief. There is sufficient sense of place, of Hampstead on one rather gloomy evening and in particular of Florence, but the locales do not loom so large as the London of *Antic Hay* or the California of *After Many a Summer*. A fair proportion of the novel consists of dialogue, and the dialogue in turn mainly consists of natural exchanges rather than conversational set-pieces. Through these orthodox devices of the story-teller Huxley conveys his message as effectively as he has ever done, so that it is not surprising that when he was asked which of his novels he was most happy with he chose *Time Must Have a Stop*.

'I personally think the most successful was *Time Must Have a Stop*. I don't know, but it seemed to me that I integrated what may be called the essay element with the fictional element better there than in other novels. Maybe this is not the case. It just happens to be the one that I like best because I feel that it came off best.'[15]

It is possible that Huxley made special efforts to integrate the 'essay element' with the 'fictional element' as a response to the widespread criticism of Propter's monologues. And it should not be overlooked that Bruno is different from Propter not only in playing his part in the action of the novel but also in having a distinctly more charitable nature. Indeed the essence of Bruno's outlook is charity, rather than proselytizing fervour, and this fact probably has something to do with the superiority of this novel to *After Many a Summer*. For Huxley himself has returned to viewing his characters generally with greater enthusiasm and affection. Eustace Barnack is as happy a contrivance as any of his hedonistic predecessors; Veronica Thwaile approaches the standard of the earlier temptresses; Sebastian is, to say the least, convincingly developed (though his conversion is minimally accounted for, in flashback), and some of the minor people—John Barnack, Mrs Gamble—are satisfactory satiric inventions. It is worth adding that the scene of the Poulshot household, stands comparison in terms of hilarity with some of the scenes in *Crome Yellow* and *Those Barren Leaves*.

When taking the manuscript of this novel to a typist, Huxley told Christopher Isherwood that it was a 'curiously *trivial* story, told in great detail, with a certain amount of squalor'.[16] Despite the misgivings or diffidence or deprecating humour in this remark, it is

M

in a sense a trivial story (though not a 'curiously' trivial one), but a good deal of the point lies in the contrast between the *Comedie Humaine* and the *Divina Commedia*. It would surely be difficult to argue against the assertion that *Time Must Have a Stop* is Huxley's best performance in fiction in the last twenty-seven years of his career.

9

Ape and Essence (1948)

Shortly after the publication of his ninth novel Huxley wrote in a letter :

'You are probably right in what you say about the form of *Ape and Essence*. And yet there was no other form that would do. I tried at first to write it "straight"; but the material simply wouldn't suffer itself to be expressed at length and in realistic, verisimilitudinous terms. The thing had to be short and fantastic, or else it could not be at all.'[1]

Ape and Essence is a fable and its form, however ingenious, is not the product of a mere desire for ingenuity. It is different from *Brave New World* and *Island* (the two other novels with which it is most likely to be classified) at least in respect of credibility. Both the 'dystopia' of 1932 and the Utopia of 1962 depend a good deal upon simple naturalistic effects, but this is less true of *Ape and Essence*, which on one level owes whatever disturbing power it has to macabre elements usually found in improbable tales of horror. For all the humorous or satirical effects, it relates in the mind of the reader to traditional images of the demoniacal, the sinisterly ugly, the menacingly irrational. Graves are dug up and innocent scapegoats are tormented or buried alive. There is slavery, human sacrifice, unrestrained bestiality, rampant superstition, widespread deformity; and all in a landscape of ruins and desert. In one sense, since it is a fable and not a prediction, there is no need for anyone to 'take it seriously', but Huxley's main object was to undermine the feeling of security of those who cannot take evil seriously. Complacent secularism is attacked through a vision of the sort which, in its traditional forms, complacent secularism would ridicule.

However, the fantastic section of the novel is approached by way of a realistic introduction. The first part, called 'Tallis', comprises a brief satire on Hollywood and a number of touches which anticipate the material of the second, much longer part. The method should probably be regarded as a variant of the regular method by which through the ages authors have prefaced visionary tales. The medieval allegorists, Bunyan, Coleridge and, in more recent times, Henry James, William Morris, and H. G. Wells—to offer just a few examples—have all thought it desirable to move into the main, supernatural story via some comparatively humdrum proceedings during which, for instance, the dreamer settles to his sleep or one of the company looks up the intriguing manuscript. In much this way, and partly perhaps for the same reason, Huxley has his first narrator (who is a *persona* of the author) talk with Bob Briggs at the film studio and later travel with Briggs to the Tallis ranch.

In terms of narrative the first part deals primarily with the discovery of William Tallis's rejected film-script, and Huxley, one feels, has devoted about the right amount of space (twenty-four pages) to ramifying this simple tale. If this part were distinctly shorter, containing for instance either no Bob Briggs or an attenuated Bob Briggs and less reference to the Hollywood of which Briggs is so representative a character, the effect would be perfunctory. Something of substance, an ample 'curtain-raiser' including material which would foster the reader's eagerness for Part Two, was required. What Huxley has provided in addition to the satire on Hollywood and the glimpses of Tallis's script is a tone whose cynicism faintly foreshadows what is to follow. This tone, which is calculated to suggest that such a prospect as Tallis envisages is not to be scoffed at, is already perfectly present in the first paragraph.

'It was the day of Gandhi's assassination; but on Calvary the sightseers were more interested in the contents of their picnic baskets than in the possible significance of the, after all, rather commonplace event they had turned out to witness. In spite of all the astronomers can say, Ptolemy was perfectly right: the centre of the universe is here, not there. Gandhi might be dead; but across the desk in his office, across the lunch table in the Studio Commissary, Bob Briggs was concerned to talk only about himself.' (p. 1)

Placing Gandhi against the picnickers on Calvary and then focusing more sharply upon one particular *homme moyen sensuel* is a means of conveying neatly the point which will continually be made by varying methods throughout the novel. We later learn from the Arch-Vicar that it was not so much the sheer quantity of evil working through the human race before and during the third world war that led to Belial's triumph; it was rather the loss of recognition of spiritual qualities. Belial conquered because people no longer believed in him. The reference to Gandhi begins this theme, and the author's opening tone, conveying a wearily amused acceptance of egotism, likewise sets the tone of almost all that follows.

The theme is developed throughout Part I, though for the moment it is developed in a minor key. Bob Briggs's timid dreams of adultery and the milieu in which he lives are repeatedly set against more impressive names and activities from the past. Briggs is contrasted with Beddoes, Byron, Keats and Shelley not for the sake of humour alone but as a reminder of the audacity and spiritual grandeur which those romantic poets, in the midst of their human failings, possessed. In a similar vein Briggs is caused to compare what he imagines to have been his sexual compulsions with the compulsions felt by Luther, and a little later comes the joke about Christ. Briggs has asked his producer, Lou Lublin, for an increase in salary, to which request Lublin has replied: 'Bob . . . in this Studio, at this time, not even Jesus Christ himself could get a raise' (p. 3).[2] This leads the narrator—that is, for practical purposes Huxley himself—to imagine the scene of Christ before Lublin as it might have been painted by Rembrandt, by Breughel, and by Piero della Francesca.

The nature of the pessimism of *Ape and Essence* is made plain by the features I have mentioned. If Part II is about an imaginary nadir in the history of the human race, Part I is about an actual state of affairs which Huxley saw as possibly impelling us towards some sort of nadir. The notion of Christ as an employee begging for a rise in salary; the loss or debasement of the qualities found in Renaissance painting; the Prufrockian vacillations of a Bob Briggs as compared with the awful daring of many moments of surrender on the part of some romantic poets; the fact, which we a little later discover, that the studios are making a picture called 'Catherine of Siena' in which the emphasis is upon some insignificant love-affairs in the saint's life : all these matters compose the theme of vanishing spirituality.

Into this ethos comes fortuitously the film-script of 'Ape and Essence', written by a misanthrope, William Tallis. In this way Huxley has divided the presentation of his material between at least two *personae*. The first *persona* is a pyrrhonic observer, and it is he who, along with Briggs, takes an interest in the rejected script. The second *persona* is named Tallis, and his embitterment is itself the subject of amused comment.

A further complication is that Tallis's script contains a narrator, whom we may call the 'second narrator' and whose views, while certainly coinciding with those of Tallis, may or may not always be taken to coincide with the first narrator's or with Huxley's. It is likely that Huxley worked in this manner with the object of distancing himself from attitudes which he sometimes possessed during and just after the Second World War but did not wish to be devoured by. Probably he was tempted by the pessimism ascribed to Tallis and sought alleviation in the pyrrhonism of the first narrator, but also tried, in the interests of reason and true non-attachment, to transcend both types of response. I shall contend that the resultant mixture is unpleasing in a quite different way from that which Huxley had in mind.

We are told in effect that the script of *Ape and Essence* was written out of personal guilt, because its author had left his German-Jewish wife and daughter for an American actress, and thus abandoned them to the Nazis. But critics can be excused for seeing only undue pessimism, since the disowning of Tallis within the novel scarcely begins to exorcize his baleful spirit.

The opening pages of 'The Script' contain a curious mixture of naturalism and satiric allegory. In the 'present', which is the year 2,108, a four-masted schooner called the *Canterbury* is approaching the coast of California at the end of its voyage from New Zealand. The coming of this ship with its party of scientists constitutes a straightforward though humorous tale. Something over a hundred years earlier occurred the third world war (conducted with both nuclear and biological weapons) and this event is depicted allegorically. In the early pages of Part II allegory predominates but is interrupted here and there by the straightforward tale. This unusual combination of elements is acceptable because the reader is imagining a film-performance and therefore feels no desire to jib at the sort of fantastic effects which are quite common in the cinema. But of course such features as a cinema-audience consisting of baboons are not simply the result of the author's desire to amuse himself, though no doubt he obtained amusement from them. Huxley wished to portray the historical event which forms the background to the main story of Dr Alfred Poole as a means of telling the reader what is wrong with the world now, in the twentieth century. Allegory was chosen, in all probability, because a realistic depiction of the third world war would have obscured the explanation of its cause in terms of human psychology. Being fascinated by scenes of widespread destruction is not the best way of understanding the nature of the spiritual decline which led to the destruction. Accordingly we who are 'in the cinema', so to speak, are shown another cinema full of baboons whom we no doubt resemble. On the screen appear baboon-actors in full, sadistic control of human beings with the faces of Faraday, Einstein, and Pasteur. Two Einsteins, each one enslaved by a different army, are fairly soon obliged by their captors to inaugurate the catastrophic war.

On the simplest level the fable here represents the opposition between scientific discovery and its misuse, but the following lines given to the sardonic narrator make it clear that Huxley is making a more comprehensive comment.

'Surely it's obvious.
Doesn't every schoolboy know it?
Ends are ape-chosen; only the means are man's.
Papio's procurer, bursar to baboons,
Reason comes running, eager to ratify;
Comes, a catch-fart with Philosophy, truckling to tyrants;
Comes, a pimp for Prussia, with Hegel's patent History;
Comes, with Medicine to administer the Ape-King's aphrodisiac;
Comes, rhyming and with Rhetoric, to write his orations;
Comes with the Calculus to aim his rockets
Accurately at the orphanage across the ocean;
Comes, having aimed, with incense to impetrate
Our Lady devoutly for a direct hit.' (pp. 32f.)

The fundamental opposition is between ends, which are 'ape-chosen', and means, which are man's. It is not that some ends are bad, but that to allow images of the future to crowd out or distort perceptions of the present is always bad. The proper use of the mind is for free disinterested enquiry or for free disinterested response to each moment of experience. Hence, the names of Einstein and Pasteur are introduced not just because their work, pre-eminently, has made nuclear and biological warfare possible, but also because those scientists represent the creative spirit in contrast to the tendency to stultify thought by presuming to know in advance what conclusions thought should reach. The implication is that man's spirit, his 'glassy essence' as Shakespeare's Isabella calls it, is characterized by transparency, so that it lets in truth. Wishes and fears, including what are thought of as noble aspirations, are apeish because they throw up a barrier. Huxley's view is that in the present century more formidable barriers containing fewer chinks are being erected than ever before because we have concluded that mind (as opposed to spirit) is the sole instrument and arbiter of truth. But since the mind has an inclination to propose objectives, we are often driven into frenzied imbecility by a tendency to subvert or ignore the given truths of experience in an effort to reach imagined destinations.

Such is the underlying argument of the book, expressed mainly by an onslaught on some popular modern assumptions. Nowhere else in Huxley's writings is there such unmitigated derision as in the opening pages of 'The Script', and it is the form which has made expression of the derision possible. There is no sense of the local or particular, except that we are dealing with twentieth-century manifestations. The entire world is implicated because, in the allegorical sections, there are no idiosyncratic characters but only ape-performers, three representatives of the creative spirit in bondage, and one narrator, who, while reminding us of the glassy essence, shows little confidence that anyone will pay proper attention. Baboon-housewife, baboon-stockbroker, baboon-singer, baboon-soldiers and baboon-audience make up the whole of mankind, for the enchained scientists did their work in the past. (Contemporary scientists, says the narrator, are all in the pay of baboonery.)

Everything is subjected to ridicule including, naturally enough, the medium of Hollywood film (a debased product, the narrator suggests) in which the ridicule is supposed to be cast. In fact Huxley presents a film within the film and by this means is able unobtrusively to imply that we are all engaged in watching the lunatic antics of one another. The baboon-singer and the baboon-marshalissimos on the screen are not different from the audience but are merely, for the moment, playing different roles. Although the marshalissimos give the actual orders for the twin Einsteins to press switches, they have been urged on by a representative of the Church, and behind these leaders lie the peoples of the world, some of whom happen to be actors in the film while others are members of the audience. We, the readers of the novel, are in a manner being entertained by the larger film whose subject is ourselves. Since Swiftian comparisons are apt, it's as if the monkey which carries off Gulliver and Gulliver himself might be thought of as two aspects of human nature, the monkey-aspect now being in full control.[3] It

182

is the fantastic form of this section of the novel which aids Huxley to make his further point that individuals all responding with full alertness to their individual experiences have distinctive faces, but the predominance of the monkey-aspect imposes faces as little distinguishable as the faces of monkeys. There is an overwhelming unison in singing as in war, so that by the rapid shifts of scene or by cinematic musical accompaniment Huxley can both present his ironic contrasts (between, for example, a choral rendering of 'Onward Christian Soldiers' and the picture of the Einsteins pressing the switches) while at the same time fostering the notion that there is no fundamental contrast : apehood is all.

A short way into 'The Script' the allegory concludes with the words : 'A choking scream announces the death, by suicide, of twentieth-century science.' From now on the straightforward tale of human beings acting in the year 2,108, is continued without interruption. The first step (now that preliminaries concerning the coming of the *Canterbury* are over) is the presentation of a comic, though sympathetic, protagonist, Dr Alfred Poole, who, in being initially both ineffectual in practical affairs and the victim of a possessive mother's upbringing, is more reminiscent of Jeremy Pordage than of Huxley's other heroes, though he plainly has a little in common with Denis Stone and Bernard Marx as well. The choice of Alfred Poole as hero is a considerable determinant of the tone of the book, for it ensures the absence of tragic elements (such as are provided by Orwell's Winston Smith in *1984*) and some alleviation of the pessimism.

The narrator's introductory description of Poole makes it clear that he belongs to the category of likeable bunglers, the shy, sensitive, clumsy men who are inevitably put upon by bullies, tricksters, and predatory women. A man of this kind, as he has appeared in countless light-hearted plays and films and in such novels as Wells's *The History of Mr Polly* and Kingsley Amis's *Lucky Jim*, traditionally proceeds through humiliating vicissitudes to a final acquisition of a nice heroine and escape from an uncongenial milieu. Poole's progress is exactly of this sort. The progress is conducted in three phases which, in an orthodox presentation, might be distinguished as chapters. The first phase comprises the events of part of Belial Day (the day on which the New Zelanders set foot on the coast of California). The second phase consists of the happenings of Belial Night, which are described in such detail and include so long a conversation between Poole and the Arch-Vicar as to take up about a third of this part of the story, or almost a quarter of the whole novel. The third phase begins on the following morning and covers a period of some eight weeks, at the end of which Dr Poole and his Loola set off on their desperate flight to join the community of 'Hots' living near Fresno. The activities of Belial Night thus occupy the centre of the main story and in fact they are placed not much beyond the middle of 'The Script' taken as a whole. In this way the most exciting and memorable part of the novel may be thought of as an apex in Part II to which earlier matters lead up and from which later matters fall away. If, however, we observe the shape of the entire novel, also bringing into view Part I, 'Tallis', we see that the portrayal of Belial Night occurs in roughly that penultimate position which Huxley so often favoured in his novels for the placing of the most startling material.

A closer examination of the structure of 'The Script' from the point at which the allegory is concluded reveals that there are twelve major scenes of varying lengths and a few minor scenes which act purely or mainly as links. The first major scene in the story of Alfred Poole, which comes shortly after we have been told of his nature and, very briefly, shown his capture by ruffians, might well be dubbed by a film-producer, the 'gravedigging scene'. The camera first takes a panoramic picture of southern California and then moves rapidly downwards to focus upon one place : 'a large rectangular graveyard, lying between the ferro-concrete towers of Hollywood and those of Wilshire Boulevard' (p. 46). Here are workers, overseen by a Chief, hauling up an old twentieth-century coffin with the object of utilizing whatever utilizable goods may be found inside it. Poole is brought among this party, and there follows a dialogue which constitutes our first explanation of the new society. In this way several things are concisely achieved. We gather that there is no technology (even properly-woven clothes must be plundered from graves), that the Devil has taken over, that sexual activity is restrained in some curious fashion, and that it is the custom to bury alive unsatisfactory people. At the same time Huxley is making fun of the opulence and complacency of Hollywood as it was at the time of writing and had been for about thirty years. (The particular cadaver now robbed once housed the spirit of the Production Manager of Western-Shakespeare Pictures Incorporated.) In addition a fundamental point in Huxley's definition of evil begins inconspicuously to emerge : this is to the effect that evil thrives upon, and is perhaps a concomitant of, fear. We shall later more fully

184

appreciate that Belial is a non-entity expressing the general will which matches nobody's real will, and that worship of Belial is the terrified denial of individuality.

The first scene concludes as Poole is pulled out of the grave in which he was about to be buried alive. The second scene, while slightly advancing our knowledge of local customs, principally comprises an introduction to the heroine, who is distinguished from her fellows by a tendency to identify herself with sufferers. At this point she and Poole strike up a promising friendship.

Poole's guide, and ours, to the ways of the community remains for the time being the Chief, who, in the third scene, comments upon the burning of books to fuel the ovens of the bakery and upon the teachings of the Satanic Science Practitioner, and later takes charge of the preparations for the purification ceremonies. We learn more at this stage about the local belief that women are vessels of the unholy spirit (since they arouse desire and frequently produce deformed babies), but these are subordinate matters conveyed with an increasing sense that we are fast reaching the melodramatic and expository heights.

The method of the long scene of the events of Belial Night is one of portraying monstrosities along with an elaborate commentary conducted by the Arch-Vicar. In other words, Belial-worship is demonstrated while its history and psychological meaning are explained by the most able mentor. The Arch-Vicar is the familiar intelligent apologist, like Orwell's O'Brien in *1984* or like Huxley's own Mustapha Mond, but he is less impressive than Mustapha Mond in being liable to moments of pique or jealousy. His superiority over the mass of the people lies only in his greater understanding of the evil which he serves and helps to perpetuate. The contrast between him and the Chief, who has continued to be Poole's guide up to this point, is the traditional contrast between the subtle ecclesiastic and the more blunt-witted leader of the secular arm, as represented, for example, (though with differences in national characteristics and in objectives as well) by Shaw's Earl of Warwick and his Peter Cauchon.

The entire scene, which, from the night-time chanting of the priests to Poole's reading of 'Epipsychidion' in the fresh morning, takes up forty-five pages, is an intensification of some main features of the book, and remains in the mind as an image of the book. The Arch-Vicar's lengthy exposition dominates in the memory over the narrator's sporadic remarks, which it often resembles in subject-matter though not in manner. The force of the collective, which is shown or implied throughout the novel, here reaches its ultimate expression in such incidents as that of the sadistic chanting by the thousands seated, tier upon tier, in the Los Angeles Coliseum. Gross and ugly matters, which Huxley so frequently includes in most parts of the work, now receive special emphasis, so that our abiding impression of the physically repellent reflecting spiritual malformation is obtained chiefly from this scene. In addition, Huxley has devised a liturgy which exemplifies his attitude towards his material at this point and in other parts of the book. An orthodox Christian form of worship is inverted, principally to show that now, in AD 2108, evil is espoused openly instead of furtively, as in the past. But the humour at the expense of Belial-worship barely conceals humour at the expense of Christian ritual as well. For all Huxley's religious inclination, he never had much use for the Church and its ceremonies, which he seems to have regarded as intrinsically absurd and contrary to the great principle of vigilance to the moments of individual experience. Organized worship, whether it purports to be for good or (as here in *Ape and Essence*) for ill is automatically suspect.[4] The chief point, nevertheless, is the complete surrender to evil, which is closely associated with a thoroughly degrading kind of fear. The hint is that we, living in the twentieth century are moving towards a state in which honest expression of our desires would take some such form as this liturgy. The comedy lies in the plain avowal of degradation, which cuts through the hypocrisies of ordinary life in humorously unrealistic fashion. For in life, now or in any conceivable future, men—I am speaking of the majority, not, for example, of such a rare creature as Dostoevsky's Stavrogin—may practise evil while disguising the fact from themselves, or, more rarely, they may actually worship evil as well, but do so (as in witchcraft and black magic) with self-deceiving solemnities and glorifications. Practitioners of witchcraft presumably could not bring themselves to describe their deity in such disparaging terms as 'blowfly' and 'worm'.

The priestly chanting and the following incidents of impaling deformed infants upon butcher's knives—the whole taking place in torch-lit darkness before ranks of 'massed gargoyles'—curiously combine the sinister and the comic. Slight modifications could produce either a positively grand-guignol effect or an effect of farce. Huxley assumes a manner of jovial relish as a means of expressing his distaste for the nastiness and silliness of mankind. The most obvious comparison is with Swift, especially with the 'Voyage to the Country of the Houyhnhnms', but it is also apt to recall *Candide*.

Poole's conversation with the Arch-Vicar, which shortly follows the chanting and the first killings of deformed babies, is a continuation of the comic element (though, of course, it contains a perfectly serious message) and thus differs from the Savage's conversation with Mustapha Mond in *Brave New World*. The Arch-Vicar has gross manners which consort oddly with his learned address and high, eunuch's voice. He gorges, greasy-handed, on pigs' trotters swilled down with wine, and delivers what amounts to a fairly polished lecture with his mouth full. Poole (like Bernard Marx of *Brave New World* rather than the Savage) is alternately sycophantic and self-assertive. In this way the dialogue is amusing even while it seriously expresses Huxley's own views (or the views he held in his more pessimistic moments) of the trend of world-history since the seventeenth century.

' "As I read history," he says, "it's like this. Man pitting himself against Nature, the Ego against the Order of Things, Belial" (a perfunctory sign of the horns) "against the Other one. For a hundred thousand years or so the battle's entirely indecisive. Then, three centuries ago, almost overnight, the tide starts to run uninterruptedly in one direction. Have another of these pig's feet, won't you?" ' (p. 90)

The Arch-Vicar's subsequent remarks are an enlargement, with historical illustrations, of this point. Belial is winning all the battles and has all but won the war, because Man, dressed (by the scientific method) in a little brief authority, has obscured and even begun to deny the existence of his glassy essence which unites him with the Order of Things. Here once again, as in *After Many a Summer* and to a lesser extent in other late novels of Huxley, is the Faustian theme.

The Arch-Vicar's words are at first punctuated by and later replaced by the noise of the activities below, in the arena. Among the thousands gathered there fear gives way to orgiastic copulation (much to the Arch-Vicar's envious disgust) and out of the portrayal of bestiality Huxley begins at last to produce his positive theme. Up to this point it has not been in the least apparent that any hopefulness could emerge, since Poole and his Loola have seemed to be quite mediocre, quite lacking the spark to surmount their environment. But simply by flinging themselves into the spirit of the orgy each discovers a new personal dimension : Loola finds that she has monogamistic yearnings and Poole realizes that the senses can be the gateway to the divine.

The matter is expressed partly by two contrasting pieces of poetry, the first an adaptation of the Cardinal's words in Act V, Scene V of the *Duchess of Malfi*, and the second an extract from 'Epipsychidion'. It is important to examine these pieces of poetry because in them, I believe, Huxley goes to the root of his attitude towards his material.

It will be recalled that Webster's Cardinal is troubled with a guilty conscience just before Bosola enters to kill him. Webster's marvellous image of a 'thing arm'd with a rake' (which in the play is at once a premonition of Bosola with his sword and the emergence into consciousness of deeply-buried impulses in the Cardinal's own mind) is used by Huxley in the following way.

> '*When I look into the fishponds in my garden,*
> (And not mine only, for every garden is riddled
> With eel-holes and reflected moons), *methinks*
> *I see a Thing armed with a rake that seems,*
> Out of the ooze, out of the immanence
> Among the eels of heaven, *to strike at me*—
> At Me the holy, Me divine! And yet
> *How tedious is a guilty conscience*! How
> Tedious, for that matter, an unguilty one!
> What wonder if the horror of the fishponds
> Draws us towards the rake? And the Thing strikes,
> And I, the uneasy Person, in the mud,
> Or in the liquid moonlight, thankfully
> Find others than myself to have that blind
> Or radiant being.' (p. 115)

The rough meanings of these lines is that man's nature is not fundamentally divided, that good and evil are not manichaeistically opposed, but inextricably bound up together. When a man looks into his mind (his 'fishponds') he sees both the Thing armed with a rake and the 'eels of heaven', which are slippery impulses to truth and goodness. He observes both 'mud' and 'liquid moonlight'. The eels could not exist without the mud which is a necessary part of their element; the sinister Thing from the depths is as unavoidable as the reflection of heavenly radiance upon the surface. People are drawn towards the rake because they find it supremely difficult to tolerate their essential ambivalence.

The lines are uttered by the narrator at the point where Poole is pulled into the orgy of Belial Night. Their application to the narrative is clear; in the California of the year 2,108, a whole people has descended into the mud, but, paradoxically, it is there that two of the people, Poole and Loola, find also the eels of heaven. Poole has hitherto avoided the flesh on the assumption (drilled into him by his mother) that his nature is divisible and that he must eschew the evil part. Now he is degraded and the surprising result is his discovery of an impulse to love. This movement in Poole's mind is not stated directly by the author, presumably because he did not wish to impair the satirical tone of the novel. In fact humour still plays over the lines of poetry given to the narrator and over Poole's reading of Shelley the following day.

> 'Warm fragrance seems to fall from her light dress
> And her loose hair; and where some heavy tress
> The air of her own speed has disentwined,
> The sweetness seems to satiate the faint wind;
> And in the soul a wild odour is felt
> Beyond the sense, like fiery dews that melt
> Into the bosom of a frozen bud.' (p. 122)[5]

It is most remarkable to Poole that a 'wild odour' can be felt 'in the soul' and 'beyond the sense' because he has previously been led to believe that the senses are the enemy of the soul. While the scene is not wholly an interlude in the satirical sequence it does unobtrusively inform us of the way Huxley has descried of facing the fact of the mud. Individuals should welcome the mud; they should resist not evil. Despite differences in meaning and emphasis, this solution has a long tradition, for it can be traced back to Heracleitus and to Socrates as he appears in *The Symposium*. Something similar is plainly expressed by Donne (especially in 'The Extasie'), by Blake (especially in 'The Marriage of Heaven and Hell'), by Dostoevsky, Baudelaire, Lawrence and Jung.

The scene we are now considering looks forward to the concluding page on which appears a quotation from 'Adonais', and ultimately it looks forward to the final chapter of *Island* where, in a deeply impressive vision, Huxley presents a conjunction of Chartres and concentration camp, of Christmas tree decorations and charnel house.

But we are some way from the end of the novel. The positive theme has been stated and from now on will not be much enlarged, but both the rhythm of the structure and the acceptability of the narrative demand that the final escape of Poole and Loola be post-poned. Accordingly, the later pages of 'The Script' constitute a comparatively 'quiet' counter-movement in which Poole finds that his love for Loola endures and that the Shelleyan way of viewing such love holds up.

Huxley takes advantage of the need for a fairly substantial con-cluding section to present some relevant animadversions on man's exploitation of the natural resources of the earth, but the most important additions to the narrative are sporadic assertions of the positive message. The Narrator's tone becomes noticeably less sar-donic and more fervent.

'And is there perhaps a hint of that which, in the *Ave Verum Corpus*, in the G-minor Quintet, lies beyond the world of *Don Giovanni*? Is there a hint already of what (in Bach, sometimes, and in Beethoven, in that final wholeness of art which is analogous to holiness) transcends the Romantic integration of the tragic and the joyful, the human and the daemonic? And when, in the darkness, the lover's voice whispers again of

> "a mortal shape indued
> With love and life and light and deity,"

is there already the beginning of an understanding that beyond "Epipsychidion" there is "Adonais", and beyond "Adonais" the word-less doctrine of the Pure in Heart?' (pp. 149f.)

The way out of the morass is personal rather than collective, for the personal reaches out to the universal whereas the collective reaches out to the internecine. Right progress is, as Socrates advo-cated, from love of carnal beauty (*Don Giovanni*) to tokens of absolute beauty ('Epipsychidion' and 'Adonais'), beyond which there is a final, unrealizable stage of full knowledge of absolute beauty.

Poole progresses as far as an appreciation of 'Adonais'. As he and Loola sit beside the grave of their supposed creator, he appears to be convinced that there is a 'light whose smile kindles the Universe,' a 'Beauty in which all things work and move'. But Huxley cannot end on precisely that note. The fugitive couple eat and (recalling the deplored picnickers on Calvary with whom the novel opened) Poole scatters an egg-shell over Tallis's grave. In other words, the author of 'The Script' has contrived to kill himself off before the end of the story and to have his characters treat his grave with disrespect. In this way, by a characteristic conjunction of the high aspirations of romanticism and a burst of mockery, Huxley perhaps tried to combat his own Tallis-like pessimism, which has often been regarded as the sole mood of the novel.

But the spirit of Tallis has loomed too large. We should not have to read the novel carefully in order to realize fully (let alone remember) that it has a positive theme and a hopeful outcome. Huxley so stressed the ghoulish elements because the seminal part of his imagination was working in this way at that time (the period just after the dropping of the atom bomb). He was fascinated by man's hubristic lunacies and, more specifically, by such matters as genetic deformity resulting from exposure to radiation; so fascinated that his positive theme has a fugitive and desperate air.

IO

The Genius and the Goddess (1955)

For his tenth novel Huxley chose the device of narrator, which he had not employed since the 1920s. Two of his most successful stories, 'Uncle Spencer' (1924) and 'Two or Three Graces' (1926), are presented as the productions of persons who have heard about the events or were marginally involved in them. These persons are given styles that suggest their natures but are not otherwise much characterized.

The Genius and the Goddess, a *nouvelle* of about thirty-thousand words, is for the most part in the guise of a piece of oral narration by a man who played a leading role in the events which he is now describing. This device should be seen first of all as yet another answer to a problem which Huxley had by now been faced with for some twenty years, the problem of how to pass on certainties without fracturing the work. He evidently felt the need to incorporate into his later fictions his own commentaries upon the actions. Take away Mr Propter, for example, and no one could make of the remaining events and characters of *After Many a Summer* what Huxley wished us to make of them. But in that novel the commentary and the action are more clearly separated than Huxley seems ever again to have regarded as satisfactory.

Now in *The Genius and the Goddess* the fictional element and the essay element are at one, though this has been achieved by minimizing the dramatic element. Rivers is a fully-fledged character who acts and suffers, as well as being the complete analyst of the spiritual significance of the story. He does not stand aside from the action like Mr Propter, or undergo most of his fate off stage like Bruno Rontini. He does not merely explain things as do several characters in *Island*. The message he delivers is perfectly Huxley's own even though his voice, appearance, past and present behaviour are all distinctive.

However, there is too much reportage and too little re-creation. What happens in this novel is not allowed even faintly to obscure the lessons which we, through Rivers, are encouraged to absorb. Huxley has tried to ensure that every detail of the plot, while receiving its full discursive comment, remains just sufficiently graphic, but I doubt if he has succeeded.

The attempt is made through the character of Rivers and through his relationship with the events. He is an eloquent and witty physicist whose views of himself and of the nature of human life were changed by the happenings of 1922. Furthermore, he is a man who always seeks general conclusions through the observation of particular details. We are led to imagine that the very quality of Rivers's experience in 1922 has been replaced in his memory by, or is now for convenience being subordinated to, summaries, analytical descriptions and conclusions. As a result of inventing Rivers Huxley was thus absolved from the extreme demands of naturalism. He wished to stress meaning rather than dramatic detail and knew that he was not one of the novelists who can manage both supremely well. Some further remarks made in the 'Paris Review' interview are pertinent here.

'Well, there are lots of excellent story-tellers who are simply story-tellers, and I think it's a wonderful gift, after all. I suppose the extreme example is Dumas : that extraordinary old gentleman, who sat down and thought nothing of writing six volumes of *The Count of Monte Cristo* in a few months. And my God, *Monte Cristo* is damned good! But it isn't the last word. When you can find story-telling which carries at the same time a kind of parable-like meaning (such as you get, say, in Dostoevski or in the best of Tolstoi), this is something extraordinary, I feel. I'm always flabbergasted when I re-read some of the short things of Tolstoi, like *The Death of Ivan Ilyich*. What an astounding work that is! Or some of the short things of Dostoevski like *Notes from Underground*.'[1]

Nevertheless, in other contexts Huxley seems less patient with story-telling as such,[2] and in *The Genius and the Goddess* 'parable-like meaning' occupies—and indeed, almost usurps—the very surface.

The main purpose of Rivers's opening remarks on the falsity of even the most convincing fictions is of course to introduce a story whose point is that life cannot be explained by art or science. But there is an amusing contradiction between these remarks and the particular work of art of which they form a part. Rivers asserts that 'Fiction has unity, fiction has style' (p. 1), and then proceeds to relate with manifest style a 'true' story whose unity is flawless. Rivers asserts that *The Brothers Karamazov* 'makes so little sense that it's almost real' (p. 1), thus suggesting that his own tale will inevitably have something of the Dostoevskian 'senselessness'. But in fact *The Genius and the Goddess*, while stressing the jumble of real life, has complete symmetry and coherence.

So far I have said little about the personality of Rivers, although this is naturally a principal agent of the unity of the book. In fact Rivers has two personalities, the first expressed by the voice speaking now in 1954, and the second belonging to his younger self. It will be necessary later on to say something about Rivers as a character within the story he relates; for the moment I am concerned only with the maturer Rivers whose style is the style of the novel.

He is an American, a widower of sixty whose lined face and large frame still suggest how Apollonianly good-looking he once was. He feels that he will not have a long life and recommends getting used to the idea of dying. He gives evidence of being briskly and compassionately confident in his dealings with both children and adults. His conversational manner combines chivying confidence with wit, fluency, and subtlety. He is as impressive as any of Huxley's talkers, wittier (though less funny) than Scogan or Cardan; as harshly realistic and, no doubt, to some readers (this is certainly a matter of taste) as irritating as Propter.

'Would it have been better, I wonder, if we had come out into the open, courageously called a spade a phallic symbol and handed one another our quivering entrails on a silver platter? Maybe it would. Or maybe it wouldn't. The truth shall make you free; but on the other hand, let sleeping dogs lie and, above all, let lying dogs sleep. One must never forget that the most implacable wars are never the wars about things; they're the wars about the nonsense that eloquent idealists have talked about things—in other words, the religious wars. What's lemonade? Something you make out of lemons. And what's a crusade? Something you make out of crosses—a course of gratuitous violence motivated by an obsession with unanalysed symbols. "What do you read, my lord?" "Words, words, words." And what's in a word? Answer : corpses, millions of corpses. And the moral of *that* is,

Keep your trap shut; or if you *must* open it, never take what comes out of it too seriously.' (pp. 102f.)

These words form only a portion of Rivers's commentary upon Katy's lack of interest in discussing their adulterous relationship. He is expounding what Katy, as a typical feature of her 'pagan' make-up, knew without benefit of theory, and what he, as the intellectual son of a Lutheran minister, had painfully to learn. That the story is largely made up of such commentaries helps to determine its quality; determines, for instance, that it is not in any true sense a tragedy despite the fact that the events are of the sort usually described as tragic. Rivers's breeziness (which diminishes or increases according to the subject matter but only once or twice vanishes altogether) is of course a leading vehicle of meaning. Here is a grievous story related for the most part with a kind of insouciance, and even a kind of showiness. But the 'patter', the verbal display, is partly a means of making the serious point that neither words nor experience should be taken too seriously. In the passage that I have quoted Rivers explicitly limits the importance of words and implicitly advocates a sort of nonchalance in the face of painful happenings. He says in effect that we thoughtlessly allow words to govern our attitudes to experience. If he and Katy had discussed their relationship in the terms of sinfulness, then it would have been felt as sinful. There are only two sensible responses to such a situation : the first to refrain from discussing it as far as possible, and the second to discuss it without foisting significances upon it. But as soon as words are used the danger of imposing significances is imminent and must be guarded against. By deliberately using facetious terms— 'our quivering entrails on a silver platter'—Rivers places this little episode within the great scheme of things, thus avoiding absurdity and self-centredness. His lively manipulation of words for effect (not merely here but throughout the book) is like a juggler's contemptuous skill : he is the master of his equipment, not its slave. But because words are symbols and not insignificant things like the juggler's plates or indian clubs, Rivers's control of them fosters control of his attitudes to experience as well. Thus, the joke in the above passage about lemonade and crusade is a cheapening, through glib word-play (reminiscent of the music hall), of a kind of activity which Rivers thinks people have always held too dear.

Time and again, Rivers (like other of Huxley's characters beginning with Denis Stone) discusses the nature of words, their uses and limitations, so that theoretical disquisitions combine with the example of Rivers's own manner and the example of the plot to point the moral of the whole work, which is to the effect that life is a series of unplanned happenings whose patterns can be discerned only in retrospect, and then only partially. In these ways Huxley uses art to define the boundaries of art, but more importantly to assert that people should humbly submit to experience, in full acknowledgement of predestination and in hope of receiving grace. They should resist, or use only for special purposes, the symbolizing, conceptualizing tendencies of the mind which tend to confer pattern upon the patternless.

'At every instant every transcience is eternally that transcience. What it signifies is its own being, and that being (as one sees so clearly when one's in love) is the same as Being with the biggest possible B. Why do you love the woman you're in love with? Because she *is*. And that, after all, is God's own definition of Himself : I am that I am. The girl is who she is. Some of her isness spills over and impregnates the entire universe. Objects and events cease to be the mere representatives of classes and become their own uniqueness; cease to be illustrations of verbal abstractions and become fully concrete.' (p. 46)[3]

One of the special purposes to which the conceptualizing tendencies can be put is illustrated by this very passage, that is, to postulate a general truth. The novel is made up of general truths given narrative illustrations and framed in words that recommend by their own example, by broad implication, or by direct statement, a wary attitude to words. In the same vein Huxley causes Rivers a little later to desiderate an ideal, or at least greatly improved, vocabulary, which, if it would still falsify experience, would do so to a lesser degree.

'How impossibly crude our language is! If you don't mention the physiological correlates of emotion, you're being false to the given facts . . . What we need is another set of words. Words that can express the natural togetherness of things. Muco-spiritual, for example, or dermatocharity. Or why not mastonoetic? Why not viscerosophy? But translated, of course, out of the indecent obscurity of a learned language into something you could use in everyday speech or even in lyrical poetry.' (pp. 52f.)

In the telling of his tale Rivers often tries to indicate the 'physiological correlates of emotion'. He cannot recreate the 'natural togetherness of things' since there are no adequate words, but his manner throughout implies both a theoretical awareness of this togetherness and an absence or lessening of the kinds of moral judgement which our present vocabulary fosters.

'Meanwhile [Rivers remarks] one can only record the fact that, on the verbal level, morality is simply the systematic use of bad language.' (p. 94)

Partly because we do not sufficiently recognize that behaviour is connected with bodily conditions we are prone to inappropriate forms of censure and approval. Rivers continually implies that none of the characters had any true choice of conduct. Henry and Katy Maartens, Ruth and Rivers himself all contribute to the tragedy and do so in consequence of unavoidable mental (or neuro-physiological') states. Rivers attacks the 'sin' rather than the 'sinner' and regularly implies that the cure is an increase in knowledge.

So far I have been emphasizing a harmony produced by the mere device of narrator, by the narrator's present personality as expressed through his opinions, and by the narrator's style of conversation. Also contributing to the harmony is the characterization which is likewise made to seem expressive of the narrator's cast of mind, but in the process, unfortunately, loses immediacy.

Roughly speaking, the stress is upon psychological categories and states of mind rather than upon persons, even though at least one of the persons was drawn from life. In reply to a correspondent who was at the time playing the part of Katy Maartens in a stage-version of *The Genius and the Goddess*, and who had complained that she could not make sense of the part, Huxley explained at length that the character of Katy owed a good deal to his observations of Frieda Lawrence.

'Frieda's attitude towards life was much the same as Katy's. She was profoundly matter-of-fact, accepting events as they were given, in all their painful or delightful confusion. She had little patience with idealism or exalted ethical systems. Her essential view of life was expressed in Shakespeare's words in *King Lear*—"Ripeness is all". This ripeness of realism made some people feel, at a first meeting, that she was rather rough and even a little heartless . . . Another characteristic was her child-likeness . . . Finally, she had the most sovereign disregard for what people might think or say about her . . .

'This is the person who, as a young girl, fascinated Henry when he saw her in California, and who, as a mature woman, fascinates John Rivers from the first moment he enters the Maartens household. I have done my best in the play to make the character of Katy do and say nothing incompatible with this person. There are details which might, perhaps, be improved; but I feel that in essence, this person I knew and then re-imagined in another context is solidly there.'[4]

And yet the Katy of the novel is less 'solidly there' than any of Huxley's other major female characters, except, perhaps, for Susila in *Island*, and the reason is that the author, through Rivers, offers more of an 'anatomy' than a dramatization. Katy's looks are conveyed mainly in general terms. She has 'the face of a goddess disguised as a healthy peasant girl', of 'Hera playing the part of a milkmaid.' She is Wagnerian; her hands are not 'spiritual, Blessed-Damozellish appendages', but hands competent to perform practical tasks (p. 39). We learn something of her upbringing and we gather a few facts about her methods of dealing with children and literary tastes (distaste for H. G. Wells and Henry James; approval of Lawrence). Katy acts of course, and acts decisively, but her actions too are reported rather than brought to life. The most important scene in the novel is the one in which Katy comes in the night to Rivers's bed, but if we compare this with sexual episodes in other of Huxley's novels (for instance, Veronica Thwaile's visit to Sebastian's bedroom) the unusual technique of this book is immediately emphasized. Of all the pictures of Katy, only one, the picture of her lying dead beside her car, compares in vividness to the depictions of all the principal female figures in the earlier novels.

Katy's character is simply and almost unanalysedly that of 'goddess'. She gives a far greater impression of simple (though intelligent) goodness than seems to be attributed to Frieda Lawrence in the letter which I have quoted. She is admired because (in addition to her beauty) she is without egotism and uses her considerable intelligence in direct practical ways, resisting premature conceptualization and holding no moral prejudices. She is almost a female version of the 'simple man', Fénélon's depiction of whom Huxley includes in *The Perennial Philosophy*.[5]

But of course Huxley delineates the vulnerability as well as the estimableness of a 'goddess' in order to show the vulnerability of all human beings. Katy is Huxley's supreme 'pagan', for her conflicts are exclusively concerned with solutions to practical problems and she does not suffer from a sense of guilt. There is no gulf between her wishes and her actions, and, apart from momentary feelings of irritation or dismay, she wastes no time in desiring alternatives to the situations in which she finds herself. Huxley earlier found it possible to envisage acceptance of life only in such a character as Anne Wimbush, who evades painful thought and responsibility, or in such figures as Mark Rampion, Mr Propter and Bruno Rontini, who discourse more than they act. Now there is a plain division between a good character who discourses (Rivers) and another good character for whom speculative talk is superfluous because the proper end of philosophical speculation—practical wisdom and goodness—has already been reached. Katy's imperfection as a human being lies in the limits of her knowledge rather than in moral shortcomings. To adapt Eliot's phrases, she fares forward rather than attempting to fare well, and her wisdom consists of humility.[6]

The methods used for presenting Katy are used for presenting the other characters as well, with the result that aspects of the book are reminiscent of seventeenth-century character studies; of the *Anatomy of Melancholy*, Bacon's *Essays* and Earle's *Microcosmographie*. Where Earle discusses the character of the modest man and Bacon describes the nature of jealousy, Huxley, through Rivers, analyses a phase of adolescence and this 'anatomy' seems to constitute the ground-plan of the figure of Ruth Maartens.

'When you're a child, your mind is a kind of saturated solution of feeling, a suspension of all the thrills—but in a latent state, in a condition of indeterminacy. Sometimes it's external circumstances that act as the crystallizing agent, sometimes it's your own imagination. You want some special kind of thrill, and you deliberately work away at yourself until you get it—a bright pink crystal of pleasure, for example, a green or bruise-coloured lump of fear; for fear, of course, is a thrill like any other, fear is a hideous kind of fun.' (pp. 27f.)

Only once or twice does Rivers support his direct portraiture of Ruth by this kind of general comment, but the comment thoroughly accords with the rest of the portraiture because Ruth is not sharply individualized. The sort of touches which impart vividness to a Lucy Tantamount are absent. Ruth is constituted of states of mind normal for a girl of her age, and more sharply defined mainly in respect of her being an American living in the early 1920s whose parents are clever and knowledgeable. At fourteen she is fascinated by Edgar

Allan Poe and writing poetry in which typical rhyming words are gloom and tomb; about a year later she has moved on to a phase of Wilde and Swinburne and the poetry has to do with yearning and burning, lips and whips. Ruth's appearance is shadowy to us, and her conversation we rarely hear, and then only in undistinguished snatches. The stage of her development, a stage in which intense, floating emotions are cultivated in emulation of literary models, is what causes her contribution to the tragedy.[7] Therefore, in accordance with the author's limited aims, it is almost all we know about her, and almost all we need to know.

The other characters are presented in much the same manner, so that the whole narrative principally consists of a placing together of four different psychological categories and a few accidental circumstances in such a way as to produce an unforeseen but inescapable end.

If Ruth is the category of adolescent girl whose mind is a 'saturated solution of feeling', Henry is the more familiar Huxleyan category of great intellect allied to emotional inadequacy. He is less distinct than his predecessors (Shearwater, Lord Edward, Peter De Vries) although he is more fully analysed. The emphasis is overwhelmingly upon how his mind works and there is comparatively little reference to his physical appearance or reproduction of his conversation. Huxley is mainly interested in describing the phenomenon of a genius who is hypochondriacal, childishly self-centred and pubertally enthusiastic over pornography. Rivers remarks in a characteristic metaphor :

'Henry's universe was modelled on the highball. It was a mixture in which half a pint of the fizziest philosophical and scientific ideas all but drowned a small jigger of immediate experience, most of it strictly sexual.' (p. 70)

This is a small but adequate sample of Rivers's general manner of describing (or defining) Henry Maartens. Each item of Henry's behaviour is reported and commented upon in such a way that the commentary all but forces out our pictures of him and his actions. Henry remains only just sufficiently substantial while serving to promote a body of critical analysis or definition which points 'outwards' from the book to life.

The fourth of the psychological categories brought together in this novel is embodied in the youthful Rivers. The mature Rivers deals with his younger self as he deals with the other characters, that is mainly by general definition rather than through the reproduction of peculiar details. At twenty-eight he was the Puritanical Man or the Man of Principle, educated to this condition by a mother who favoured but could not properly love him (or anyone else). He had been encouraged to view his life as a series of hurdles, and to conduct himself in obedience to certain inelastic rules. Thus, there is the simple rule that adultery is wrong, and Rivers's acceptance of this rule is demolished by taking part in a particular act of adultery whose immediate consequences are miraculously good. 'Le Cocu Miraculé', comments the recipients of Rivers's story. 'What a subject for a French farce!' (p. 100)

Rivers's traits are not so plainly fitted to form a contribution to the finale as are the traits of the other three main personages. His role is passive except in one fatal instance : it is he who with characteristic honour insists on leaving the Maartens household and in this way brings about the actual occasion of the accident. This fact is not unimportant, but it is probably true that Rivers is given his particular nature to provide further contrast and because only a reformed puritan or convert to 'paganism' would have been impressed by the events in such a way as to cause him now to tell the story homiletically.

The chain of episodes which the behaviour of these four characters (only trivially supported by Beulah and Timmy) produces is the most consistently ironic that Huxley ever composed. The narrative is designed to give the impression that life is, in Rivers's words, a series of 'booby-traps'.

'Fun—every kind of fun. Sex fun, eating fun, power fun, comfort fun, possession fun, cruelty fun. But there's either a hook in the bait, or else when you grab it, it pulls a trigger and down comes the bricks or the bucket of bird lime or whatever it is that the cosmic joker has prepared for you.' (p. 50)

In reading the other novels one is allowed to imagine that reasonable alternative choices could have been made, and that such choices would almost certainly have led to better results. Gumbril might well have foreseen that dallying with Myra would endanger his friendship with Emily; Elinor Quarles might sensibly have suspected that an *affaire* with Webley would bring no good; Anthony Beavis could have sensed some bad consequence of not being frank

201

with Brian Staithes. Many other examples could be offered. But in the present novel even the best people (Katy and Rivers) make what seem to be the best choices only to bring about catastrophe. Accordingly, *The Genius and the Goddess* is the least reassuring of the novels, if one begins it with vestiges of an assumption that the personal future is moderately predictable.

To summarize all the 'fun' and all the 'booby-traps' would be to summarize almost the entire narrative, but it may be useful to recall the main sequence. If (to begin with an accident) Katy's mother had not fallen ill, necessitating Katy's absence in Chicago; if, during this period, Ruth had not been ignored by a high-school footballer and therefore turned to Rivers; if Rivers had handled Ruth's passion for him more tactfully; if Henry, so childishly missing his wife, had not grown jealous of the young doctor from Johns Hopkins and caused himself to become ill, thus obliging his wife to return home exhausted and in need of reinvigorating sexual activity; if Katy's regained strength and confidence had not made her, in a moment of thoughtlessness, humiliate her daughter; if Ruth had been allowed to go with Katy and Rivers to prepare the country house for Henry's convalescence; if Ruth had not presented the accusatory poem; if the disposition of people in the two cars had been different; if an argument had not been raging as one car approached a crossroads, then Katy and Ruth would not have been killed and the subsequent lives of the other people would have been radically different. No link in the chain is removeable. But the emphasis is upon what Huxley at this stage regarded as the futility of considering alternatives, an activity which, like pondering the might-have-beens of history, is merely an amusement. When Rivers's hearer asks if Henry Maartens would have lived to eighty-seven without his medical pills, he is told (in a way that further emphasizes the main point of the novel) that he has asked a meaningless question.

In mentioning the principal links in the chain I have not sufficiently indicated the manner in which Huxley has ensured that every incident is natural, unavoidable and 'senselessly' functional. Perhaps it is unnecessary to choose more than one example. On the morning that the Maartens children return home from a fortnight's sojourn at the house of a friendly neighbour, Katy characteristically notices every manifestation of their period of freedom from her authority. Uncharacteristically, however, she indulges in boisterous denunciations of their failings. Perhaps she feels cocksure and somewhat thoughtlessly joyful over her success in restoring both Henry and herself to normal health. Whatever the reason, Katy's mood leads her to throw away Ruth's cosmetics and this in turn leads to Ruth's fatal accident. The episode possesses in itself, and in the disparity between itself and its consequences, the senselessness which Huxley, through Rivers, asserts is a regular property of life but seldom a property of fiction.

I have not yet mentioned all the means by which the features of this short novel are held together. In the chain of events each link fits smoothly with its neighbours, but some links additionally contain foretastes and echoes. Ruth's literary tastes, for instance, of which much is made in the early part of the novel, are not solely a way of characterizing her and explaining her subsequent behaviour; they are also, in their details, prophetic. Ruth is sentimentally enraptured by death and in particular by death in dark woods, by the idea of being blown away into nothingness by the wind on a dark night, by the prospect of being buried alive (as in 'The Fall of the House of Usher'). At the end of the novel Ruth dies in an ambulance, but our last picture of her is as a bundle lying among the leaves of a dark wood. Similarly, Ruth fancies herself in the role of Salome and in another, quite different sense she becomes a *femme fatale*.

It is not purely a part of the narrative thread that Henry should keep in his wall-safe, behind a portrait of Katy, a collection of pornographic books. The delights of the books are matched, so we gather, by the activities of Henry and Katy, and Rivers later discovers that such eroticism lies 'behind' the actual beauty of Katy as well as behind the painting of her. These same delights which Rivers, in consequence of his upbringing tends to believe will entail some kind of punishment, in fact materially help to produce the concluding sufferings. Of course a further irony lies in the fact that it is mainly Henry's belief that Katy must be enjoying similar voluptuousnesses with the doctor from Johns Hopkins (who turns out to be a cripple) that forces him to force her to return home and there commit elaborate adulteries with Rivers.

In addition to these correspondences within the story of the Maartens family there are correspondences between the story and elements in the larger story which is the entire novel. Rivers is given something of a history stretching after, as well as before, 1922, and there are two incidents that interrupt his narration. All elements are knit into one insistent theme. Rivers's marriage to a girl named Helen enhances his substantiality, but Helen is included mainly, it seems, to stress a point about the art of living and the art of dying.

'Helen knew how to die because she knew how to live—to live now and here and for the greater glory of God. And that necessarily entails dying too (sic) there and then and tomorrow and one's own miserable little self. In the process of living as one ought to live, Helen had been dying by daily instalments. When the final reckoning came, there was practically nothing to pay.' (pp. 10f.)

We have noticed Huxley obscurely driving towards this conception in the early novels and clearly expressing it from the time of *After Many a Summer*. Taking no thought for the morrow and dying in order to live constitute the proper form of acceptance, so that the example of Helen reinforces the example of Katy.

Other matters extraneous to the main story are similarly related to it in theme. There are two well-placed digressions which provide relief from a concentrated tale while giving thematic support. Just over a third of the way through the book when Rivers is fairly launched upon his narrative, he is interrupted by his grandson, Bimbo, who has had a nightmare and needs comforting. Immediately before the denouement Rivers is again interrupted by the return home of his daughter, Molly, and his son-in-law. The first digression enables Huxley to make the point that this child is bound for a life of 'booby-traps' in the form of 'fun', and the second digression gives him the opportunity to assert that no amount of applied child-psychology, common-sense and love can guarantee that a person will grow up to be wholesome and contented (for Molly has an unhappy temperament). These digressions, therefore, are calculated to aid the argument of the main story that nothing avails and that humility is the only wisdom.

For all its points of resemblance to some of Huxley's other writings (and its obvious place in the development of his ideas), *The Genius and the Goddess* contains statements and clear implications which in one respect go beyond anything Huxley wrote before or afterwards. In 1955 his view of the human lot seems to have been closer than usual to that view of T. S. Eliot which is expressed with particular force by the fourth part of 'East Coker'. Eliot's words are strikingly different from any Huxley ever used, or ever would have used, but the belief which they convey that suffering is a preordained and essential characteristic of human life appears to have possessed Huxley at this period.

'The whole earth is our hospital
Endowed by the ruined millionaire,
Wherein, if we do well, we shall
Die of the absolute paternal care
That will not leave us, but prevents us everywhere.'

Huxley was contemptuous of the concept of original sin,[8] and the God of whom Rivers speaks is neither paternal nor caring, but for the first and only time in Huxley's writings there is a sense of complete resignation. All pleasure, all that is not pain, is simply 'bait'. This is the only work in which he speaks of predestination in what seems to be the theological sense, and states that predestination and the possibility of grace are alone of fundamental importance in the career of an individual. Knowledge does not liberate; nor does it indicate ways to a better future.

Nowhere else does Huxley suggest that between an enlightened and affectionate upbringing of a child and an ignorant, unloving upbringing there is, apart from the frames of mind of the parents, nothing to choose. In *Time Must Have a Stop*, as in *Eyeless in Gaza*, he plainly argues that virtuous consideration of the consequences of actions will probably lead to better things; in *The Genius and the Goddess* he tries to demonstrate that there is no such probability. If the pessimism or fatalism of *The Genius and the Goddess* were transferred to the subject-matter of *Island* we could find that, by some inexplicable means, the spoilt Murugan would have turned out to be good and the unspoilt Mary Sarojini to be bad.

It is probable that in the years 1954 and 1955 Huxley's thinking strayed from its normal path. Pessimistic to some degree he may always have been, but the pessimism was—as we have seen—usually accompanied either by sheer pleasure in the process of living, intellectual high spirits, boundless curiosity, or alternatively, by a fairly hopeful search for better things. Normally he held both the old-fashioned belief that knowledge liberates and the quasi-existentialist assumption that man determines, within limits, his character and his fate. Most unacceptably all this is thrown overboard in *The Genius and the Goddess*, a novel contrived to demolish hope. In the absence of a full biography it is tempting to conjecture that this temporary mood was caused by the long illness and the death, in 1955, of Maria Huxley.

I I

Island (1962)

Island was not Huxley's last work, for, in addition to the short book, *Literature and Science*, published just before his death, it was followed by at least one paper, 'The Politics of Ecology; The Question of Survival', one essay called 'Shakespeare and Religion', and the first chapter of another novel.[1] Nevertheless, *Island* gives an impression of culmination because every important problem which ever occupied Huxley has been manœuvred into it and, seemingly, solved within the limits of present knowledge.

During the writing of *Island* he received treatment for cancer of the tongue. It was also in the period of writing the book that the Huxleys' house near Hollywood was burned down, and of this occurrence he wrote in a letter: 'I took it as a sign that the grim reaper was having a look at me'.[2] Ronald W. Clark, the biographer, conveys the impression that Huxley attached special significance to this novel and took extraordinary pains over it. Mr Clark writes:

'All his years of distress, all his experiences and all his learning, now seemed to contribute to this story of "a society in which a serious effort is made to help its members to realize their desirable potential". It was the story of a non-existent but plausible state of life, yet it was strangely different from *Brave New World*, and *Ape and Essence*. The difference was not only that here at last Huxley was describing a society with which he felt personal sympathy. It was not merely that he drew for it on his own experiences, recreating the death of Maria with a tenderness which he normally reserved for real life and tended to keep from his novels. It is possible that he took more trouble over the book, sensing that it might be his last. It is possible that his feeling of personal identification with this picture of life as he felt it should be lived helped to raise his professional ability to a higher level, so that again and again one finds in it what C. E. Montague once called "a splinter

206

of perfection in the art of letters". Whatever the cause or causes, *Island* describes a society not merely credible but so real that the reader may wonder when some lone discoverer among the eastern archipelagos will find his vessel swept towards its shores.'[3]

Some of these appreciative words run counter to the bulk of critical opinion, but, whatever the literary merits of *Island*, is is certainly the result of a special kind of effort. Huxley had always been fascinated by physical pain and by death : in Pala even the worst physical pains can be much mitigated, if not abolished, by hypnosis or yogic techniques, and the 'art of dying' is a general accomplishment. From at least the time of *Proper Studies* the author had been concerned with present and historical inadequacies in education and the social system. His utopia takes account of all the faults, and provides remedies which do not overlook the facts of human nature. In Pala drugs take their proper, wholly beneficial place. Sexual activity is presented as being as exciting as it ever was but no longer containing possibilities of degradation. Palanese art, admittedly, is not magnificent, but fine painting at least is compatible with the relative absence of conflict and suffering. The interconnectedness of experience and of all nature is generally and profoundly appreciated. Religion has its due place and function. Lying behind much of the Palanese excellence is the solution to Huxley's fundamental problem of dualism. Mind and body, or, to speak more precisely, mind-body and spirit, are no longer felt to be separate and opposed. In consequence the best natives of the island are Huxley's ultimate 'pagans'.

So far I have been writing summarily of the main features of the utopia. Only in proceeding through the stages of this study will it be possible to show how comprehensively Huxley has met, in one story, the difficulties of a lifetime. But at this point it is also worthwhile to indicate briefly the range of reference to the author's personal affairs and family background.

It seems very likely that the fictional Westerner whose work and influence in the nineteenth century contributed much to the formation of the model society has something in common, not only with James Esdaile, an English doctor who practised in India in the 1840s[4] but also with T. H. Huxley, whose brilliant wide-ranging curiosity was like that ascribed to Dr MacPhail. It is probable also that Dugald, the former husband of Susila, is based upon Huxley's brother, Trevenen, who committed suicide in 1914. Further, just

o

as in *Antic Hay* and *Eyeless in Gaza* there is the death of the mother, here is the death of a mother-figure, Will Farnaby's Aunt Mary; and here, most impressively of all, are the dying moments of Lakshmi which, as Mr Clark points out and as Laura Archera Huxley makes plain in detail, owe so much to the last weeks of Maria Huxley's life.

These features of the novel help to explain why Huxley attached so much importance to *Island* and why he was hurt by its reception. Sir Julian Huxley writes:

'The outcome of this deep and many-sided concern with human affairs and human possibilities was his last full-scale book, *Island*. This he regarded as one of his major contributions to serious thought, and he was saddened and upset by the incomprehension of so many of its reviewers, who treated it as a not very successful work of fiction, and science fiction at that.'[6]

Huxley had done his best to produce a work which brought to fruition the explorations of a lifetime (and which continued the efforts of his most talented forebears), but many reviewers merely saw a rather inept novel. It is best to approach *Island* not, as one approaches most novels, with expectations that personal relationships, conflict, and interesting characterization will dominate, but rather as one approaches, say, *News from Nowhere*. Morris, rather than Butler (despite the allusions to *Erewhon*) is the best comparison, because for once satire plays only a small part.

Huxley, unlike all his predecessors, was concerned both to portray his conception of excellence and to give a detailed account of the psychology of achieving it. As always in tackling this *genre*, the basic technical problem must have been how to convey information and ideas without holding up the narrative too often or for too long at a time. Presumably, as Huxley worked at his novel the problem was at its most intractable, for he had an immense amount of information to convey. Much of the story is devised (as is the story of *News from Nowhere*) for the purpose of allowing various people to explain the ways of the ideal community, but the physical environment of Pala, most of its people, and some of the happenings compose a series of pleasing images which unquestionably strengthen the advocacy of the ideas. If Huxley had confined his ideas to essays (and of course a number of them are to be found in essays) they would have had considerably less appeal.[7] The commentary is accompanied at almost every turn by what are designed to be aesthetically impressive pictures, and, in fact, commentaries and pictures are fairly thoroughly merged. It is possible and valuable (as Mr Peter Bowering has shown[8]) to extract the ideas from their context, but it is the whole context which most deserves our attention. One reason for this is that Huxley has done a remarkable thing in causing goodness and wisdom to appear both attainable and worth attaining. Conversely, the few bad people in the novel have not the slightest tinge of attractiveness, which is not to say that they are unrealistically ogrish, but that they are merely silly even when they are recognizably the sort of people who often hold power in the world.

Island begins and ends with the word, 'Attention', uttered by mynah birds, and, while the explicit exhortation within the novel is that people should concentrate upon the fleeting moment, it is possible that Huxley is also obliquely urging us on the first page to read and on the last page to remember, not simply as literary critics or recipients of an entertainment. The first mynah bird arouses Will Farnaby from his sleep of exhaustion; the last one suggests among other things that Will has awoken from his sleep of unenlightenment. In the beginning Will is cynical and frightened (as he has been all his life), but at the end, despite the coup and the shooting of Dr Robert MacPhail, he is no longer so. He is an alien intruder to start with, a yahoo come among houyhnhnms, and he remains in treacherous touch with the yahoo world outside Pala. By the close his nature has altered, but fresh, more menacing yahoos have taken over. The frame of the novel thus illustrates Huxley's usual mixture of optimism and pessimism. A perfect world is feasible : the majority either will not let it come about or will prevent it from surviving. Goodness is realizable, but good people, must, as always, be isolated or exist in beleaguered groups. Huxley quotes Buddha : 'I will show you sorrow, and the ending of sorrow', and indicates by narrative and style that the two states are to be thought of not as consecutive but as simultaneous. It is when the sorrowful blows fall most thickly in the closing chapters that Will Farnaby's mind and the author's tone are at their most serene. This is the primary reason why the novel is organized as it is.

Almost immediately after the first mynah bird has spoken we are plunged into the past life of Will Farnaby. His nature, which is explained mainly by reference to his past, is more important to the plot and therefore more intricately developed than the natures of visitors to utopias have traditionally been. In place of such straightforwardly decent, intelligent, open-minded visitors as Butler's and

Morris's narrators we have a guilt-ridden journalist, whose nearest counterpart in Huxley's earlier fiction is Anthony Beavis. Will's traits emerge rapidly in the course of the first three chapters as he remembers (convincingly in the circumstances) the death of his wife and his *affaire* with a woman called Babs, and as he talks first with the child, Mary Sarojini, and later with the adults, Dr Robert Mac-Phail, Vijaya, and Murugan. In these ways a swift introduction to Pala, dramatic rather than narrative in form, is accomplished while the hero is being characterized. There is no unseemly rush to reach the main expository sections of the book but there is no waste of time either, for, amid the images of tropical vegetation and of graceful, intelligent inhabitants it is so necessary for Huxley to acquaint us with a hero who 'won't take yes for an answer' (p. 20). The island offers a continual affirmative and this to many readers is bound to be such a suspect position that Huxley requires a sceptical man of ability who has suffered, sometimes as a result of his short-comings and sometimes quite gratuitously, to register all the obvious doubts. There is a further point arising from the fact that *Island* is not only a portrait of a perfect society but also a plea to individuals within any existing society to improve themselves. For this reason Huxley has produced a hero not much given to hopes of self-change and has shown us the beginnings of his transformation.

There are of course other matters in the early chapters, some of which are worth mentioning since they illustrate a feature of the method of the book. Huxley clearly set out to dramatize as well as to explain as many as possible of the techniques and customs of the Palanese. He brings Will Farnaby to the island as a badly scared and injured man, and this leads to the situation in which Will, instead of being promptly deported, lies in bed and receives various informative visitors through the course of five chapters. But at this stage of the novel Will's fears and pains, the mental suffering which is the result of having seen snakes and the physical suffering from his injured knee, are eased by disciplines with which every Palanese child is reared. The varied uses which Huxley makes of his hero's infirmities are representative of the economical methods of the novel. So much is included so briefly. Similarly, by the simple expedient of having Murugan accompany MacPhail and Vijaya to Will lying in the forest we are told, in the midst of everything else in Chapter Three, about the vulnerable political situation of Pala.

Writers of utopian fictions do not usually aim at credibility, but

Huxley has done so, not simply by making his community politically vulnerable but also by presenting believeable—though not, with the possible exception of Will Farnaby, rounded—characters. Even the best Palanese have only relatively sound minds in relatively sound bodies, and no one is free from personal difficulties. The epigraph to the novel is from Aristotle : 'In framing an ideal we may assume what we wish, but should avoid impossibilities.' Accordingly, Huxley has depicted the efficient tackling of problems rather than their total annihilation. The various talks at Will Farnaby's bedside, for example, are full of present difficulties (as well as historical accounts of difficulties overcome) and these are not confined to Will himself and the native dissidents, Murugan, the Rani, and Mr Bahu. Part of the aim is to focus upon several painful emotions and to show the best and the worst ways of dealing with them. This is the point of including here the private sorrows of two Palanese, Susila whose husband has lately died, and Dr Robert MacPhail whose wife is now dying. These two have unavoidable griefs which they bear willingly but do not brood over. Their strength lies in an awareness, gained through life-long training, that good and bad are not opposing principles but part and parcel of each other. Will, on the other hand, has some unpleasant memories to face and some other problems which are merely muddles to be sorted out, but his main difficulty (which does not fully emerge until later in the novel) lies in his assumption that the bad is both opposed to the good and also the stronger force. Even at his age Will is educable because he knows that his ego should not seek to subordinate the rest of the universe. Murugan and his mother are incorrigible because they do not know this, and Bahu is simply, but very intelligently, a worldly wiseman.

I have been bringing out the least explicit element of an early part of the book. On the surface a story is moving forward and a good deal of information is being imparted. It is here that the three dissidents sound out Will Farnaby's potentialities on a collaborator, and here also we learn about the technique of birth control and enhancement of sexual pleasure (*maithuna*), the mutual adoption clubs, and the history of Pala in the nineteenth century. In addition, Will's past life is further delineated and what purport to be small extracts from the old Raja's booklet are presented. (The reading of the booklet, which is in the form of a series of propositions rather like the axioms in Spinoza's *Ethics*, constitutes Huxley's last variation of a technique which began with the 'History of Crome' and has continued through all the extracts from diaries and notebooks.)

211

These early chapters are representative of the whole novel in being a feat of lucid compression. One detects behind this book a high degree of systematic planning the object of which was evidently to include examples of every species of human problem, and to vary the means of presentation in order not solely to absorb the reader but also to assault his defences of habit and scepticism, first with one weapon then with another. Thus, in Chapters Four to Eight we have, in turn, a glimpse of the intelligence and fortitude of Susila, the brief assertiveness of the Raja's *Notes*, the satire as Murugan, the Rani and Mr Bahu pay their call, the pleasantly naïve and chatty explanation of *maithuna* by two young practitioners, Susila's straightforward account of the mutual adoption clubs, Will's detailed reminiscences, and Dr MacPhail's broken historical 'lecture'. The methods vary according to the subject-matter. But the subject-matter is also unified by its parallels and contrasts. The topic of sexuality, for example, is treated by reference to the guilt-free pleasures of Nurse Appu and Ranga, Will Farnaby's recollections of the sordid, and the relationship, like that of Hadrian and Antinous, between Murugan and Colonel Dipa. Similarly, the Rani's possessive remarks and the ill result of her possessiveness in the shape of Murugan are calculatedly placed near the account of the mutual adoption clubs.

The events up to this point have occurred during the afternoon of Will's arrival on Pala and on the following day. By what is presumably the third day he is able to get up from his bed, and so from now on he can be taken to various institutions on the island and have their functions explained to him, just as Butler's narrator is shown such places in Erewhon as the law courts, the musical banks, and the colleges of unreason. It is while this is happening, even more than at other stages of the novel, that critics' complaints are justified. For instance, John Atkins writes in an introduction to the revised edition of his book, *Aldous Huxley*:

'And of course the author, reflecting from time to time that he is writing a novel, throws in the odd physical touch ("Psycho-physical means to a transcendental end," said Vijaya, raising his voice against the grinding screech of the low gear into which he had just shifted). But the novelist's duty of making a vital selection of experience is not performed. It is casual and arbitrary.'[9]

It is true that in the central parts of the novel no story of any consequence is unfolded. The beginning, comprising amongst other matters a fairly detailed introduction to several characters, and the end, which contains descriptions of exciting experiences, are not lacking in the properties of good narrative. But in the middle Will is simply taken one day to the uplands of Pala where he sees the work of the climbing school and a ceremony at the Shivapuram temple, and the next day to Vijaya's house and to the school house. At these places or *en route* to them a good many of the accounts of Palanese ways are given. It is difficult to imagine what other course the author could have adopted, since he had set himself the task of including, somewhere or other, all the following matters: the proper use of drugs; the benefits of regular manual work; the workings of a co-operative economy; the need for birth-control; ways of producing rival but non-profit-making newspapers; techniques for minimizing crime and delinquency; the value of mountaineering; the proper function of religious ceremony; sex-education for children; the nature and place of art; a portrait of a happy family; methods of teaching persons of different temperament and ability so that all subjects connect with one another and with common experience. Since Huxley's evident aim was to be compendious rather than selective, he could not have accommodated more narrative without inflating the novel over much, but the result at this stage is that commentary is supported by only the most perfunctory story. Nevertheless, the Shiva ceremony is amply portrayed; the methods of schooling are shown as well as analysed; there are clear impressions of people performing tasks, playing games, rapt in religious experiences.

Even in these central chapters the choice of setting and episode is not 'casual and arbitrary', as Mr Atkins puts it, because though there is little sense of events pressed into being by the sheer force of characters and circumstances, there is, certainly, a carefully planned matching of the graphic with the discursive in many of the scenes, and of each scene with others, so that the whole is a network designed to promote one way of life while alternative and much commoner ways are shown up as inadequate, ludicrous, or wicked. The arrangement is quite intricate and too plainly contrived to fulfil the requirements of the novel proper, but it produces effective advocacy. Every positive argument with its attendant images is linked with others elsewhere in the book in such a way that consolidation through variety and extension rather than tedious repetition is the effect gained. A full description of any single topic (for example, the prevention of crime) would entail references to a fair proportion of the novel, because *Island* is not a hotch-potch of proposals for the good life casually attached to an indifferent story, but a structure in which one's appreciation of each item is enhanced, directly or indirectly, by knowledge of many other items.

In this way the novel is a structure of close inter-relationships, and only the most trivial steps in the story are superfluous to Huxley's didactic purpose. If Will Farnaby has a bad fall, this is so that we can be shown how to deal with physical shocks; if a praying mantis comes on the scene, this is so that Will—and therefore the reader—can be taught in the final chapter how to accommodate even the apparently gratuitous horror of the mantis. Murugan is presumed to be homosexual solely to emphasize by contrast the wisdom of normal Palanese upbringing and the native methods of training in sexual activity. The Rani's theosophy constitutes both a touch of satire for our entertainment and an illustration of false spirituality. Vijaya is given physical strength partly in order to show how strength need not lead to bullying or contempt for the frail. Conversely, the *maithuna* instructress, Mrs Rao, is plump and 'very stupid upstairs' because it is necessary for us to realize that such traits need not be disadvantages. In particular, the concluding deaths of Lakshmi and Dr MacPhail occur so that the reader, having been 'trained', so to speak, by the earlier sections of the novel in a mode of acceptance of such experiences, can properly accept them.

In the foregoing remarks there are implications that some of the effects of *Island* are cumulative, and it is true that the closing chapters form a climax, not simply in the usual sense that a sequence of events bears fruit, but also in the unusual sense of a fusion and heightening of all the preceding ideas. And these ideas form a summit towards which Huxley can now be seen to have been struggling (often without knowing his direction) since at least 1920.

The fourteenth chapter is about innocence, feelings of guilt, and death. The narrative concerns three deaths which Will Farnaby has found particularly distressing, and the last hours of Lakshmi, Dr Robert MacPhail's wife. The subject of guilt is dealt with by reference to Will's bad behaviour leading to the death of his wife, Molly, and by the play, 'Oedipus in Pala'. It will be clear that we are dealing with one of Huxley's recurring preoccupations, which first appeared in *Antic Hay* when Gumbril brooded over what he felt to be a contradiction between his mother's goodness and the fact that she died young and painfully. In effect Huxley, in the closing sections of his final novel, provides a way of coming to terms with the harrowing deaths in his previous writings.

As Will Farnaby privately recollects or speaks aloud his tale of the deaths of his wife, his aunt, and his childhood pet, we receive what almost amounts to a summary, in tone and substance, of so much that has gone before. His wife had great charity but he preferred the vulgarity and lasciviousness of his mistress. Hence the quarrel which caused Molly to run from the house and have an accident in her car. Lying behind this story are several others from the death of Little Phil to Katy Maartens's car-accident, which all have to do with the death of a good person coming at a time when some other person is bound to feel either responsible or at least that he or she survives unworthily.

The most impressive part of the sequence of Will Farnaby's recollections concerns his Aunt Mary. She was completely good and therefore, as it seems, completely punished, first by giving birth to a deformed child, next by having her young husband killed in France, and finally, after years of good works, by contracting cancer of the breast. The detail here of the corruption of Aunt Mary's soul alongside the corruption of her body, together with the cynical commentary upon the story of her life ('only God can make a microcephalus idiot'—p. 234) is a neat recapitulation of the essential point of such varied earlier episodes as the following: the story of Sir Hercules Lapith; the history of the Monster in *Antic Hay*; the tale of Grace Elver; the death from meningitis of Little Phil; Bruno Rontini's cancer of the throat, and, in particular, the deaths of Gumbril's and Anthony Beavis's mothers. The different qualities of these episodes do not obscure their similarity in being about 'undeserved' death, so that it is reasonable to conjecture that each served in varying degree as an objective correlative for the emotions aroused in Huxley by the deaths of his mother and brother. Sir Julian Huxley has recently written:

[At the funeral] 'Trev and I were on the verge of tears, and Aldous, then at the critical age of fourteen, stood in stony misery. We know now, from several of his early novels, what sense of irreparable bereavement occupied his mind and soul; I am sure that this meaningless catastrophe was the main cause of the protective cynical skin in which he clothed himself and his novels in the twenties.'[10]

At first in Chapter Fourteen of *Island* the emotional and metaphysical problem is simply but forcefully stated. The next stage in the sequence is Huxley's debunking of conventional answers that point to the Fall and to God's mysterious ways. The God of the play, 'Oedipus in Pala', is a vain tyrant who repeatedly proclaims his Otherness, chuckles over the misfortunes of Thebes and revels in the citizens' supplications. What is clearly implied by this representation is Huxley's opinion not only of a classical god visiting a city with plague because of an unwitting act of incest, but also of a Christian God who punishes men for failing to rise to standards which He has ensured are beyond the limits of the possible. The entire penitential aspect of Christianity (and perhaps of post-Christian quasi-religious, philosophical, and political faiths) is being dismissed as an aberration, a product of unenlightenment. Suffering remains but it has nothing to do with guilt and punishment. Consequently the next scene is an illustration of guiltess suffering and a demonstration of the 'art of dying'.

' "It's dark because you're trying too hard," said Susila. "Dark because you want it to be light. Remember what you used to tell me when I was a little girl. 'Lightly, child, lightly. You've got to learn to do everything lightly. Think lightly, act lightly, feel lightly. Yes, feel lightly, even though you're feeling deeply. Just lightly let things happen and lightly cope with them.' I was so preposterously serious in those days, such a humourless little prig. Lightly, lightly—it was the best advice ever given me. Well, now I'm going to say the same thing to you, Lakshmi . . . Lightly, my darling, lightly. Even when it comes to dying. Nothing ponderous, or portentous, or emphatic. No rhetoric, no tremolos, no self-conscious persona putting on its celebrated imitation of Christ or Goethe or Little Nell. And of course, no theology, no metaphysics. Just the fact of dying and the fact of the Clear Light. So throw away all your baggage and go forward. There are quicksands all about you, sucking at your feet, trying to suck you down into fear and self-pity and despair. That's why you must walk so lightly. Lightly, my darling. On tiptoes; and no luggage, not even a sponge-bag. Completely unencumbered." ' (p. 257f.)

These words, and others spoken a little later by Dr Robert Mac-Phail which emphasize joy and love by reference to the sound of gay music coming through the night air, constitute a total contrast to common conceptions of what should take place at a death-bed. But of course Huxley is not endeavouring to minimize the fact of dying, in the way that he earlier satirized in *Brave New World*. On the contrary, the assumption is that reactions of struggle, grief, penitence, solemnity, are attempts to detain the departing ego, and as such form a kind of evasion, though a form which increases the pain. Every facet of the novel is against the belief that joy or pleasure can be won only by refusal to face facts. In *Brave New World* Linda died happily because she was drugged and distracted; the Savage, on the other hand, wanted Linda and everyone else to welcome suffering as a token of continuing freedom. The scene which closes the fourteenth chapter of *Island* is a resolution of Huxley's earlier dilemma in that Lakshmi dies happily precisely because she is fully aware of what is happening. With the help of her husband and daughter-in-law she attains for a few moments a state in which, while neither disregarding nor falsifying any element in her situation, she sees her normal consciousness as an obfuscation of reality. At the same time Huxley includes a touch of poignancy, and does so with an effectiveness that he has matched perhaps only twice before—in the story of Sir Hercules and in the death of Little Phil.

From now on in the novel, there is a welcome increase in narrative pace and a submerging of exposition beneath narrative. Almost all the unfamiliar ways of Pala have already been conveyed, but what remains is the most important factor, for it is a representation of the vision of life upon which local customs are based. Will Farnaby and the reader have been impressed by their observations but total conviction can come—if at all—only through sharing this native vision.

It should be emphasized at this point, before we consider the details of the drug-taking, that Huxley has anticipated certain criticisms. First, he makes it quite plain that he is not advocating the indiscriminate use of drugs that has become commoner in the years since the publication of *Island*. On the contrary, the drug which Huxley has invented is supposed to be beneficial only because it is part of a carefully defined, non-existent context of social, psychological and cultural habits. Will Farnaby is allowed to take the drug under controlled conditions, despite his quite different background, because he is only 'mildly schizoid'. Secondly—and this topic is much more fully dealt with in *Heaven and Hell* (1956)— Huxley is not implying that valuable quasi-mystical experience can be obtained by swallowing a pill. The fictitious drug is merely an adjunct to years of training in what Huxley would call 'seeing reality', so that it reinforces rather than contradicts the regular Palanese vision of life.

There are three stages in the experience which Will Farnaby undergoes as a result of taking the *moksha*-medicine. The first consists of an absence of the sense of time and a relegation of the sense of self. Will is aware that time is passing because a chiming clock tells him so, but chronometry seems wholly pointless. Similarly, he is aware, through flickering memories, of his normal modes of thinking and feeling, but these modes now appear unreal and even disgusting. As Will listens to Bach's Fourth Brandenburg Concerto he begins to think of his usual states of consciousness as acting as a 'muddy filter'. It follows of course (though Huxley does not at this point say so) that the precise nature of the muddiness of each individual's filter is unique, and that reality, in lying beyond individuality, is the same for everyone. Here is Huxley's final word on a theme which first appeared, though briefly and tentatively, in *Crome Yellow* when Denis Stone experienced a loss of the normal sense of self. In *Antic Hay* Gumbril spoke to Emily of a 'crystal quiet' within the mind, full acknowledgement of which would entail the death of the 'regular, habitual, daily part' of an individual. It should be remembered, too, that a leading purpose of the design of *Point Counter Point* was to place together what we may now describe as the 'muddy filters' of many characters with the implication that truth cannot reside within the normal workings of any particular consciousness. Huxley then sought universality but could only theorize about it, expressly in the words of Claude Bernard read by Lord Edward Tantamount and implicitly through the architecture of the novel. I have traced this theme *en passant* in several previous chapters and at this point wish only to emphasize that even in the novels after *Eyeless in Gaza* the existence of universal reality has been more argued for than demonstrated. The demonstration in this final chapter of *Island* is an extension of the sort of non-fictional experiences recounted in *The Doors of Perception* and *Heaven and Hell*, but it is a considerable extension.

Laura Archera Huxley tells us in *This Timeless Moment* that 'in the years between 1953 and 1963, Aldous had about ten or twelve chemically induced psychedelic experiences.'[11] She reproduces snatches of conversation and events (such as the occasion of Huxley's listening to Bach's Fourth Brandenburg Concerto after having taken the drug LSD) which have a clear bearing on *Island*. She tells us that Huxley 'wrote to Dr Albert Hoffman, the discoverer of LSD, "in *Island* the account of individual psychedelic experiences is first-hand knowledge"'.[12] From these facts it would seem that after 1954, when *The Doors of Perception* was published, Huxley's experiences with drugs grew richer and more revealing, for little in the earlier book is so impressive as the description in the closing pages of *Island*. But, of course, there is the important difference that the words in *Island* are designed to fulfil a special, fictional purpose, and it is this purpose that I am concerned with. Although Huxley's account is based on 'first-hand knowledge', he has also used the devices of a novelist, by causing Will Farnaby's experience to form a climax, by giving it complete coherence and inclusiveness, and by expressing it in language that would be unfitting in a non-fictional work.

The second stage of Will's experience occurs when, on Susila's instructions, he reluctantly opens his eyes. What happens now is even more reminiscent of *The Doors of Perception* and, in the fiction, of Denis Stone's moment of vision in *Crome Yellow*, for it consists of seeing objects directly without the distorting, blurring effects of words and concepts.

'His attention shifted from the geometrical constructions in brown agate to their pearly background. Its name he knew, was "wall"; but in experienced fact it was a living process, a continuing series of transubstantiations from plaster and whitewash into the stuff of a supernatural body—into a god-flesh that kept modulating, as he looked at it, from glory to glory. Out of what the word-bubbles had tried to explain away as mere calcimine, some shaping spirit was evoking an endless succession of the most delicately discriminated hues, at once faint and intense, that emerged out of latency and went flushing across the god-body's divinely radiant skin. Wonderful, wonderful! And there must be other miracles, new worlds to conquer and be conquered by. He turned his head to the left and there (appropriate words had bubbled up almost immediately) was the large marble-topped table at which they had eaten their supper. And now, thick and fast, more bubbles began to rise. This breathing apocalypse called "table" might be thought of as a picture by some mystical Cubist, some inspired Juan Gris with the soul of Traherne and a gift for painting miracles with conscious gems and the changing moods of water-lily petals.' (p. 270)

These perceptions, which seem to be like the perceptions of a very responsive young child to whom even a common wall is still 'apparell'd in celestial light' are of a kind the value of which Huxley (following so many other writers) often stressed. In the essay, 'Knowledge and Understanding', he writes:

We are humanized by imitating others, by learning their speech and by acquiring the accumulated knowledge which language makes available. But we understand only when, liberating ourselves from the tyranny of words, conditioned reflexes and social conventions, we establish direct, unmediated contact with experience.'[13]

The language used throughout a good part of the final chapter of *Island* constitutes a necessary and impressive attempt to express what, by its very nature, must lie near the outer limits of the verbally expressible. Through the medium of drugs (and aided by his lifelong aptitude for contemplation) Huxley had apparently regained some of the childhood capacity for 'direct, unmediated contact with experience', and then, for the purpose of persuading the reader to a way of life, struggled against the 'tyranny of words' on ground where the tyranny is nearly absolute. In reading the above passage (which, it should be stressed, is only a very small part of a sequence that flows in the same striking way for about twelve pages) one absorbs what must be a clear impression of the observations and feelings ascribed to Will Farnaby. The movement of the texture and colour of the wall is rendered in such a way that most normally imaginative readers could not fail to visualize adequately and with conviction a process which they have never actually observed, though faint, mingled recollections of some paintings and some films probably assist the effect of Huxley's words. The phrases, 'god-flesh' and 'god-body's', have the kind of originality which strikes some familiar chord. The references to Traherne and Juan Gris, with the assertion that Will's experience goes beyond an imaginary combination of their talents, further enable us to form a roughly accurate conception of what Will is seeing. The attempt, one feels, is as successful as it could possibly be.

After this point, while Will is still undergoing what I have called the second stage of his experiences, Huxley presents a surprising reversal of effects. Whoever supposed that the *moksha*-medicine was going to produce only an intensely pleasurable vision now finds that this is not at all its function. *Moksha* is a Sanskrit word meaning liberation, and the drug that Huxley has invented liberates the user from bondage to his ego. But while this means that the attractiveness of attractive or neutral things such as walls and tables is not diminished by the usual sense of their relationship to oneself and by the concepts under which they are normally submerged, it also means that the repellent nature of ugly or frightening things is likewise unmodified. There is no softening of the impact of either the heavenly or the hellish. Huxley's aim in the final pages is to confront the reader with the most complete nakedness of beauty and horror that the 'tyranny of words' will permit, and then to indicate how beauty and horror can be reconciled.

Here it must be pointed out that Will Farnaby's 'hell' is highly individual. It seems that the heavenly vision is the same for everyone, but the hellish vision takes on the idiosyncracies of the particular unenlightened person. At first, however, as the unpleasant phase of Will's vision begins to unfold, he sees and feels what any person who falls well short of sainthood might see and feel. On one side of the room in which he and Susila are sitting there appears a lizard; on the other side, a male and a female specimen of *Gongylus gongyloides*, or praying mantis. Will then has an enlarged, unrelieved sight of the female mantis eating the male mantis as a normal conclusion to the act of copulation. Following this, the lizard flashes across the floor and eats the remaining mantis. Huxley's presentation of these simple but unnerving images of the 'Essential Horror' is as memorable as any of his earlier descriptions of the gruesome.

'And now one of the nightmare machines, the female, had turned the small flat head, all mouth and bulging eyes, at the end of its long neck—had turned it and (dear God!) had begun to devour the head of the male machine. First a purple eye was chewed out, then half the bluish face. What was left of the head fell to the ground. Unrestrained by the weight of the eyes and jaws, the severed neck waved wildly. The female machine snapped at the oozing stump, caught it and, while the headless male uninterruptedly kept up his parody of Ares in the arms of Aphrodite, methodically chewed.' (p. 273)

It is the scrupulous rendering of the facts of this process interspersed with expressions of feeling ('nightmare machines', 'dear God!') which makes the passage an epitome of all the offensive or outrageous happenings which Huxley has insisted upon facing in novel after novel. Here is pure horror which the human mind is compelled by its nature to try to explain, but cannot. A little later in the chapter Huxley will state how the activities of these insects should ideally be comprehended. But first Will finds a stream of unpleasant personal recollections flowing uninvited through his mind. They consist of scenes of war, murder, marching brownshirts, the last days of his Aunt Mary, and his sexual activities with Babs (now seen as similar to the activities of the *Gongylus gongyloides*), the whole accompanied by sounds of the Bach concerto, which is still being played, and by a fluctuating, indeterminate sense of cheapness and vulgarity. This medley constitutes Will Farnaby's personal hell, and it enters his consciousness as a result of the unregenerate frame of mind in which he began the experiment, just as Eustace Barnack's recollections of vice and weakness form a part of his experiences on the *Bardo* plane. The *moksha*-medicine has simply but devastatingly enabled Will to see the object (any external feature or any feature of his own make-up) as in itself it really is. The doors of perception have been cleansed, but the cleansing has produced a more lucid vision of beauty and horror as opposites.

Interestingly enough, when Huxley offers a final prescriptive and descriptive message of reconciliation, he does so through the eyes of Will Farnaby after the influence of the drug has worn off. The problem is to see beauty and horror as indissolubly one; the method, Susila states, is to combine contemplation and compassion. Will has an access of compassionate feeling as he looks at Susila's face and the result is expressed in these words:

' "It isn't the sun," he said at last, "and it isn't Chartres. Nor the infernal bargain basement, thank God. It's all of them together. And you're recognizably you, and I'm recognizably me—though, needless to say, we're both completely different. You and me by Rembrandt, but Rembrandt about five thousand times more so." He was silent for a moment; then, nodding his head in confirmation of what he had just said, "Yes, that's it," he went on. "Sun into Chartres, and then stained glass windows into bargain basement. And the bargain basement is also the torture chamber, the concentration camp, the charnel house with Christmas tree decorations. And now the bargain basement goes into reverse, picks up Chartres and a slice of the sun, and backs out into this—into you and me by Rembrandt. Does that make any sense to you?" ' (p. 279)

The imagery is selected with precision. Rembrandt is chosen because of his gift for making light shine out of darkness and darkness appear at the heart of light. The conjunction of charnel house and Christmas tree, of Chartres and concentration camp could scarcely be matched as a test of the validity of the clear, unifying vision which has been Huxley's objective—as we can now see more clearly than ever—throughout his career. The moments depicted in the closing pages of *Island* comprise the greatest imaginable success because the union that Huxley represents, though a product of art, is not a merely artistic harmony. The minutely receptive reader shares momentarily the way of looking ascribed to Will Farnaby.

Accordingly, the ironic ending of this novel, while being a repetition of a formal device with which all but two of Huxley's novels have closed, has a changed significance. Irony is not banished (for that, on Huxley's part, would be evasion and falsehood) but is taken up into a larger vision.

Conclusion

We can be sure that if Huxley had lived on his thought would have progressed, so the definitive air of *Island* is an illusion. He never stood still. There is a sense of finality in the utterances of Propter, yet *Island* is a far cry from *After Many a Summer*, and indeed from *The Genius and the Goddess*, published only eight years before the author's death. Few thinkers can have been more capable than Huxley of continuing lively curiosity and of changing direction whenever the facts indicated a need for change.

But—as I have regularly implied—it is an exaggeration, if not a downright error, to see Huxley as a thinker who happened, for accidental or tactical reasons, to take up the writing of fiction. He wrote 'novels of ideas', but this phrase should not be allowed to suggest either too great a shortage of the true novelist's talents or cerebration carried on with only minimal interference from the feelings. The mistaken notion that Huxley's works lack feeling is aided by his own ways of seeing himself, earlier in his career as an 'amused, Pyrrhonic aesthete',[1] and later as one striving for non-attachment. The truth of the matter is subtly different, for analysis of the novels reveals that (as no doubt many responsive readers have always felt) there was in varying degrees a holding at bay of emotions, and that these restrained emotions help to determine meaning and value. Lawrence may have been wrong to imagine that Huxley endangered his sanity by writing *Point Counter Point*, but such a view is a useful corrective to excessive notions of 'coldness' and uninvolvement;[2] and just as Mark Rampion is not Lawrence but 'just some of Lawrence's notions on legs',[3] so Philip Quarles is not Huxley but a considerable contraction of Huxley.

Huxley was not what is normally understood as an 'emotional' man. He once wrote :

'My own nature, as it happens, is on the whole phlegmatic, and, in consequence, I have the greatest difficulty in entering into the experiences of those whose emotions are easily and violently aroused.

Before such works of art as *Werther*, for example, or *Women in Love*, or the *Prophetic Books* of William Blake I stand admiring, but bewildered.'[4]

However, complex emotions, of whatever strength, inform the novels, and it is for these emotions that Huxley in inventing his various devices, including the larger structures, found 'objective correlatives'. At one end of the sequence, the design, the incidents, the people and the language of *Crome Yellow* make up the formula for a particular compound of feelings, including sadness; while, at the other end, *Island* expresses bereavement. Neither the intellectual ideas which the novels are so full of, nor the technical ideas which Huxley thought up or adapted are merely sportive. He had an exceptional capacity for using ideas creatively, as expressive of the whole man. In this way, the tricks of *Eyeless in Gaza* should be recognized as reflecting full-blooded concerns with time, death and spiritual rebirth; and the fantastic effects of *Ape and Essence* as methods of organizing a mood of dejection into a countervailing hope of change through the very carnality gross representations of which have helped to express the dejection. *Brave New World* is as much about personal problems as it is about problems of society.

One detects in Huxley's writings—alongside the Pyrrhonism which he gives to Philip Quarles and the searching for non-attachment which he gives to Calamy, Anthony Beavis and Sebastian Barnack—a kind of Stoicism arising from a conviction that, since the individual is a tiny fragment of the cosmic process, it is bad to 'make a fuss' about personal feelings. Instead of having an inclination to rage or repine about any shocking feature of the human condition, he continually recommended, either by direct statements or implicitly through his manner, a mixture of insouciance and intellectual honesty. But Huxley's emotions, though stoically restrained, never appear to have been evaded in the fiction, so that even *Brave New World*, the novel in which ideas seem most flagrantly to crowd out feelings, owes its distinction not only to its celebrated ingenuities but also to emotional pressures which, we can be sure, produced the main ingenuities, and which are amply (though inconspicuously) expressed by construction and style.

With whom, in the end, can Huxley be usefully compared? Comparisons with Swift quickly become more misleading than useful because of Swift's indignation. Likewise, for all his Voltarian sense of the ridiculous, the passion which in Voltaire was directed against clericalism and injustice is lacking in our author. On the other hand, Peacock is too worldly and too comfortable to be regarded as a forerunner, except in a few technical ways and in readiness to discern nonsense. No other English writer of fiction comes readily, or even laboriously, to mind as a serious aid to the placing of Huxley.

T. S. Eliot's remark, which I quoted at the beginning of this book, that Huxley's 'place in English Literature is unique', should not be regarded as a careless compliment to be corrected by some better scholar. Perhaps part of the reason why Huxley evades helpful, as opposed to pedantic or facile, classification lies partly in his willingness to 'try on' other men's life-styles and other men's artistic techniques. It will not, I hope, be taken either as promoting Huxley beyond his merits or as confirming certain low opinions of his writing, if I say that he borrowed too freely from various territories to be neatly trapped in one of them. But it goes without saying that his amoeboid capacity did not dilute the flavour of his own personality.

He was a religious man who felt twentieth-century problems in the quick of his being long before many people became fashionably and often rather spectatorially aware of them. I doubt if it is possible to think of one contemporary spiritual or social crux which Huxley was not urgently concerning himself with forty years ago. The general assumption that his answer after the mid-thirties was mysticism is true, though it may give rise to misunderstandings. He never became a fully-fledged mystic, but remained a professional writer (the two vocations probably are incompatible). His profound interest in the mystical, continually reinforced or modified by the most up-to-date finding of psychologists (for, unlike most literary men, he was not content with smatterings of Freud, Jung and Adler) did not force out enthusiasm for the reform of institutions. He was what many aspire to be, the complete liberal, being the embodiment, except in physical capacities, of his grandfather's famous definition of a liberal education.[5] It will be possible for a long time to come for people to retrace the steps in Huxley's search without any feeling that they are dealing with long-solved doubts and difficulties, and this fact alone will keep his fiction alive. But it will chiefly endure for the usual reasons of form and (in its own curious way) fidelity to nature.

Notes

PART I

Introduction

A Variety of Fiction

1   T. S. Eliot, *Aldous Huxley 1894–1963* (ed. Julian Huxley), Chatto & Windus, 1965, p. 30
2   idem, p. 32
3   Northrop Frye, *Anatomy of Criticism*, Princeton University Press, 1957, Princeton, New Jersey, p. 308f.
4   See *Point Counter Point*, Collected Edition, Chatto & Windus, 1963, p. 410 :
    'But then I never pretended to be a congenital novelist.' (The whole of Chapter 22 is relevant.)
    Huxley's reply to interviewers was : 'I don't think of myself as a congenital novelist—no.' *Writers at Work*, The *Paris Review* Interviews Second Series, (int. Van Wyck Brooks), Secker & Warburg, 1963, p. 171
5   op. cit., p. 310
6   *Letters of Aldous Huxley* (ed. Grover Smith), Chatto & Windus, 1969, letter no. 510, p. 538
7   *Eyeless in Gaza*, Collected Edition, Chatto & Windus, 1955, p. 520f.
    (It might be argued that *Ulysses* meets these requirements, but Bloom's visceral sensations and the like are part of a highly organized pattern, and the main point is that in life no such patterns exist or are discernible.)
8   *After Many a Summer*, Collected Edition, Chatto & Windus, 1968, p. 225
9   *The Genius and the Goddess*, Chatto & Windus, 1955, p. 7
10 *Literature and Science*, Chatto & Windus, 1963, p. 99
11 Keats's remarks about negative capability occur in a letter of the 21st to the 27th December, 1817. See *The Letters of John Keats* (ed. Hyder Edward Rollins), Cambridge University Press, 1958, Vol I, letter no. 45, pp. 191ff.

12 E. M. Forster, *Aspects of the Novel*, Edward Arnold & Co., 1927, p. 85

13 idem, pp. 75ff.

14 *Point Counter Point*, p. 410

15 *Eyeless in Gaza*, p. 144f.

16 In his *Enemies of Promise*, Routledge & Kegan Paul, 1938, p. 53f., Mr Connolly reproduces two passages from *Eyeless in Gaza*, providing italics for all the otiose or stale expressions. Mr Connolly believes that a publisher's contract, under which Huxley had to produce two books a year, had a bad effect.

17 R. P. Blackmur, *Language as Gesture*, Harcourt Brace Jovanovich, New York, 1935, p. 6

Chapter One

Crome Yellow

1 Huxley himself, along with many reviewers and critics, thought of his first novel in this way. In a letter of the 28th June, 1921 he wrote to his father : 'I am working hard at my Peacockian novel.' See *Letters*, no 185, p. 198

2 J. B. Priestley, *Thomas Love Peacock*, Macmillan, 1927, p. 135

3 idem, p. 140

4 idem, p. 141

5 *The Letters of Percy Bysshe Shelley* (ed. Frederick L. Jones), Oxford University Press, 1964, Vol. II, p. 98, Letter 501, June, 1819. The reference is to *Nightmare Abbey*, but Shelley's subsequent remarks indicate that he thought that all Peacock's writings possessed these qualities in some degree.

6 Alexander Henderson, *Aldous Huxley*, Russell & Russell, New York, 1964, p. 133f. (First published, London, 1936.)

7 It seems likely that Huxley obtained the idea of comical ingenuity in the construction of privies from reading Sir John Harington's 'The Metamorphosis of Ajax', which was first printed in 1596.
   See *Sir John Harington's A New Discourse of a Stale Subject called The Metamorphosis of Ajax* (ed. Elizabeth Story Donno), Routledge & Kegan Paul, 1962.

8 No doubt several examples could be found in this novel of Huxley's tendency (which is apparent in many of the novels) to adapt literary sources to his own purposes. I have noted what may be the use of Sir John Harington's work, and in note 21 draw attention to the use of the sermon by the Rev. E. H. Horne. There is also, in the incident of Mr Scogan's telling fortunes, a modification of the fortune-telling scene in *Jane Eyre*. (See *Letters*, p. 640.)

9 Her appearance, though not perhaps her nature, is that of Lady Ottoline Morrell. See the illustrations in *Ottoline* (ed. Robert Gathorne-Hardy), Faber & Faber, 1963

10 In *Rotunda*, 1932 where it is called 'The Dwarfs'; and in *Twice Seven*, 1944, and in *Collected Short Stories*, 1957, in each of which it is entitled 'Sir Hercules'.

11 Alexander Henderson, op. cit., p. 135

12 In this poem Huxley gives to Sir Hercules an early unscientific grasp of some of the notions of evolutionism. Forty years after the appearance of the *Origin of Species* Hardy caused his Jude Fawley and Sue Bridehead to resemble the Darwinian partial mutations, or sad-fated 'rare precursors of the nobler breed'.

13 See *Writers at Work*, p. 176

> 'And there is something of Norman Douglas in Old Scogan of *Crome Yellow*. I knew Douglas quite well in the twenties in Florence. He was a remarkably intelligent and highly educated man, but he had deliberately limited himself to the point where he would talk about almost nothing but drink and sex. He became quite boring after a time.'

But it has often been convincingly assumed that there is something of Bertrand Russell in Scogan.

14 Sir Kenneth Clark in *Aldous Huxley 1894–1963*, p. 15f. points out that Gombauld's half-finished picture, which will, it is hoped, display these qualities, is Caravaggio's 'Conversion of St Paul'.

15 Cyril Connolly, *The Modern Movement*, André Deutsch and Hamish Hamilton, 1965, p. 47

16 In this respect and in its possession of three towers Crome does not resemble the 'Manor House' at Garsington where Huxley, as a guest of the Morrells, spent some time in the War-years and in 1920.

17 For example, *The Doors of Perception*, Chatto & Windus, 1954, p. 18

> 'Visual impressions are greatly intensified under the influence of mescalin and the eye recovers some of the perpetual innocence of childhood, when the sensum was not immediately and automatically subordinated to the concept. Interest in space is diminished and interest in time falls almost to zero.'

It was not until 1953 that Huxley, having taken a mescalin tablet, shared briefly the vision that has so often been described in literature and mystical writings. But it seems likely that Denis's modest vision is a representation of a type of experience that occurred to Huxley in his youth.

18 *Aldous Huxley 1894–1963*, p. 17

19 idem, p. 21

20 The assumption that Dorothy Carrington was the model for Mary Bracegirdle and Mark Gertler the model for Gombauld (though no doubt there were considerable differences between the originals and their fictional counterparts) is borne out by Grover Smith in his edition of the *Letters*, op. cit., pp. 108 and 211. Letter no. 97 (p. 109) is interesting in relation to Ivor Lombard's night in the roof with Mary Bracegirdle.

> '. . . while of nights, I have been sleeping out on the roof in company with an artistic young woman in short hair and purple pyjamas . . . while early in the morning we would be awakened by a gorgeous great peacock . . .'

21 The following words appear in small print after the close of Chapter 9 (p. 62)

> 'The sermon attributed to "Mr Bodiham" in Chapter IX is a reproduction of the substance of an Address, given by the Rev. E. H. Horne, in A.D. 1916, to a meeting of clergy, and then published. It is now reprinted as an Appendix in a small book by him, entitled *The Significance of Air War* (Marshall, Morgan & Scott).'

See also the *Letters*, no. 169, p. 185 :

> 'The Sermon, by the way, is lifted almost without alteration from a really superb tract I came upon the other day.'

22 Cyril Connolly so describes it in his *The Modern Movement*, p. 47
23 Angus Wilson, 'The House Party Novels', The *London Magazine*, August, 1955, p. 56
24 D. S. Savage, *The Withered Branch*, Eyre & Spottiswoode, 1950, p. 133
25 Jocelyn Brooke has written of Huxley's early works, though not specifically of Denis or *Crome Yellow*, that

> 'The effect was intoxicating : like the great Knockespotch, that imaginary genius described in *Crome Yellow*, Mr Huxley had "delivered us from the dreary tyranny of the realistic novel"; like Knockespotch again, he preferred to study the human mind, not "bogged in a social plenum", but "freely and sportively bombinating".'

Jocelyn Brooke, *Aldous Huxley*, Longmans Green, 1954, p. 6. (Denis Stone is not the first futile young hero, since Norman Douglas's *South Wind* containing Denis Phipps appeared in 1917.)

Chapter Two

Antic Hay

1 Huxley himself was an unenthusiastic schoolmaster in 1916 at Repton and from 1917 to 1919 at Eton.

2   Harold F. Brooks has produced a number of particularly perti-
     nent instances in his essay, 'Four Quartets: the structure in
     relation to the themes', Eliot in Perspective (ed. Graham Martin),
     Macmillan, 1970, p. 133f.
3   This is a fair representation of historical facts. Wren had the
     support for his plans of Charles II, and an Act of 1667 empowered
     the Mayor and Sheriffs of London to regulate, through a jury,
     the details of building and demolition. But the provisions of the
     Act were not enforced, and parishes and individual citizens pro-
     ceeded to build in accordance with what they believed to be their
     own interests. I have taken this information from Michael
     Harrison, London Growing, Hutchinson, 1965.
4   See Howards End, Chapter Five. Interestingly enough, there is a
     slight similarity between the meanings which Huxley and Forster
     attribute to the pieces of music which they describe. Mozart and
     Beethoven are both interpreted as saying that the bad (to Helen
     Schlegel the goblins of pettiness and malice) is never annihilated.
5   Compare T. S. Eliot's words : 'Human kind cannot bear very
     much reality.' ('Burnt Norton')
6   'Burnt Norton'
7   It has recently been made clear, by Sir Julian Huxley in his
     autobiography, Memories, William Heinemann, 1968, and by the
     publication of the Letters, that Huxley was here thinking of the
     death of his own mother, Julia Arnold, which occurred when he
     was fourteen.
8   It is in the essay 'Sir Christopher Wren', that Huxley makes
     plain his own preference for order and proportion in architecture.
     He writes : 'But it is in England that the golden mean of reason-
     ableness and decency—the practical philosophy of the civilized
     man—has received its most elegant and dignified expression.'
     'Sir Christopher Wren', On Art and Artists, Chatto & Windus,
     1960, p. 278. (This essay first appeared in On The Margin in
     1923.)
9   Compare the procedure in his plays of Shaw who often surrounds
     a hero or heroine whose views are right by persons whose views
     are wrong. (Candida and Major Barbara are interesting excep-
     tions.) Something similar happens in all Huxley's novels from
     Point Counter Point onwards : in Antic Hay, as we have seen, the
     correct way is not neatly represented by a single character.
10   It is likely that Coleman's choice of mistress reflects, though
     flippantly, Huxley's conception of the relationship between
     Baudelaire and Jeanne Duval. See the essay 'Baudelaire' in Do
     What You Will.
11   Compare the parallelism in Part II of The Waste Land ('A Game

of Chess'). While there are several obvious differences between Huxley's point and Eliot's, both authors broaden a theme of sterility by juxtaposed references to different social classes.

12   Gumbril's behaviour at this moment is a perfect example of Jean-Paul Sartre's notion of 'bad faith', which Sartre defines as 'a certain art of forming contradictory concepts which unite in themselves both an idea and the negation of that idea'. Sartre's illustrations make plain that in practice this means a limiting or controlling of awareness in certain ways in an attempt to prevent dissatisfaction with oneself.
       See Jean-Paul Sartre, *Being and Nothingness* (tr. Hazel E. Barnes), Methuen, 1957, pp. 55–67

13   It is common for critics of Huxley to assert, in one form or another, that his response to the body is sometimes so abnormal that it can be dismissed by sensible persons. The following remark is an example of this assumption :
          '. . . but there is in *Crome Yellow* and *Those Barren Leaves* none of the pathological wallowing in physical disgust that began to darken the picture in *Point Counter Point* and *Eyeless in Gaza,* and has now become so tedious.'
       Angus Wilson, 'The House Party Novels', The *London Magazine,* p. 55, August, 1955

14   L. P. Hartley, The *Spectator,* December 22nd, 1923. p. 998f.
15   Evelyn Waugh, 'Antic Hay', The *London Magazine,* 2nd August, 1955, p. 53

Chapter Three

Those Barren Leaves

1   This does not preclude Miss Thriplow's also being a Huxleyan version of Katherine Mansfield.
      Cyril Connolly in his *The Modern Movement,* p. 47, states :
          'He was to describe her [Katherine Mansfield], not too sympathetically, in *Those Barren Leaves.*'

2   In this respect *Point Counter Point* is the novel which most resembles *Those Barren Leaves,* but Philip Quarles is something of a hero in the later novel in spite of the fact that his is not the central role of all the other heroes from Denis Stone to Will Farnaby.

3   It is not certain that Huxley consciously echoed Marvell. In a letter he wrote : '. . . a reference among other things to Canning's parody of Darwin, *The Loves of the Triangles,* incidentally an excellent description of the loves of these particular characters—

perhaps of *most* love, in so far as all love is between entities which obey Euclid rather than Lobatchevsky and "never meet".'
Letters, no. 323, p. 344

4 Even Rousseau, according to Bertrand Russell, 'appealed to the already existing cult of sensibility, and gave it a breadth and scope that it might not otherwise have possessed'.
History of Western Philosophy, George Allen & Unwin, second edition, 1961, p. 652 (first published, 1946)

5 'Religion and Literature', *Selected Essays*, Faber & Faber, 1951, p. 398

6 There are no such addresses in any of the other novels, and when they occur in the short stories (for example, 'Uncle Spencer' and 'Two or Three Graces') Huxley is writing in the character of a narrator.

7 Elizabeth Bowen in her *Collected Impressions*, Longmans Green, 1950, p. 147, refers to Huxley's 'unnecessary incidents [so called by other critics] like the dog on the roof in *Eyeless in Gaza*, or the moron's death in *Those Barren Leaves*'. Miss Bowen continues : 'Strictly, those two incidents are necessary; they are the moral pivots of the two books.'

8 The description of *Candide* in *The Oxford Companion to French Literature* (ed. Sir Paul Harvey and J. E. Heseltine), Oxford University Press, 1959, concludes with the following words :
'We may see in the last words the moral either that work within his proper sphere is man's consolation for his unhappy lot; or that practical work is more profitable than vain philosophical speculation.' (p 101f.)
Huxley's essay, 'On Re-reading Candide', first appeared in *On the Margin* (1923). One small point about *Candide* might be worth mentioning : there is in it reference to a Pope's daughter (sic) who is betrothed to the Prince of Massa-Carrara.

9 One critic, at least, has seen in the story of Chelifer and Barbara Waters the influence of *Du Côté de Chez Swann*. See Peter Bowering, *Aldous Huxley: A Study of the Major Novels*, The Athlone Press, 1968, p. 64f.

10 Ronald W. Clark, *The Huxleys*, William Heinnemann, 1968, p. 138

11 Christopher Isherwood, *Aldous Huxley 1894–1963*, p. 159

12 idem, p. 158

13 Compare the following remarks by Huxley :
'Well, the poet would certainly get an extraordinary view of life which he wouldn't have had in any other way, and this might help him a great deal. But, you see (and this is the most significant thing about the experience), during the experience you're not really interested in doing anything practical—even

writing lyric poetry. If you were making love to a woman, would you be interested in writing about it? Of course not. And during the experience you're not particularly interested in words, because the experience transcends words and is quite inexpressible in terms of words. So the whole notion of conceptualizing what is happening seems very silly. *After* the event, it seems to me quite possible that it might be of great assistance; people would see the universe around them in a very different way and would be inspired, possibly, to write something about it.'
Writers at Work, p. 169

14 For comparison see Nancy Cunard's *Grand Man*, Secker & Warburg, 1954. Cardan's appearance and attitudes may well be caricatured versions of Norman Douglas's. On the other hand, Cardan is extraordinarily mannered and fluent in conversation whereas Douglas seems often to have been jerky and colloquially bawdy.

15 Compare Keats's remarks on the 'poetical Character' :
'When I am in a room with People if I am ever free from speculating on creations of my own brain, then not myself goes home to myself : but the identity of every one in the room begins to press upon me that, I am in a very little time annihilated—not only among Men . . .'
The Letters of John Keats, Vol. I, letter no. 318, p. 387

16 It is reasonable to deduce a kind of wariness from Huxley's practice; and such was his reputation for audacity in the nineteen-twenties that it is not surprising that expressions of enthusiasm for older values are hedged around by disarming gestures. In his introduction to *The Letters of D. H. Lawrence* (Heinemann, 1932) he writes :
'Before tea was over he asked me if I would join the colony, and though I was an intellectually cautious young man, not at all inclined to enthusiasms, though Lawrence had startled and embarrassed me with sincerities of a kind to which my upbringing had not accustomed me, I answered yes.' (p. XXIX)

17 op. cit., p. 134

18 op. cit., p. 66

19 Leonard Woolf, The *Nation and Athenaeum*, January 24th, 1925, p. 584

Chapter Four

Point Counter Point

1 From the 'Chorus Sacerdotum' at the conclusion of *Mustapha*. Greville's point is that we cannot evade the contradictions, for

Nature has implanted them to make virtue hard to attain :
    'If Nature did not take delight in blood,
    She would have made more easy ways to good.'

2 '. . . your Rampion is the most boring character in the book—a gas-bag.' *The Collected Letters of D. H. Lawrence* (ed. Harry T. Moore), William Heinemann, 1962, vol. 2, p. 1096

    Huxley himself wrote that 'Rampion is just some of Lawrence's notions on legs. The actual character of the man was incomparably queerer and more complex than that.' *Letters,* no. 317, p. 240

3 *Music at Night,* Chatto & Windus, 1931, p. 21

4 *Do What You Will,* Chatto & Windus, 1929, p. 51

    (Other essays in this volume, as its title suggests, bear out the theme.)

5 In an interview Huxley remarked, '. . . I have great difficulty in inventing plots. Some people are born with an amazing gift for story-telling; it's a gift which I've never had at all.' *Writers at Work,* p. 171

6 Apart from presenting the features of his own mind that especially interested him at this stage, Huxley does include other auto-biographical details : the son left with relatives, the return from Bombay, some of the arguments presumably, and, of course, physical disability (Philip's lameness as a substitute for near-blindness). It is worth remarking, also, that Juliette Huxley has written that, 'Aldous, in the persons of Philip Quarles and Walter Bidlake, reveals some facets of his own character.' *Aldous Huxley 1894–1963,* p. 43

7 For a detailed discussion of the literary consequences of the friend-ship between Huxley and Lawrence see Chapter Four of Jerome Meckier's *Aldous Huxley: Satire and Structure,* Chatto & Windus, 1969. Mr Meckier considers that Quarles is a picture of Huxley as Huxley felt himself to be seen by Lawrence.

8 For comparison see especially Part II, 'The London Years' of Harry T. Moore's *The Intelligent Heart,* William Heinemann, 1955, and Lawrence's series of poems, 'Look! We have come through!'

9 Apart from the parallels between Philip Quarles and Huxley himself, and between the Rampions and the Lawrences, it has been widely accepted since the publication of the book that John Bidlake is based on Augustus John, Burlap on Middleton Murry, and Lucy Tantamount on Nancy Cunard. Some people have aligned Webley with Sir Oswald Mosley (although in 1928 Mosley was still a junior minister in the Labour Government). Naomi Mitchinson has stated that her father was 'in a sense the original

of Lord Edward in *Point Counter Point*' (*Aldous Huxley 1894–1963*, p. 53), and, as a minor instance a certain Indian liberal, according to the editor of the *Letters* (p. 254), appears as Mr Sita Ram in Chapter Six.

10 From a letter of 18th January, 1927, we gather that Huxley had just read François Porche's recently-published *Vie de Baudelaire* and had been fascinated by it. *Letters* No. 258 p. 282

Huxley implies the second of the origins by causing Rampion to say to Spandrell : 'Laugh away, old Dostoievsky ! But let me tell you, it's Stavrogin who ought to have been called the Idiot, not Mishkin. He was incomparably the bigger fool, the completer pervert' (p. 564). (These words suggest questionable interpretations on Huxley's part of *The Idiot* and *The Devils*.)

11 From 'Une Charogne'.

12 *The Devils of Loudun*, Chatto & Windus, 1952, p. 364

13 *Point Counter Point*, p. 373. Compare *Eyeless in Gaza*, p. 9, ' "And I would," he said aloud, as he put the picture down, "I would wish my days to be separated each from each by unnatural impiety".' The uses and abuses of memory are, of course, a leading topic of *Eyeless in Gaza*, and continued to occupy Huxley to the time of *Island*.

14 A. E. Dyson, 'Aldous Huxley and the Two Nothings', 'Critical Quarterly', Winter, 1961, p. 298f.

15 op. cit., p. 45

16 Preface to *On Art and Artists* (ed. Morris Philipson), Chatto & Windus, 1960, p. 7

Chapter Five

Brave New World

1 An interesting book about modern 'anti-utopias' is *The Future as Nightmare* by Mark R. Hillegas, Oxford University Press, New York, 1967. Mr Hillegas contrasts our century with earlier periods. He argues that the stories of H. G. Wells, despite the optimism of some of them, have constituted the chief literary influence upon the authors of 'anti-utopias'.

2 Kingsley Amis, *New Maps of Hell*, Victor Gollancz, 1961, p. 18

3 See *Writers at Work*, p. 165

'Well, that started out as a parody of H. G. Wells' *Men Like Gods*, but gradually it got out of hand and turned into something quite different from what I'd originally intended. As I became more and more interested in the subject, I wandered farther and farther away from my original purpose.'

4   Northrop Frye, writing of what he calls the 'second phase' of satire, places Huxley in a line of descent as follows :
    'Lucian's attitude to Greek philosophy is repeated in the attitude of Erasmus and Rabelais to the scholastics, of Swift and Samuel Butler I to Descartes and the Royal Society, of Voltaire to the Leibnitzians, of Peacock to the Romantics, of Samuel Butler II to the Darwinians, of Aldous Huxley to the behaviourists.' op. cit., p. 230
5   This is what A. E. Dyson must have in mind when he writes :
    'The novel is similar in structure to Book IV of Gulliver, particularly in that the direction the irony seems to be taking is devastatingly reversed half-way through, and everything thrown in the melting-pot again.' op. cit., p. 300
6   Nevertheless, Huxley seems to have felt that the portrait of the Savage was one of 'the literary shortcomings of twenty years ago.' He writes in the foreword of 1946 :
    'For the sake, however, of dramatic effect, the Savage is often permitted to speak more rationally than his upbringing among the practitioners of a religion that is half fertility cult and half *Penitente* ferocity would actually warrant. Even his acquaintance with Shakespeare would not in reality justify such utterances.' (p. viii)
7   Laura Archera Huxley, *This Timeless Moment*, Chatto & Windus, 1968, p. 262
8   idem, p. 23
9   *Ape and Essence*, Chatto & Windus, Collected Edition, 1967, p. 43
    It recalls also the essay 'Tragedy and the Whole Truth' in *Music at Night* (1931), and Huxley's view, expressed in *Writers at Work* (p. 178), that a higher form than tragedy would be a form in which tragic and comic elements are fused.

Chapter Six

Eyeless in Gaza

1   Huxley once wrote to a correspondent :
    'In the case of the other character I started with the story of the betrayal by the friend, which was based upon a case which I had heard. The character was, of course, definitely Trev's. [That is, Trevenen Huxley, who committed suicide in 1914.] If I preserved the stammer and insisted on the ascetic obsession, it was for this reason : that it is, artistically speaking (and perhaps there are also profounder, ethical and psychological

reasons as well), all but impossible to represent an entirely good character that is without weakness.'
Letters, no. 402, p. 409

2 op. cit., p. 303

3 In a letter of 28 May, 1961, Huxley wrote : 'I read *Du Côté de Chez Swann* in 1915, in the original Mercure de France edition.' *Letters,* no. 867, p. 913

4 An example is when Rivers, in *The Genius and the Goddess,* on being reminded that the 'Muses are the daughters of Memory', replies, 'And God . . . is not their brother. God isn't the son of Memory; He's the son of Immediate Experience. You can't worship a spirit in spirit, unless you do it now. Wallowing in the past may be good literature. As wisdom, it's hopeless.' (p. 9)

5 Compare Elinor Quarles's reproach to her husband that he lacks 'natural piety'. See *Point Counter Point,* p. 373, and p. 90 of this study.

6 See *Ends and Means,* Chatto & Windus, 1937, p. 3f.

7 op. cit., p. 117

8 Compare Blake's mythology, which might have influenced Huxley, consciously or otherwise, at the time of writing these words, for he has previously (p. 144) spoken of Blake as the first to see man as a succession of states. Blake's myth has it that the Fall was a contraction from spirituality into materiality and that the Council of God decided, while Fallen Man lay stretched out on the Rock of Ages, that the body should be the limit of materiality for mankind.
See especially 'Vala', 'Night the Eighth', *Poetry and Prose of William Blake* (ed. Geoffrey Keynes), The Nonesuch Press, 1941, p. 331.

9 In *The Rainbow* Ursula Brangwen observes a 'plant-animal' through a microscope, and concludes :
'It intended to be itself . . . Self was a oneness with the infinite. To be oneself was a supreme gleaming triumph of infinity.'
The Rainbow, William Heinemann, Phoenix Edition, p. 441

PART II

Chapter Seven

After Many a Summer

1 op. cit., p. 142

2 *Aldous Huxley 1894–1963,* p. 154

3 Jocelyn Brooke, op. cit., p. 26

4 Derek Verschoyle, The *Spectator*, 13 October, 1939

5 See *Writers at Work*, p. 166 : 'No they've never had any effect on me, for the simple reason that I've never read them.'

6 See below, p. 175

7 No better list of references for Propter's teaching could be found than the list that Huxley himself in effect provided by compiling *The Perennial Philosophy*, but for the socio-economic aspects it is useful also to read Gerald Heard's *Pain, Sex and Time*, New York, 1939.

8 See, for instance, Julian Huxley, *Essays of a Humanist*, Chatto & Windus, 1964; *The Humanist Frame*, (ed. Julian Huxley), Allen & Unwin, 1961, and *Objections to Humanism*, (ed. H. J. Blackham), Penguin Books, 1965.

9 T. S. Eliot, 'Little Gidding'

10 'Swift', *Do What You Will*, Chatto & Windus, 1929, p. 100

11 John Wain, 'Tracts against Materialism', The *London Magazine*, August, 1955, p. 60

12 The characters, whatever else their deficiencies, are not impossible, as Huxley has in effect pointed out. In a letter to his son he mentioned a description given to him of a visit to the *ménage* of William Randolph Hearst and Marion Davies and commented, 'The reality sounds more gruesome, and also more improbable, than the fictions of *After Many a Summer*'.
Letters, no. 561, p. 593.

13 Compare Blake's words '*Unorganized Innocence: An Impossibility.* Innocence dwells with Wisdom, but never with Ignorance'.
The Poetry and Prose of William Blake (ed. Geoffrey Keynes), The Nonesuch Press, 1941, p. 372

14 op. cit., p. 149

15 Propter tells Jeremy Pordage that the latter is 'A bit of a murderee ... as well as a scholar and a gentleman.' (p. 20)
Compare Spandrell telling Lucy 'It takes two to make a murder. There are born victims, born to have their throats cut, as the cut-throats are born to be hanged.' (*Point Counter Point*, p. 209)
Compare also Lawrence's Birkin telling Gerald Crich, 'It takes two people to make a murder : a murderer and a murderee. And a murderee is a man who is murderable. And a man who is murderable is a man who in a profound if hidden lust desires to be murdered.' (*Women in Love*, William Heinemann, Phoenix Edition, 1961, p. 27)

16 Here I am merely reflecting Huxley's position (supported by a number of quotations in various chapters of this study) without attempting to examine it in the light of the numerous modern

works on 'self', 'not self', 'consciousness' and allied concepts. Well-known works, such as Gilbert Ryle's *The Concept of Mind* and Sartre's *Being and Nothingness* do not seem to contradict the Huxleyan position.

17 *King Lear*, Act III, Scene IV. (The mad Edgar who uses these terms, of course also uses others which are less applicable to Gonister.)

18 *Letters*, no. 431, p. 44

Chapter Eight

Time Must Have a Stop

1 See below, p. 175
2 'The Circus Animals' Desertion'
3 See *Point Counter Point*, p. 39, and p. 93 of this study.
4 However, the Arden Edition of *King Henry IV, Part I* follows the punctuation of the Quartos of 1598 and thus gives a simpler reading of the lines to the effect that thoughts, life and time all stop at death. In his last essay, 'Shakespeare and Religion' (which he was still dictating on the day before his death) Huxley again commented upon Hotspur's remarks, clarifying though not altering the gloss in *Time Must Have a Stop*.

See *Aldous Huxley 1894–1963*, p. 174f. These were Huxley's last words as a writer.

5 op. cit., p. 168
6 On the subject of power, consider the theme of *Grey Eminence*, and for Huxley's attitude towards introverted self-torment see the essay, 'Pascal', in *Do What You Will*, and the second half of *The Devils of Loudun*.
7 In addition to the essay, 'Chaucer' (in *On the Margin and Essays New and Old*), there are the following remarks :

'And there's another really sublime writer [Homer has just been mentioned] who has this quality—Chaucer. Why, Chaucer invented a whole psychology out of absolutely nothing : an incredible achievement. It's one of the great misfortunes of English literature that Chaucer wrote at a time when his language was to become incomprehensible. If he had been born two or three hundred years later I think the whole course of English literature would have been changed. We wouldn't have had this sort of platonic mania—separating mind from body and spirit from matter.'

Writers at Work, p. 178

8 See *Aspects of the Novel*, pp. 165ff.

9   Peter Bowering has made detailed references to these omens : op. cit., pp. 163ff.

10   idem, p. 161

11   idem, p. 167

12   A quite different explanation is offered by Sir Oliver Lodge in his book, *Raymond*. In Chapter Twelve of that book, entitled 'On the Contention that all Psychic communications are of a Trivial Nature and deal with Insignificant Topics', Sir Oliver maintains that the spirit of the departed communicates matters which seem trivial to an outsider but are loaded with emotional associations for former intimates. Furthermore, 'the idea that a departed friend ought to be occupied wholly and entirely with grave matters, and ought not to remember jokes and fun, is a gratuitous claim which has to be abandoned. Humour does not cease with earth-life. Why should it?'
Sir Oliver J. Lodge, *Raymond*, (tenth edition), Methuen, 1918, p. 349 (first published, 1916)

13   In a letter to publishers Huxley described *Time Must Have a Stop* as 'a piece of the *Comédie Humaine* that modulates into a version of the *Divina Commedia*. About half way through the story, which I have deliberately kept light, with events on a small scale minutely described, the principal comic character dies, and all that follows takes place against the background of his post-humous experience, which is, of course, wholly and disquietingly incompatible with the life he was leading and which goes on among those who survive him.'
Letters, no. 480, p. 498f.

14   D. S. Savage, op. cit., p. 155

15   *Writers at Work*, p. 172

16   *Aldous Huxley 1894–1963*, p. 158

Chapter Nine

Ape and Essence

1   *Letters*, no. 568, p. 600

2   The remark was made in real life during the casting for the film-version of *The Gioconda Smile*. See *Letters*, no. 541, p. 572

3   In a letter of 10 August, 1945 (written, that is, on the day following the day of the dropping of the atomic bomb on Nagasaki) Huxley said :

    'National states armed by science with super-human military power always remind me of Swift's description of Gulliver being carried up to the roof of the King of Brobdingnag's palace by a gigantic monkey: reason, human decency and spirituality, which are strictly individual matters, find themselves in the clutches of the collective will, which has the mentality of a delinquent boy of fourteen in conjunction with the physical power of a god.'

Letters, no. 505, p. 532

4   In Huxley's writings there are many remarks hostile to organized religion. Apart from such fictional references as Gumbril's response to the service in the school chapel and the depiction of the funeral of Grace Elver, consider the following words from the essay, 'Knowledge and Understanding', *Adonis and the Alphabet*, 1956, p. 63 :

'Artificial piety based on conditioned reflexes merely transfers intellectual pride from the bumptious individual to his even more bumptious Church.'

In *Island* Vijaya is caused to say in effect that religion is necessary to man but its forms must be treated with great circumspection. See *Island*, p. 178f.

5   From 'Epipsychidion'

Chapter Ten

The Genius and the Goddess

1   op. cit., p. 172
2   See especially Mark Staithes's words in *Eyeless in Gaza* (p. 520f.) and Mr Propter's views as reflected upon by Pete Boone in *After Many a Summer* (p. 225). See also my remarks in the Introduction, pp. 12ff.
3   Compare Huxley's remarks, quoted on p. 219f. of this study, in the essay 'Knowledge and Understanding'. Many similar comments occur in his later writings, and the educational techniques damatized in *Island* include training in the proper use of words.
4   *Letters*, no. 780, pp. 831f.
5   *The Perennial Philosophy*, Chatto & Windus, 1945, p. 130f.
6   See 'The Dry Salvages' :
'Not fare well,
But fare forward, voyagers';
and 'East Coker' :
'The only wisdom we can hope to acquire
Is the wisdom of humility.'
7   In considering the characterization of Ruth, compare T. S. Eliot's remarks in his essay, 'The Use of Poetry and the Use of Criticism', about the adolescent tendency to write 'under a kind

of daemonic possession by one poet'. In addition there are Eliot's opinions expressed in the essay, 'Hamlet', that adolescents are often filled with emotions that seem unrelated to, or in excess of, the actual situations in which they are placed. (Eliot argues that Shakespeare's Hamlet, without the excuse of adolescence, feels for his mother a degree of disgust which seems to us excessive.)

8 See Chapter Fourteen of *Island*.

Chapter Eleven

Island

1 The paper was a contribution to the proceedings of the Center for the Study of Democratic Institutions; the essay appears in *Aldous Huxley, 1894–1963* and in Laura Archera Huxley's *This Timeless Moment*. The first chapter of the new novel also appears in Laura Archera Huxley's book.

2 See Ronald W. Clark, op. cit., p. 354

3 idem, p. 355

4 See *This Timeless Moment*, p. 7f.

5 See the second chapter of *This Timeless Moment*.

6 Sir Julian Huxley, *Aldous Huxley 1894–1963*, p. 23f.

7 The most pertinent essays are 'The Education of an Amphibian' and 'Knowledge and Understanding', both of which appear in the volume, *Adonis and the Alphabet*, and 'Human Potentialities' which is a contribution to the volume, *The Humanist Frame* (ed. Julian Huxley), Allen & Unwin, 1961.
Laura Huxley writes :
   '*Island* was difficult : its message could have been conveyed in a form other than a novel, but Aldous felt that by fusing the message with a story, he would reach a larger and more varied audience.' op. cit., p. 273

8 op. cit., Chapter XI

9 John Atkins, *Aldous Huxley*, (revised edition) Calder & Boyars, 1967, p. xxxii. (First edition published 1956)

10 Sir Julian Huxley, *Memories*, George Allen & Unwin, 1970, p. 70. In a letter of August, 1914 Huxley wrote of his brother's suicide :
   'There is—apart from the sheer grief of the loss—an added pain in the cynicism of the situation. It is just the highest and best in Trev—his ideals—which have driven him to his death— while there are thousands who shelter their weakness from the same fate by a cynical, unidealistic outlook on life. Trev was

not strong, but he had the courage to face life with ideals—
and his ideals were too much for him.'
Letters, no. 48, p. 61f.

11 op. cit., p. 131
12 idem, p. 146 (The letter to Dr Hoffman is not reproduced in the *Letters*.)
13 'Knowledge and Understanding', *Adonis and the Alphabet*, Chatto & Windus, 1956, p. 52f.

Conclusion

1 The description is used in the foreword to the Collected Edition of *Brave New World*, p. viii. Huxley seems to refer to himself specifically at the time of writing *Brave New World*, but its application can almost certainly be extended.
2 See Richard Aldington, *Portrait of a Genius, But . . .* , William Heinemann, 1950, p. 321. Aldington states that Lawrence prophesied that Huxley would be in a lunatic asylum within a year. Lawrence's feeling seems to have been that the writing of *Point Counter Point* must have involved facing stark realities with great, though morbid, courage.
3 *Letters*, no. 317, p. 340
4 *Ends and Means*, Chatto & Windus, 1937, p. 166f.
5 'That man, I think, has had a liberal education, who has been so trained in his youth that his body is the ready servant of his will and does with ease and pleasure all the work that, as a mechanism, it is capable of; whose intellect is a clear, cold logic engine, with all its parts of equal strength, and in smooth working order; ready, like a steam engine, to be turned to any kind of work, and spin the gossamers as well as forge the anchors of the mind; whose mind is stored with a knowledge of the great and fundamental truths of Nature and of the laws of her operations; one who, no stunted ascetic, is full of life and fire, but whose passions are trained to come to heel by a vigorous will, the servant of a tender conscience; who has learned to love all beauty, whether of Nature or of art, to hate all vileness, and to respect others as himself.'
T. H. Huxley, 'A Liberal Education; And Where to Find It,' *Lay Sermons, Addresses and Reviews*, Macmillan, 1880, p. 34f.

Bibliography

(The place of publication is London unless otherwise stated.)

The Novels of Aldous Huxley

NOTE: All the novels are published by Chatto & Windus.

	First Editions	Editions Used
Crome Yellow	1921	1963
Antic Hay	1923	1949
Those Barren Leaves	1925	1960
Point Counter Point	1928	1963
Brave New World	1932	1967
Eyeless in Gaza	1936	1955
After Many a Summer	1939	1968
Time Must Have a Stop	1944	1966
Ape and Essence	1948	1967
The Genius and the Goddess	1955	1955
Island	1962	1966

Criticism and Reference

Aldington, Richard. *Portrait of a Genius, But . . .* , William Heinemann, 1950

Amis, Kingsley. *New Maps of Hell*, Victor Gollancz, 1961

Atkins, John. *Aldous Huxley*, Calder & Boyars, revised edition, 1967

Blackham, H. J. (ed.). *Objections to Humanism*, Penguin Books, 1965

Blackmur, R. P. *Language as Gesture*, Harcourt Brace Jovanovich, New York, 1935

Blake, William. *Poetry and Prose* (ed. Geoffrey Keynes), The Nonesuch Press, 1941

Bowen, Elizabeth. *Collected Impressions*, Longmans Green, 1950

Bowering, Peter. *Aldous Huxley: A Study of the Major Novels*, The Athlone Press, 1968

Brooke, Jocelyn. *Aldous Huxley*, Longmans Green, 1954

Brooks, Harold F. *Eliot in Perspective*, (ed. Graham Martin) Macmillan, 1970

Clark, Ronald W. *The Huxleys*, William Heinemann, 1968

Connolly, Cyril. *Enemies of Promise*, Routledge & Kegan Paul, 1938

Connolly, Cyril. *The Modern Movement*, André Deutsch, Hamish Hamilton, 1965

Cunard, Nancy. *Grand Man*, Secker & Warburg, 1954

Eliot, T. S. *Collected Poems 1909–1962*, Faber & Faber, 1963

Eliot, T. S. *Selected Essays*, Faber & Faber, 1951

Forster, E. M. *Aspects of the Novel*, Edward Arnold, 1927

Forster, E. M. *Two Cheers for Democracy*, Edward Arnold, 1951

Frye, Northrop. *Anatomy of Criticism*, Princeton University Press, Princeton, New Jersey, 1957

Greville, Fulke. *Poems and Dramas of Fulke Greville* (ed. Geoffrey Bullough), Oliver & Boyd, 1939

Harington, Sir John. *Sir John Harington's A New Discourse of a Stale Subject called The Metamorphosis of Ajax*. (ed. Elizabeth Story Donno), Routledge & Kegan Paul, 1962

Harrison, Michael. *London Growing*, Hutchinson, 1965

Heard, Gerald. *Pain, Sex and Time: A New Outlook on Evolution and the Future of Man*, Cassell, 1939

Henderson, Alexander. *Aldous Huxley*, Russell & Russell, New York, 1964 (First published, London, 1936)

Hillegas, Mark R. *The Future as Nightmare*, Oxford University Press, New York, 1964

Huxley, Aldous. *Letters of Aldous Huxley* (ed. Grover Smith), Chatto & Windus, 1969

Huxley, Aldous (ed.). *Letters of D. H. Lawrence*, William Heinemann 1932

Huxley, Julian (ed.). *Aldous Huxley 1894–1963*, Chatto & Windus, 1965

Huxley, Julian. *Essays of a Humanist*, Chatto & Windus, 1964

Huxley, Julian (ed.). *The Humanist Frame*, George Allen & Unwin, 1961

Huxley, Sir Julian. *Memories*, George Allen & Unwin, 1970

Huxley, Laura Archera. *This Timeless Moment*, Chatto & Windus, 1968

Huxley, T. H. *Lay Sermons, Addresses and Reviews*, Macmillan, 1880

Keats, John. *The Letters of John Keats* (ed. Hyder Edward Rollins), Cambridge University Press, 1958

Moore, Harry T. (ed.). *The Collected Letters of D. H. Lawrence*, William Heinemann, 1962

Lawrence, D. H. *The Rainbow*, William Heinemann, Phoenix Edition, 1961

Lawrence, D. H. *Women in Love*, William Heinemann, Phoenix Edition, 1961

Lodge, Sir Oliver J. *Raymond or Life and Death*, Methuen, tenth edition, 1918

Meckier, Jerome. *Aldous Huxley: Satire & Structure*, Chatto & Windus, 1969

Moore, Harry T. *The Intelligent Heart*, William Heinemann, 1955

Morrell, Lady Ottoline. *Ottoline The Early Memoirs of Lady Ottoline Morrell*, (ed. Robert Gathorne-Hardy), Faber & Faber, 1963

Priestley, J. B. *Thomas Love Peacock*, Macmillan, 1927

Russell, Bertrand. *History of Western Philosophy*, George Allen & Unwin, second edition, 1961 (First published, 1946)

Sartre, Jean-Paul. *Being and Nothingness* (tr. Hazel E. Barnes), Methuen, 1957

Savage, D. S. *The Withered Branch*, Eyre & Spottiswoode, 1950

Shakespeare, William. *The First Part of King Henry IV*, Arden Edition, Methuen, 1960

Shelley, Percy Bysshe. *The Letters of Percy Bysshe Shelley* (ed. Frederick Jones), Oxford University Press, 1964

The Oxford Companion to French Literature (eds. Sir Paul Harvey and J. E. Heseltine), Oxford University Press, 1959

Writers at Work, The *Paris Review* Interviews, second series (intr. by Van Wyck Brooks), Martin Secker & Warburg, 1963

The *Critical Quarterly*, vol. 3, no. 4, Winter, 1961

The *London Magazine*, August, 1955

The *Nation and Athenaeum*, 24 January, 1925

The *Spectator*, 22 December, 1923, 13 October, 1939

Index